THE GRECIAN TASTE

THE GRECIAN TASTE

Literature in the Age of Neo-Classicism
1740—1820

JOHN BUXTON

. . . those minds that nobly could transfuse
The glorious Spirit of the Grecian Muse.

Byron: *English Bards and Scotch Reviewers*

BOOKS
10 East 53d St, New York 10022
(a division of Harper & Row Publishers, Inc.)

First published 1978 by
THE MACMILLAN PRESS LTD
London and Basingstoke

Published in the U.S.A. 1978 by
HARPER AND ROW PUBLISHERS. INC.
BARNES AND NOBLE IMPORT DIVISION

Printed in Great Britain

Library of Congress Cataloging in Publication Data

Buxton, John, 1912—
   The Grecian taste.

   Bibliography: p.
   Includes index.
   1. English literature — 18th century — History and
criticism. 2. Neoclassicism (Literature) 3. English
literature — 19th century — History and criticism.
I. Title.
PR445.B88   820'.9'006   78—909
ISBN 0—06—490845—3

Contents

List of Plates

Preface

In the autumn of 1972 a series of exhibitions in London and elsewhere illustrated the phase of taste known to art historians as 'neo-classicism'. These were the two exhibitions, at the Royal Academy and at the Victoria and Albert Museum, entitled 'the Age of Neo-Classicism'; the Lady Hamilton exhibition at Kenwood; the exhibition of 'Early Neo-Classical Furniture in Britain 1755–80' at Osterley Park; and 'The True Style' exhibition at the Holburne Museum in Bath. Ancillary to these was the bicentenary exhibition of the Hamilton Collection at the British Museum. In Florence, earlier in the same year, I had visited an exhibition entitled 'Cultura neoclassica e romantica nella Toscana Granducale' held in the Pitti Palace. These exhibitions covered the years 1750–1830, with very few works of art made before or after those dates.

I thought it would be of interest to consider the work of English writers in this same period and to inquire how this conformed to the same neo-classical taste which was so vigorously affecting architecture, sculpture and painting, and the domestic arts of furniture, silver, china and dress. These writers would, no doubt, respond to the taste of the age in a variety of ways, just as the architects and painters did, but there would be common factors. Besides, writers might be more articulate about the aesthetic theories that lay behind neo-classicism, and indeed several of them, most notably Akenside, Blake and Shelley, wrote much on this subject.

This book derives from a series of lectures delivered in the University of Oxford in Michaelmas Term, 1972, when my audience could, if they wished, visit the exhibitions to which I referred them. But a man reading a book by his fireside does not respond in the same way as to a lecture, and very little of what I then said have I here transcribed. I have not much revised my opinions, but I have curtailed some parts of the argument and expanded others; I have been rather more generous in quotation than is acceptable in a lecture; I have, reluctantly, omitted one writer, but have included two others whose work I had not then considered carefully enough.

JOHN BUXTON

1 Introduction

Der gute Geschmack, welcher sich mehr und mehr durch die Welt ausbreitet,
hat sich angefangen zuerst unter dem griechischen Himmel zu bilden.

Johann Joachim Winckelmann, *Gedanken über die Nachahmung
der griechischen Werke in der Malerey und Bildhauer-Kunst,* 1755

'Good taste was first formed under Greek skies.' With these words
Winckelmann proclaimed a new era in European taste. A generation
earlier the aristocratic members of the Society of Dilettanti had
responded, at their Sunday dinners in London, to the toast of 'Grecian
Taste and Roman Spirit'. Their President, when proposing this, had
been garbed in a scarlet toga, in accordance with a resolution of the
Society, passed on 1 February 1741, 'That a Roman dress is thought
necessary for the President of the Society', which was supplemented a
month later by a further resolution, 'That it should be Scarlet'. The
Society, by its enlightened patronage of archaeological exploration in
the eastern Mediterranean, did much to effect the change to Grecian
taste; but the scarlet toga remained the dress of their President until
1790, when someone stole it. Only then was the Roman toga
superseded by a Greek chlamys, specially designed by Richard Payne
Knight; and the primacy of Grecian taste was not only acknowledged
but exhibited at the meetings of the Society.

Few well-born Englishmen could much earlier have evaded the
powerful Augustan tradition in which they had been nurtured in
order to assert the unique superiority of Greek civilization; but the
son of a Prussian cobbler was not thus inhibited, and his bold but
sensitive intelligence broke through to a realization of what others
could but grope after. Mengs' portrait of Winckelmann at the
entrance to the exhibition, 'The Age of Neo-Classicism', in Burling-
ton House in 1972 proclaimed to every visitor the responsibility of
this one man of genius for the Grecian taste which prevailed in
Western Europe from 1760 to 1820, during the years which, for
Goethe, formed the century of Winckelmann. Never before had the
taste of educated men owed so much to the vision of one man.

The word 'neo-classicism', however, was first introduced to our wondering forefathers in *The Times* of 6 May 1893: 'A man must be a scholar,' they were warned, 'before he can make neo-classicism even tolerable in art.' The adjective 'neo-classical' had been coined a few years before, but none of these 'neo-' compounds was invented until the Victorian era. In the age of neo-classicism the word in common use was 'Grecian'—'One must have taste to be sensible of the beauties of Grecian architecture,' said Horace Walpole; 'one only wants passions to feel Gothic.' Lord Kames likened the man who prefers 'a rude Gothic tower before the finest Grecian building' to the man who 'prefers the Saracen's head upon a signpost to the best tablature of Raphael'. Thomas Warton, contemplating Sir Joshua Reynolds' painted window in the chapel of New College, might regret his introduction into this 'Gothic pile' of 'Grecian groupes', and his complimentary politeness could not deceive Sir Joshua. Elsewhere, in a note on *Il Penseroso* Warton contrasted old St Paul's, 'a most stately and venerable pattern of the Gothic style', with Wren's replacement. 'We justly admire and approve Sir Christopher Wren's Grecian proportions. Truth and propriety gratify the judgment, but they do not affect the imagination.' Blake ranged himself with Warton in making the same contrast: 'Grecian is mathematic form, Gothic is living form.' (But he was by no means consistent in his preference.) And Sir Walter Scott, introducing into the Gothic landscape of Loch Katrine the Lady of the Lake, described her in the accepted terms of ideal beauty, with

> locks flung back, and lips apart,
> Like monument of Grecian art.

Even in far away India English officers recruiting sepoys preferred those whose looks invited the complimentary epithet 'Grecian'.

'Grecian', then, was the word in common use to describe the taste of the age. And it has other advantages over 'neo-classical': it is unambiguous, whereas 'neo-classical' could equally well refer to classical Rome as to classical Greece. It defines the change of taste, which substituted Athens, or, more often, Alexandria*, for Rome: 'Grecian' invites our attention to the Greek world, but 'neo-classical'

---

* Joseph Warton, in *An Essay on the Writings and Genius of Pope*, 1756, names the age of Ptolemy II as the second of five recorded ages in which literature and the fine arts have reached perfection; it 'has never yet been sufficiently taken notice of'.

leaves us adrift in the Ionian Sea, between Italy and Greece. Besides, although the art historians, following judiciously in the footsteps of their Adam, Winckelmann, use the term 'neo-classicism' with precision, literary historians and critics do not. They use it of Sir Thomas Wyatt's satires; of Spenser's metrical experiments, and of his pastoral; of Campion's songs; of Milton's heroic poem, of Dryden's criticism, of Pope's satires; with the result that, in a literary context, the word has become so imprecise as to be without meaning. A word that is undefined in terms of chronology, of idea, of manner, might as well be abandoned; and 'Grecian', which can be defined in all these contexts, which has the advantage of contemporary usage, and which denotes what differentiates the taste of the time from that of the preceding Augustan or succeeding Romantic, should be preferred. 'Post-Augustan' and 'Pre-Romantic' are derogatory, and unde-served: writers of the last half of the eighteenth century were not failing to match Dryden and Pope or to anticipate Wordsworth and Coleridge. They had no such ambition. Their purpose, and their performance, were distinct and independent, neither Augustan nor Romantic, but Grecian.

The finest achievements of the Renaissance had come when the rediscovered art of the classical past was brought into contact with a living vernacular tradition. Inevitably, this process had begun in Italy, where the classical tradition of Rome (which itself derived from Greece) had never been wholly superseded, where architectural monuments remained for all to see and where the language bore a recognizable similarity to Latin; in architecture, sculpture and painting trans-Alpine Europe never attained the mastery of the Italians. But the equilibrium between classical and vernacular in Northern Europe could not last, and soon the self-consciousness which characterizes all our attempts at classicism led to a con-temptuous rejection of the vernacular element and the substitution of a chaste, and therefore sterile, form. Milton's rejection of rhymed verse for *Paradise Lost* as 'the invention of a barbarous age, to set off wretched matter and lame metre', may be compared to John Evelyn's haughty dismissal of Gothic 'crinkle-crankle' in Henry VII's chapel at Westminster Abbey. Political accident rather than a logical sequence of aesthetic preferences led to the almost total omission in England of anything that may be properly termed 'baroque'—the poetry of Richard Crashaw may be offered as an exception, whose exotic quality proves the rule—and, as Mario Praz has said, 'the most faithful disciples of Palladio were English; in fact English Palladianism spans the interval between the extreme classicism of the Cinquecento and the neo-classicism of the anti-baroque reaction in eighteenth century Europe.'

The literary taste which coincides with Palladianism is that of the Augustans, who looked to Virgil and Ovid, to Horace, Persius and Juvenal, as Palladio had looked to Vitruvius. Again, their preferred form was satire, the one kind which the Romans claimed that they had not derived from Greece but had invented for themselves. Francis Atterbury no doubt spoke for his contemporaries when, in commending Waller's poems in 1690, he asked the rhetorical question 'whether in Charles II's reign English did not come to its full perfection, and whether it has not had its Augustan age as well as the Latin'. Such complacency was certain to invite challenge in due course, but the genius of Dryden and of Pope prolonged the Augustan age, of which Waller was the acknowledged precursor, far into the eighteenth century. Horace Walpole, in a letter to Richard West written a few months after he returned from the Grand Tour, observed that 'Pope has half a dozen old friends that he has preserved from the taste of last century.'

The Augustan tradition was clearly becoming exhausted, and a choice might be made between the two elements which had been held in equilibrium in the Elizabethan age. The vernacular tradition would be revived by Walpole himself in the Gothic frivolities of Strawberry Hill; in paintings such as Francis Hayman's 'Lecherous Friar' or his 'Dance of the Milkmaids on May Day'; in Bishop Percy's oddly eclectic *Reliques of Ancient English Poetry*, even in the spurious *Ossian* and the no less spurious *Rowley Poems*. But the declining classical tradition, in architecture and painting and literature, needed refreshment from original ancient sources. These, fortunately, were suddenly and copiously augmented in the middle years of the century, by the discovery of Herculaneum in 1739, of Pompeii in 1748, and of the temples of Paestum about the same time. The temples, though not concealed for seventeen centuries under layers of volcanic ash, and always visible from the sea, were encircled by malarial swamp and just as inaccessible and unknown (except to a few illiterate shepherds)as the two ancient towns at the foot of Vesuvius. Publication of the discoveries at Herculaneum began in 1755, and the great interest they aroused in England was recognized in the decision to allot five hundred copies of the splendidly illustrated volumes of *Le Pitture antiche d'Ercolano* to the English market. No doubt their purchasers were those rich young English milords who made the

Grand Tour before inheriting their estates, and who had founded for convivial reminiscence of their months in Italy the Society of Dilettanti; but these were the men whose opinions dominated the taste of the age no less than its politics. Indeed, as will appear, the two interests were not unrelated. Horace Walpole, the son of the Prime Minister, was at Herculaneum with Thomas Gray a few months after its first discovery. 'As you walk,' Gray wrote to his mother,

> you see parts of an amphitheatre, many houses adorned with marble columns, and incrusted with the same; the front of a temple, several arched vaults of rooms painted in fresco. Some pieces of painting have been taken out from hence, finer than anything of the kind before discovered, and with these the king has adorned his palace; also a number of statues, medals, and gems. . . .

At Pompeii excavation began in 1767, but there the major finds were not made until the nineteenth century. The first publication of the temples of Paestum also came in the 1760s, but for many years their primitive Doric was considered 'rude and unpleasing'.

The recovery of Greek learning in the fifteenth century direct from the original texts, and no longer mediated through Latin or Arabic, had been of primary importance and could not be matched, though it would be supplemented, in the eighteenth century. But the discoveries of Greek statues by such indefatigable excavators as Gavin Hamilton and Thomas Jenkins far surpassed those of the fifteenth and sixteenth centuries. Now to the marbles and bronzes was added a large fund of painting, in the Hellenistic frescoes of Herculaneum and Pompeii, in mosaic floors derived from Greek paintings, and, perhaps most influential of all, in the excavated Greek vases of which Sir William Hamilton formed his two famous collections. And whereas the discoveries of the Renaissance had been made for the most part in or about Rome, many of the new discoveries were made in Naples and in Southern Italy, in the country once known as Magna Graecia, whose ancient culture had been predominantly Greek, not Roman.

Thus the middle years of the eighteenth century witnessed a renewal of those Greek influences which had prompted the first Renaissance; and though there were no new literary discoveries to rival those of the fifteenth century the reorientation of taste in the visual arts inevitably led to some reconsideration of Greek literature. Besides, there were advances in Greek scholarship through the labours of such men as Bentley and, later, Porson; and many works

were now for the first time translated into English. Only now were all
the plays of the Greek tragedians made English: the first translation of
any play by Aeschylus was published in 1777, and only one play of
Sophocles and one of Euripides had been published in English before
the eighteenth century. Complete versions of Pindar, of Theocritus
and of the *Argonautica* of Apollonius Rhodius now appeared for the
first time. Plato, hitherto represented in English only by two or three
dialogues (including the spurious *Axiochus*), now began to attract
translators; so too did the Neo-Platonists, Plotinus, Porphyry and
Proclus, whose works were first made English by Thomas Taylor, the
friend of Blake and of Peacock. Perhaps most significant of all,
Pausanias' *Description of Greece* was translated by Sir Uvedale Price,
the protagonist of the Picturesque, in 1780. Some years later Thomas
Taylor (whose enthusiasm for Greek civilization led him, it was said,
to offer sacrifices to the gods of Olympus in his house in Walworth)
published another translation, which was the one used by Byron. For
the possibility of visiting Greece and seeing the remaining monuments for oneself had become much more attractive since the 1750s.
Then, the Society of Dilettanti had sent out to Athens two young
architects, James Stuart and Nicholas Revett, to make detailed
drawings of the antiquities they found there; they remained in Greece
for nearly four years, and the first volume of their monumental
Antiquities of Athens was published in 1762, seven years after their
return. The second volume, which contained their drawings of the
temples on the Acropolis, did not appear until 1789, but long before
that 'Athenian' Stuart, as he became known, had strongly influenced
architectural taste in England. That he never attained the popularity
of 'Bob the Roman', Robert Adam, was due more to his own
idleness than to aesthetic preference: he would not bother to compete
with a far more industrious Scot.

Stuart and Revett went to Greece in 1751 not as disinterested
archaeologists but with the declared intention to improve the taste of
their fellow-countrymen. 'Many authors,' they wrote,

> have maintained these remains of Antiquity, as Works of great
> magnificence, and most exquisite taste; but their Descriptions are
> so confused, and their Measures so inaccurate, that the most expert
> Architect could not from these Books form an idea distinct enough
> to make exact Drawings of any one building they describe. Their
> works seem rather calculated to raise our admiration than to satisfy
> our curiosity, or improve our taste. . . . Athens, the mother of

Elegance and Politeness, whose magnificence scarce yielded to that of Rome, and who for the beauties of a correct style must be allowed to surpass her, as much as an original excels a copy, has been almost entirely neglected.

And they had no doubt that their own work would 'meet with the Approbation of all those Gentlemen who are lovers of Antiquity, or have a taste for what is excellent in the Arts'; as indeed it did. Any improvement in English taste in the Whig society of the time must begin with those who could afford to employ architects to design their houses, and who would commission sculptors and painters and cabinet-makers to furnish and adorn them. 'The Greek Revival' forms a well-defined phase of our architectural history and comprehends not only the structure of English buildings but their decoration and furnishings. Yet we should inquire why the Society of Dilettanti sent out Stuart and Revett to Greece in the early 1750s at the very time when Winckelmann in Dresden was independently formulating his ideas on Grecian taste.

The coincidence is too remarkable to be accepted as mere coincidence. Revolutions in thought may appear, to a superficial view, to be the sudden product of an exceptional mind which has somehow generated new ideas from within itself; but most often they arise from the power of such a mind to observe that the scattered and fragmentary suggestions of others converge towards, and may be summed in, a general statement. Thus, a century after Winckelmann, and in a very different context, Charles Darwin, in *The Origin of Species*, gave a clear and summary formulation to ideas towards which many lesser minds had long been reaching. Winckelmann, who had read widely in the English authors of the Augustan age—he knew Pope's *Essay on Man* by heart—owed his greatest debt to Shaftesbury's *Characteristicks*. No doubt Addison's *Remarks on several parts of Italy* and the two Jonathan Richardsons' *Account of the Statues . . . and Pictures in Italy, France, etc.* had provided him with detailed information and had stimulated his wish to visit Italy; but Shaftesbury's concern with aesthetic principles rather than with actual works of art better suited his need before he went there. For it is an astonishing fact that when Winckelmann wrote his *Reflections on the Painting and Sculpture of the Greeks* he had seen no original works in either; and though at the end of the year, 1755, in which he published his celebrated essay Winckelmann went to Italy for the first time, and arrived in Rome, he was never to see any original work of the age of

Phidias. His appreciations of the 'Apollo Belvedere', of the 'Niobe', of the 'Laocoön', were of works already known in the Renaissance, and to which later taste has not accorded the supremacy which he gave them. 'He was like Columbus,' said Goethe, 'who had in his mind a notion of the New World before he actually discovered it.' For Winckelmann's understanding of Greek art derived from his knowledge of Greek literature rather than of Greek sculpture, and it was his especial gift to recognize in the sculpture those same classical ideals with which the literature had inspired him. Indeed, his chief contribution lies in his insistence on the unity of Greek culture. But since the principal evidences of that culture that remain are in the literature, the new movement which Winckelmann's imaginative vision began was always predominantly literary.

Shaftesbury, writing in the midst of the Augustan age, challenged the assumptions of the age, which by 'correctness' generally understood the quality of 'one who knows so well how to write like the old Latin poets'—to quote Bishop Berkeley's compliment to Pope. And as late as 1747 the extended title of Joseph Spence's *Polymetis* was *An Enquiry concerning the agreement between the works of the Roman Poets and the Remains of the Ancient Artists.* (Spence was the friend and disciple of Pope.) Yet three or four years before Bishop Berkeley wrote his letter Shaftesbury had declared,

> 'tis evident, beyond a doubt, that the *arts* and *sciences* were form'd in GREECE it-self. 'Twas there that *musick*, *poetry*, and the rest came to receive some kind of shape, and be distinguish'd into their several orders and degrees. Whatever flourish'd, or was rais'd to any degree of correctness, or real perfection in the kind, was by means of GREECE alone, and in the hands of that sole polite, most civiliz'd, and accomplish'd nation.

Such opinions foretold the coming end of the Augustan age and of the dominance of the Roman poets; Shaftesbury quoted Horace himself

vos exemplaria Graeca
nocturna versate manu, versate diurna,*

----

* Make the Greek Authors your supreme Delight;
  Read them by Day, and study them by Night.

(Tr. Philip Francis, 1749.)

to show that they too attested that the renovation of the classical tradition must be sought in Greece. There, in process of time, true and correct taste had been developed, and could be defined. 'In all the principal works of *ingenuity* and *art*, SIMPLICITY and NATURE began chiefly to be sought: and this was the TASTE which lasted so many ages, till the ruin of all things, under a universal monarchy.' Until, that is, the establishment of the Roman Empire by Augustus. The rejection of contemporary taste and its replacement by Grecian simplicity—Winckelmann's 'eine edle Einfalt'—could not have been more explicitly stated.

Yet for the Augustans there was no evident superiority of Greek works of art. The Grand Tour took them to Italy, to Florence and Pisa and Rome, sometimes to Naples and the South, but not to Greece. The majority, who never got south of Rome, were not likely to question Roman pre-eminence. Besides, they knew that many of the artists and craftsmen whom Augustus and his successors had brought to beautify the imperial city were themselves Greeks, and they therefore based their judgment of Greek art on late Hellenistic marbles or on the often feeble copies of works of an earlier period which they had seen. They had no alternative. Winckelmann himself observed that there was nothing at Rome 'in the grand Greek style except the Niobe group in the Villa Medici and the Pallas in the Villa Albani'. Even one of the few who had at that time visited Greece, Sir George Wheler, dared not break with contemporary tradition by preferring the marbles he had seen there. 'I prefer them before any place in the world,' he said, 'Rome only excepted.' Nonetheless his admiration of the Parthenon, which he saw before the Venetian bombardment of 1687, is unstinted. It was, he considered, 'absolutely, both for Matter and Art, the most beautiful piece of Antiquity remaining in the World. I wish I could communicate the Pleasure I took in viewing it, by a Description that would in some proportion express the Idea I then had of it.' But that task was left to Stuart and Revett.

However, the Society of Dilettanti, which provided the funds for their visit, included among its members several young noblemen who had themselves already been to Greece. In 1738 the fourth Earl of Sandwich and the second Earl of Bessborough went there with a few friends from Italy, to prolong the Grand Tour. They took with them an artist, Jean Etienne Liotard, who was 'to take prospects of all the remarkable places which had made a figure in history; and to preserve in their memories, by the help of painting, these noble remains of antiquity which they went in quest of'. Lord Sandwich's account of his travels was not published until 1799, seven years after his death and sixty years after his visit. In 1749 the young Lord Charlemont (James, fourth Viscount Charlemont, 1728–99) went out to Greece with the future Lord Conyngham (Francis, second baron Conyngham, died 1787), accompanied, as usual, by a classical tutor, the Rev. Edward Murphy, and again by an artist, Richard Dalton, who became the first English artist to make careful drawings of the monuments, which were published in 1751; the etchings of the sculptures of the Parthenon and of the Mausoleum were, at least, better than nothing. Lord Charlemont, Lord Sandwich and Lord Bessborough were all early members of the Society of Dilettanti. No doubt Lord Charlemont, who met James Stuart and Nicholas Revett in Rome on his return from Greece, encouraged them in their ambitions both with practical advice derived from his recent experience, and by interesting other members of the Society in providing the means to their fulfilment.

Soon after Stuart and Revett reached Athens James Dawkins and Robert Wood arrived there on their way to Palmyra and Baalbek. A plate in the *Antiquities of Athens* shows the four men admiring the monument of Philopappus on the Hill of the Muses. Dawkins and Wood continued with their expedition and published the results with admirable promptness on their return, in *The Ruins of Palmyra*, 1753, and *The Ruins of Balbec*, 1757. These sites were Roman, not Greek, but they were late Roman, not Augustan, and showed evidence of an exotic, oriental taste which was certainly not in accord with English Palladianism. Wood played a leading part in formulating plans for the Society of Dilettanti's expedition of 1764–66 to Ionia, of which Revett again was a member, together with Richard Chandler, as epigraphist, and the artist William Pars. Their results were published in two more fine volumes of *Ionian Antiquities*, 1769 and 1797, which greatly extended knowledge of Greek architecture and sculpture of the classical past. They were all the more valuable because of the continuing delay in publication of *The Antiquities of Athens*, of which the remaining volumes came out in 1795, 1814 and 1830. (The fifth and last volume, published sixty-eight years after the first, was a supplement rather than a part of the original work.) The publication of these, and of other volumes relating to Paestum, Sicily and other parts of Magna Graecia, in the later years of the eighteenth century attests the enthusiasm not only for exploration of Greek sites but also for making the results known to the educated. The findings of the archaeologists were not concealed in excavation reports in learned journals addressed to fellow-scholars; they were exhibited in sumptuous, illustrated folios to which leading members of society had been invited to subscribe. If none but they could afford to pay for such expensive books, and to wait years for the receipt of books for which they had paid, that, no doubt, was a consequence of the organization of society at the time; but it would be naive to suppose that recent discoveries of the Minoan and Mycenaean civilizations are more widely known to our contemporaries, or that their paintings, pottery and jewellery are of any influence on artists of today.

Discoveries of Greek pottery in southern Italy began to accumulate in the late eighteenth century, and these soon had considerable influence on pottery and on paintings in England. Before the middle of the century only about fifty Greek vases were known, from casual finds. They were scattered in various collections, and had not been studied. Sir William Hamilton, who went out to Naples in 1764 as British envoy, remained there until 1800, and used the opportunity provided to form two superb collections of Greek vases. The first of these was bought by the British Museum in 1772, to form the nucleus of the Greek collection there. The second, and reputedly finer, collection was partly lost when the ship that was bringing it back to England was wrecked off the Isles of Scilly in 1799*; but many vases were saved, and they were bought by Thomas Hope, the author of *Anastasius* or the *Memoirs of a Modern Greek*. Of these some, at least, eventually reached the British Museum. Sir William Hamilton followed the prevailing fashion by publishing his collections, each in four sumptuous folios. The first set, published with text by D'Hancarville (Pierre François Hugues) and with engraved and hand-painted plates by various artists, was issued at Naples in 1766–67; the second set was accompanied by a text written by Hamilton himself, and the plates, for which Wilhelm Tischbein, the friend of Goethe, was responsible, consisted of 'the simple outline of the figures on the vases'. These also were published at Naples, in 1791–95. Hamilton gave credit to Winckelmann (whose *Geschichte der Kunst des Alterthums* was published in the year in which he took up residence in Naples) and to D'Hancarville for proving that the vases were Greek, and not, as had previously been supposed, Etruscan. But Hamilton was the first to appreciate their beauty, and to understand the

---

* The wreck has recently been located, and more of this collection is likely to be recovered.

influence which Greek vase-painting might have on contemporary taste. The cheaper form of plates in the second publication was intended to make them more accessible to young and impecunious artists; and Hamilton, no less than Stuart and Revett, was intent on improving the taste of his fellow-countrymen.

Hamilton was not content with the publication of the design of his Greek vases in books, however handsome, and in 1786 his nephew Charles Greville provided him with the means for a more lively representation of Greek figures. Greville had been living since 1781 with the beautiful daughter of a Cheshire blacksmith named Amy Lyon, or Emma Hart, but after four years had decided that she was becoming rather expensive. He accordingly shipped her off to Naples, which was conveniently remote from England, with a recommendation to the English Ambassador. There Sir William, who had an eye long trained in the appreciation of Grecian beauty in works of art, found in Emma the perfection of these pleasures, and he taught her to pose in a variety of attitudes. Emma had the natural capacity of a beautiful woman for exhibiting her beauty to the greatest advantage, and her 'attitudes' were much admired by the more privileged visitors to Naples. Among these was Goethe, who described his experience in 1787, some time before Emma became Lady Hamilton. Sir William, he wrote,

> has had a Greek costume made for her which becomes her extremely. Dressed in this, she lets down her hair and, with a few shawls, gives so much variety to her poses, gestures, expressions, etc., that the spectator can hardly believe his eyes. He sees what thousands of artists would have liked to express realized before him in movements and surprising transformations—standing, kneeling, sitting, reclining, serious, sad, playful, ecstatic, contrite, alluring, threatening, anxious, one pose following another without a break. She knows how to arrange the folds of her veil to match each mood, and has a hundred ways of turning it into a head-dress. The old knight idolizes her and is enthusiastic about everything she does. In her, he has found all the antiquities, all the profiles of Sicilian coins, even the Apollo Belvedere. . . . This morning Tischbein is painting her portrait.

To the painters, whether in England or in Italy, Emma was irresistible: her vivacity delighted and challenged them; her variety, shown in her attitudes, was infinite. They did not demand more, as

Goethe did: they were content to look at her and to try to record her, and if her conversation did not match her beauty, they were not listening anyhow. In the presence of one whom they could imagine as Ariadne, or Thetis, or Medea, as a Sibyl or a Bacchante, or as Hebe, there was no need to write dramatic speeches for her. As Emma herself wrote to Sir William, 'I am a pretty whoman and one can't be everything at once; but now I have my wisdom teeth I will try to be ansome and reasonable.' At her best, she was a silent figure in a classical frieze, or, posed in the black-lined, gold-framed box which Sir William had made, a figure from a fresco at Herculaneum. She was always a subject for painters rather than for poets; and she wore her Grecian clothes with the assurance of a goddess. *Vera incessu patuit dea.* When she achieved her ambition in 1791 and returned to Naples as Lady Hamilton, Horace Walpole told Miss Berry, 'Sir William Hamilton has actually married his Gallery of Statues.' The cynical urbanity of social comment was irrelevant to the artists.

Hamilton's books contributed much to the growth of Grecian taste. In June 1769 Josiah Wedgwood celebrated the opening of his new factory with its model village at Etruria in Staffordshire by painting in red encaustic enamel on a black ground figures taken from D'Hancarville's recent publication. The name that he gave to his factory shows that Wedgwood had not yet recognized the vases in Hamilton's first collection as Greek; at that time Hamilton himself was not convinced that they were. But, Etruscan or Greek, the vases were painted with scenes from Homer and the tragedians in a style whose emphasis on outline and contour seemed designed to demonstrate the truth of Winckelmann's insight. In 1755, in the *Gedanken*, when he cannot have seen more than half a dozen Greek vases, he had called precision of contour 'the characteristic distinction of the ancients. . . . This contour', he wrote, 'reigns in Greek figures, even when covered in drapery, as the chief aim of the artist.' It is yet another example of Winckelmann's temperamental sympathy with all things Hellenic.

In England Fuseli (who had translated the *Gedanken* as *Reflections on the Painting and Sculpture of the Greeks* in 1765), Flaxman, Romney, Blake and George Cumberland were all ready to respond to this Grecian emphasis on outline, both in practice and in theory. Romney found a perfect subject in Emma, whom he painted sometimes in Grecian poses from the beginning of 1782. As early as 1778 Flaxman was designing in the Grecian style for Wedgwood, and when he was in Rome ten years later he wrote to Romney, 'Excuse my vanity for telling you my drawings have surprised some of the best English artists here, who thought they were copied from the stories on Greek vases.' So, a few years later, they were. In the 1790s he began to publish the series of volumes of engravings after outline drawings in illustration of Homer, Hesiod, Aeschylus and Dante, which were to bring him a European fame. Ingres kept his drawing of 'Prometheus visited by the Oceanides' in a prominent place in his studio in Paris, and David also made use of Flaxman's designs. The publication of Sir William Hamilton's second collection provided fresh inspiration to Flaxman, and some of his illustrations to the *Odyssey* derive from these volumes. For the English edition the engravings were done by Flaxman's friend, William Blake.

In 1796, another member of their circle, George Cumberland, published his *Thoughts on Outline* with outline drawings of scenes from Greek and Latin poetry. In this he criticized Tischbein's recently published illustrations of Hamilton's vases for using lines of unequal thickness. 'The best line I take to be that which is *fine, firm, flowing*, and *faint*, such as was used by that great man Lionardo da Vinci, and that still greater Raffael.' Blake studied his illustrations 'just as if they were antiques', he told him, and two or three years later declared that 'the purpose for which alone I live . . . is, in conjunction with such men as my friend Cumberland, to renew the lost art of the Greeks.'

Many English artists of the eighteenth century visited Italy, and a few, notably Richard Dalton, James Stuart and William Pars, went on to Greece itself. But of the English poets of the later eighteenth century only Gray and Goldsmith visited Italy, and none went to Greece until Byron led the way. Gray was in southern Italy before the new Grecian taste had begun to displace the Augustan in which he had been nurtured, and, in spite of his experiments in the Pindaric ode, Gray remained an Augustan. Goldsmith was in Italy in 1755, the year of the publication of Winckelmann's *Gedanken*, but he never reached the south, and he was too poor to have much leisure for sight-seeing: he had to earn his keep by playing the flute. His response to Italy was rather to its contemporary decadent society than to the monuments of the past, and though he probably agreed with Dr Johnson that 'a man who has not been in Italy, is always conscious of an inferioity, from his not having seen what it is expected a man should see', we do not know how far he was able to fulfil that expectation.

No English writer of the eighteenth century shared Goethe's experience of Paestum and of Sicily, the experience of conversion in the presence of Greek temples from the Palladian to the Doric, from Augustan taste to Grecian. When Goethe saw the temples of Paestum on his way south from Rome in March 1787,

> At first sight they excited nothing but stupefaction. . . . Our eyes and, through them, our whole sensibility have become so conditioned to a more slender style of architecture that these crowded masses of stumpy conical columns appear offensive and even terrifying. But . . . in less than an hour I found myself reconciled to them and even thanking my guardian angel for having allowed me to see these well-preserved remains with my own eyes.

This conversion was confirmed by his experience of Sicily, and on his way back he stopped again at Paestum. He wrote next day to Herder, 'There is nothing else I want to see in the south, especially since yesterday, when I revisited Paestum, the last vision I shall take with me on my way north, and perhaps the greatest.' Some thirty years later Shelley, after visiting Pompeii in January 1819, described a similar illumination in a letter to Peacock.

> I now understand why the Greeks were such great Poets, and above all I can account, it seems to me, for the harmony, the unity, the perfection, the uniform excellence of all their works of art. They lived in a perpetual commerce with external nature and nourished themselves upon the spirit of its forms. Their theatres were all open to the mountains and the sky. Their columns that ideal type of a sacred forest with its roof of interwoven tracery admitted the light and wind; the odour and the freshness of the country penetrated the cities. Their temples were mostly upaithric* and the flying clouds, the stars or the deep sky were seen above.

A month later he visited Paestum, and again described the scene to Peacock. 'At length we saw the sublime and massy colonnades skirting the horizon of the wilderness. . . . The effect of the jagged outline of mountains through groupes of enormous columns on one side, and on the other the level horizon of the sea is inexpressibly grand.' But Shelley, like Goethe, was somewhat surprised by the massive proportions of the Doric columns, and by the 'exceedingly

---

* Upaithric (ὑπαίθριος, -ρος) 'open to the air' seems to have been a coinage of Peacock, who used it (hypaethric) in *Rhododaphne*, 1818.

unornamented and simple architecture', which led him to speculate
on the cause of the visual effect of the Doric columns.

> But for the chastening effect of their admirable proportions their
> magnitude would from the delusion of perspective seem greater
> not less than it is; though perhaps we ought to say not that this
> symmetry diminishes your apprehension of their magnitude, but
> that it overpowers the idea of relative greatness, by establishing
> within itself a system of relations destructive of your idea of its
> relations with other objects, on which our ideas of size depend.

To this effect of self-contained, independent unity Shelley thus
attributed the power of a Greek temple to impress the beholder
without relation to any context other than the natural one of sea and
sky and mountain. Greek temples are not placed in an architectural
context of street or square. Thus was the predominantly Roman
classical tradition of the Renaissance, which had been purified of
seventeenth century accretions by the Augustans, revitalized by the
rediscovery of Greek monuments in the later years of the eighteenth
century.

Both Goethe and Shelley had read Winckelmann's work. Goethe,
at the age of nineteen, was looking forward to meeting Winckelmann
at Leipzig in 1768, but Winckelmann, who had only with the greatest
reluctance dragged himself away from Italy to visit Germany after an
absence of thirteen years, soon repented, and insisted on cutting short
his tour. At Trieste, on his way back to Rome, he was murdered, and
the momentous meeting never took place. Probably it would have
made little difference, for Goethe recognized the nature of his debt to
Winckelmann when he said to Eckermann, 'One learns nothing from
him, but one becomes something.' A meeting could hardly have
effected more. Walter Pater (who quotes this remark in his essay on
Winckelmann) sums up the relationship of these two minds when he
says that 'Winckelmann became to Goethe something like what
Virgil was to Dante,' a creature of imaginative myth rather than of
flesh and blood. He was the guide who led Goethe through the maze
of life as it presented itself to a complex and versatile imagination
which could respond to so many phases of taste, 'a reliable thread,' in
Goethe's words, 'to guide us through the various epochs of art.'
Winckelmann's single-minded dedication to the culture of classical
Greece, in which he isolated the essential qualities of simplicity and
calm, gave a coherence to his imaginative vision which might

otherwise have eluded Goethe. 'For Goethe', said Pater, 'possessing all modern interests, ready to be lost in the perplexed currents of modern thought, he defines, in clearest outline, the eternal problem of culture—balance, unity with one's self, consummate Greek modelling.' Both Goethe and Winckelmann were in rebellion against the taste of the earlier eighteenth century, Winckelmann because of the emphasis on Roman, and therefore derivative, classicism, Goethe because of the suppression of feeling in favour of form. Winckelmann taught Goethe, as he taught so many, to look to Greece for renewal. The conversion which the temples of Paestum brought about could not have happened if Winckelmann, by his prophetic writings, had not prepared the way. There the Romantic poet of *Sturm und Drang* was subjected to the purifying and reasonable spirit of Hellenism, and turned from his earlier concern with subjective self-revelation towards objective standards of beauty. The paintings of Henry Fuseli, which had so strong an appeal to him before the Italian journey, now seemed but 'the self-parody of a manneristic genius'. Goethe had come to realize that the worth of a painting or sculpture derived not from the imposition by the artist of a personal, idiosyncratic vision, but from his revelation of the underlying natural order. In this he was accepting the beliefs which had inspired the artists of Greece and of the Italian Renaissance. 'Like Nature,' he wrote, 'Raphael is always right.'

This recognition of the supremacy of Raphael is common to all the writers of the neo-classical movement. It would then have seemed as absurd to question his unchallengeable reputation among painters as, in the Renaissance, to question Virgil's supremacy among poets. William Hayley in his *Essay on Painting*, addressed to George Romney, described painting as culminating in the work of Raphael, 'who shines the finish'd Virgil of his art'. Shelley, in a letter to Leigh Hunt, declared, 'I agree with the whole world in thinking Raphael the finest painter,' and he rejected the Romantic tendency to bring Michelangelo into comparison. When Goethe was in Bologna he saw the 'St Cecilia': 'My eyes confirmed what I have always known: this man accomplished what others could only dream of.' And he was led to think of Raphael as the consummate artist to whose achievement many predecessors had contributed.

One must consider his ancestors, his masters. These were rooted in the firm ground of truth; it was their labour and scrupulous care which laid the broad foundation; it was they who vied with each other in raising, step by step, the pyramid, on the summit of which the divine genius of Raphael was to place the last stone and reach a height which no one else will surpass or equal.

Thirty years later Shelley stood before the same picture. 'You forget that it is a picture as you look at it,' he wrote to Peacock,

> and yet it is most unlike any of those things which we call reality. It is of the inspired and ideal kind, and seems to have been conceived and executed in a similar state of feeling to that which produced among the ancients those perfect specimens of poetry and sculpture which are the baffling models of succeeding generations. There is a unity and perfection in it of an incommunicable kind.

The paintings of Raphael have continued to give pleasure throughout many changes in aesthetic preference; it is an accepted proof of an artist's greatness that he should appeal always and everywhere to everyone. But it is worth inquiring, to what aspects of his universal genius neo-classical critics and painters especially responded, and why they unhesitatingly placed him above all other painters. Goethe and Shelley, no doubt, enjoyed paintings with so obvious a literary content, paintings which often seem to invite description in literary terms—the 'Disputa', the 'School of Athens', the 'Parnassus' in the Vatican, the 'Triumph of Galatea' in the Villa Farnesina, the 'Dream of Scipio' in the National Gallery. This is partly because Raphael's source often is literary; as Pope-Hennessy says, 'there is a consistent literary propulsion behind Raphael's world of forms,' and the 'Galatea' illustrates Politian's *Stanze per la Giostra*. Besides, Raphael himself was a poet. He is, in Berenson's terms, the great Illustrator, the painter who most of all invites our attention to the representative part in his pictures, the subject matter, rather than to the presentative part, the style and technique. More than any other painter he succeeds in the Renaissance ideal of concealing his artistry, at least from those who are not themselves painters. Blake indignantly wrote in the margin of Reynolds' sixth discourse, 'He who does not admire Rafael's execution cannot admire Rafael,' but that is the comment of the painter, rather than of the poet.

In his choice of subject Raphael is most of all influenced by the ancient world of Greece. Winckelmann believed that Raphael 'sent young artists to Greece, to copy there, for his use, the remains of antiquity', and certainly, during his last years in Rome, he was intent on recording the remains of the ancient city before they were destroyed, and of preserving what he could. He, more than any other, created the visual myth of antiquity, especially of Greece, and so persuasively that we can no more visualize fifth century Athens in terms other than his than we can imagine the medieval history of England in terms other than Shakespeare's. Even when Raphael chose to illustrate the Hebraic world of the Old and New Testaments he did so in the same terms. To quote Berenson again, 'imperturbably Hellenic in spirit, he has given an Hellenic garb to the Hebraic universe.' This too had its appeal to the neo-classical imagination, for more than any other painter he could fulfil the requirement that a work of art should sustain the comparison with antiquity, that, judged by standards derived from the classical art of the Greeks, it should not be found wanting. Whether such a requirement could be justified was never considered; it was taken for granted.

The phrase, 'belle comme une madonne de Raphael', became then an accepted hyperbolical compliment in France, and so it remains. But this proverbial phrase implies an un-Romantic principle of judgment in aesthetic taste. Diderot, defining *Génie* in the *Encyclopédie*, wrote, 'For something to be beautiful according to the rules of taste, it must be elegant, finished, studied, without showing it: to be of genius it must sometimes be careless and have an irregular, rugged, savage air.' Raphael's paintings had beauty so defined; Michelangelo's work revealed genius—so much of it is unfinished that *il non finito michelangiolesco* has become a stock phrase. So the Romantics tended to exalt Michelangelo, with his very unclassical manner, above Raphael, to the amazement of those who had been nurtured in neo-classicism. Shelley may speak for them all. 'With respect to Michelangelo,' he wrote to Leigh Hunt,

> I think with astonishment and indignation on the common notion that he equals and in some respects exceeds Raphael. He seems to me to have no sense of moral dignity and loveliness; and the *energy* for which he has been so much praised appears to me to be a certain rude, external, mechanical quality in comparison with anything possessed by Raphael.

The difference had been recognized in their own day, when the two men were famous rivals. Michelangelo 'claimed that his own works were the product of a sublime intuitive faculty in which reason played little part, whereas Raphael had his art not from nature but from long study'.

Raphael's powerful intellect concentrated on the ideal, but his apprehension was assisted by his sensitive response to physical beauty. In the famous letter which he wrote to Castiglione at the time when he was considering the 'Galatea' for the Farnesina he said, 'In order to paint a beautiful woman I should have to see many beautiful women, and this on condition that you would help me with making a choice; but since there are so few beautiful women and so few sound judges, I make use of a certain idea that comes into my head.' In this, whether consciously or not, he was accepting arguments used by Proclus and St Augustine to rebut Plato's objection to works of art for being at two removes from reality, an imitation of an imitation. Art, Proclus said, does not imitate objects in the world of appearances but in the world of ideas; it therefore exhibits to man's sense of sight the intellectual order that supports and controls the natural world. This concept of ideal, or intellectual, beauty was of paramount importance to the artists and writers of the age of neo-classicism, who traced its origin back to Periclean Athens and the contemporaries of Plato.

Among these was the painter Zeuxis (who figures in Plato's *Protagoras*): he received a commission to paint a picture of Helen of Troy for the temple of Hera Lacinia at Croton. Homer had never described Helen's beauty except indirectly, by recording the wondering comment of the old men on the walls of Troy when they saw her passing by. But the challenge to a painter could not thus be evaded. Zeuxis therefore sent for the most beautiful girls of Croton and chose five to serve as models. From these he selected those forms which came nearest to the imagined perfection of Helen's beauty. Raphael doubtless knew the story from Cicero's *De Inventione*, or from Pliny, and clearly his method followed the precept of Zeuxis.

In the Salon of 1789 François-André Vincent exhibited a painting of Zeuxis choosing the models for his Helen. The painter is shown seated before his canvas while the girls parade before him; on the canvas he has drawn the outline of his subject in the manner of a Greek vase-painter. The painting therefore shows a celebrated Greek painter's twofold response, to the ideal beauty of his imagination, suggested by the outline drawing, and to the actual beauty of the girls of Croton; but the dominance of the ideal is shown by the distress of models whom the painter has rejected.

Canova also sought to portray Helen of Troy—the subject was inevitably a favourite with neo-classical artists—and he executed two busts. The first, carved in 1812, he presented to a Greek lady, Contessa Albrizzi by her marriage to a Venetian nobleman, but born the daughter of a Corfiote of ancient family, Antonio Teotochi. Byron knew her, and in the autumn of 1816 saw Canova's 'Helen' in her house in Venice. He told John Murray he thought it 'without exception . . . the most perfectly beautiful of human conceptions, and far beyond my ideas of human execution'. And he wrote an epigram on the bust which well conveys the neo-classical attitude to ideal beauty.

> In this beloved marble view
>   Above the works and thoughts of Man,
> What Nature *could*, but *would not*, do,
>   And Beauty and Canova *can!*
> Beyond Imagination's power,
>   Beyond the Bard's defeated art,
> With Immortality her dower,
>   Behold the Helen of the heart!

The artists and writers of the age of neo-classicism, turning, as always, to the authority of the Greeks, had no difficulty in showing that they had been concerned with ideal beauty, τὸ καλόν, and the Greek practice was confirmed by that of Raphael. Winckelmann, in the *History of Ancient Art*, defined the term. 'The shape of beauty.' he wrote, 'is either *individual*,—that is, confined to an imitation of one individual,—or it is a selection of beautiful parts from many individuals and their union into one, which we call *ideal*. . . . The ancients purified their images from all personal feelings, by which the mind is diverted from the truly beautiful.' This we see in Vincent's painting, which shows Zeuxis disregarding the personal in his concentration on the ideal. To later, Romantic, taste this rejection of personal feeling would seem frigid.

When Shelley was in Florence in the winter of 1819–20 he decided to study the works of art in the galleries of the Uffizi, 'one of my chief aims in Italy,' he told Maria Gisborne, 'being the observing in statuary and painting the degree in which, and the rules according to which, that ideal beauty of which we have so intense yet so obscure an apprehension is realized in external forms'. He kept to his intention, spending every sunny day in the Uffizi, and there he wrote the *Notes* on the sculptures which he saw. When Thomas Medwin first published a few of these in 1833 he compared Shelley's appreciations to Winckelmann's. Shelley wrote only on sculpture, which he preferred to painting, as did most of those who were influenced by the Grecian taste. When in his letters he refers to paintings, as he not infrequently does, he disclaims any ability to respond to colour. Thus, of a painting by Correggio which he saw in Bologna, he says, 'The colouring, I suppose, must be very good if I can remark and understand it;' and of Raphael's 'St Cecilia' there, 'Of the colouring I do not speak, it eclipses nature, yet it has all its truth and softness.' This, too, was in the tradition of neo-classicism. Shaftesbury had regarded colour as subsidiary to design in painting, so that the pleasure derived from it was 'plainly foreign and *separate*, as having no concern or share in the proper delight or entertainment'. Winckelmann followed Shaftesbury in this too: 'Colour assists beauty;' he wrote, 'generally, it heightens beauty and its forms, but it does not constitute it. . . . Colour should have but little share in our consideration of beauty, because the essence of beauty consists, not in colour, but in shape.' Blake's fierce condemnation of the Venetian school and of Rubens derives from their emphasis on colour. 'Why should Titian and the Venetians be named in a discourse on art?' he wrote in the margin of Reynolds' fourth discourse. 'Such idiots are not artists.

> Venetian, all thy colouring is no more
> Than boulster'd plasters on a crooked whore.'

And of Rubens: 'To my eye Rubens's colouring is most con-temptible. His shadows are of a filthy brown somewhat of the colour of excrement; these are fill'd with tints and messes of yellow and red.' He gives his reasons for ascribing 'vulgar stupidity' to the work of Titian: 'The word Elegance ought to be applied to forms, not to colours.' ('Elegance' was the first of the qualities named by Diderot 'for something to be beautiful according to the rules of taste'.) Blake's marginalia confirm his devotion to Grecian taste.

Hostile as most of Blake's jottings are to Sir Joshua, there are occasions when he finds cause for rejoicing, as when Reynolds insists on the importance of outline, or when he writes of ideal beauty. In the Ninth Discourse Reynolds gave the clearest account of what he understood by the phrase.

> The art which we profess has beauty for its object; this it is our business to discover and to express; but the beauty of which we are

in quest is general and intellectual; it is an idea that subsists only in the mind; the sight never beheld it nor has the hand expressed it; it is an idea residing in the breast of the artist, which he is always labouring to impart, and which he dies at last without imparting.

This passage was not included in the edition of the *Discourses* which Blake used, but he would have approved it. He did not annotate the passage on ideal beauty in the Third Discourse, where Reynolds quotes Proclus. The same view of artistic creation is shared by Shelley who, in the *Defence of Poetry*, wrote, 'When composition begins, inspiration is already on the decline, and the most glorious poetry that has ever been communicated to the world is probably a feeble shadow of the original conceptions of the poet.' The derivation of Romantic notions of inspiration from the neo-classical concern with ideal beauty is apparent. 'Knowledge of ideal beauty,' wrote Blake, 'is not to be acquired. It is born with us.'

James Barry, a painter whose work Blake much admired, considered that the Greeks owed their rapid progress towards perfection in art to their concentration on ideal beauty. He was one of those who argued for the foundation of a National Gallery which should contain a collection of 'Grecian examples of art' and thereby 'contribute equally to direct the studies of our young artists, and to invigorate and perfect the taste of the public'. William Hayley, to whom Blake owed his three peaceful years at Felpham as well as many commissions, addressed to John Flaxman a poetical *Essay on Sculpture*. (Blake, whom Flaxman had introduced to Hayley, engraved the plates for this *Essay*.) There, in his tribute to Flaxman Hayley writes,

> Thou, by impassion'd Toil's repeated touch,
> For thy dear England may'st achieve as much
> As ever Grecian hand for Greece achiev'd,
> When hands gave life to all the soul conceiv'd.

This is the pure doctrine of Winckelmann, whose work Hayley frequently quotes, and whom he addresses in the fifth epistle of the *Essay on Sculpture*. He is perhaps the first English man of letters to quote from the *History of Ancient Art*. And Flaxman, whose outline drawings of Greek subjects are the quintessence of neo-classicism, spoke, in his *Lectures on Sculpture* to the Royal Academy, of the Ideal Style, which he defined thus: 'a representation of the human form, according to the distinctions of sex and age, in action or repose, expressing the affections of the soul, selected from such perfect examples as may excite in our minds a conception of the supernatural.' He too refers to the work of Winckelmann, by whom he was much influenced.

Perhaps the clearest evidence that the concept of ideal beauty in art and literature was a favourite topic of conversation in early nineteenth century society is provided by Peacock. He directs his irony at misunderstandings of the Greek idea, not at the idea itself. In the library at Crotchet Castle that successful tycoon, Mr Crotchet, eager as such persons always are to assert his fashionable taste, has recently assembled a collection of statues of Venus. The Rev. Dr Folliott is somewhat astonished by the display of nudes, and disposed to remonstrate; but his host is unabashed. He has learnt the accepted patter: 'Sir,' he says, 'the naked figure is the Pandemian Venus, and the half-draped figure is the Uranian Venus; and I say, sir, that figure realizes the finest imaginings of Plato, and is the personification of the most refined and exalted feeling of which the human mind is susceptible; the love of pure, ideal, intellectual beauty.' Nearly thirty years later, in *Gryll Grange*, Peacock reverted to the theme of ideal beauty, this time in the context of the revival of Catholic forms of worship. Mr Falconer acknowledges a special devotion to St Catharine of Alexandria. She 'presents to my mind,' he tells the Rev. Dr Opimian, 'the most perfect ideality of physical, moral and intellectual beauty.' Such devotion Dr Opimian admits to be harmless; 'it is one of the many forms of the love of ideal beauty, which, without being in itself religion, exerts on vivid imaginations an influence that is very often like it.' But by the time when Peacock wrote his last novel the Grecian taste of his youth had been transformed; and though Greek might seem 'to be the strongest chord in young Falconer's sympathies', there were many others, whose admixture makes him less representative of Grecian taste in its purity than his elders, Dr Opimian, or even Mr Crotchet.

2 Mark Akenside (1721—70)

To my compatriot youth
I point the high example of thy sons,
And tune to Attic themes the British lyre.

'Invocation to the Genius of Ancient Greece',
The Pleasures of Imagination, I, 602—604

The earliest portrayal that we possess of the author of *The Pleasures of Imagination* is in Smollett's *Peregrine Pickle*, which was published in 1751, seven years after Akenside's poem. Both men were doctors and both had their training at Scottish universities, Smollett at Glasgow and Akenside at Edinburgh; and they were born in the same year. Smollett may have been envious of Akenside's precocious success, or he may have resented some disparagement of the Scots to which Akenside had given utterance, for he had the assertive pride of a Scotsman in conflict with an Englishman. His portrait of Akenside is a caricature, but with the revealing emphasis of a master in that art who could identify and describe the essential features of his subject. He saw in Akenside 'a young man, in whose air and countenance appeared all the uncouth gravity and supercilious self-conceit of a physician piping hot from his studies'. The physician who was, in the opinion of his companion the painter, Mr Pallet (who represents Hogarth), 'a man of vast learning, and beyond all doubt, the greatest poet of the age', proceeded to demonstrate his learning with a catalogue of Greek artists. This astonished and confounded Mr Pallet, who at length 'in emphatic silence adored the immensity of his friend's understanding'. The physician 'canvassed the whole scheme of Plato's republic, with many quotations from that ideal author; touching the τò καλόν: from thence he made a transition to the moral sense of Shaftsbury, and concluded his harangue with the greatest part of that frothy writer's rhapsody', that is, with Shaftesbury's *The Moralists, a Philosophical Rhapsody*.

This identification of the chief influence on Akenside's mind with the philosophies of Plato and of Lord Shaftesbury is valid, and the doctor continues, throughout the episodes in which he takes part, to exhibit his dedication to the culture of ancient Greece. He praises Attic drama in general, and Sophocles in particular; he sings, when drunk after a banquet which he had contrived in the manner of the ancients, 'divers odes of Anacreon to a tune of his own composing'; he quotes Pindar when he confronts Mr Pallet in a duel, and again in triumph over his defeat; he quotes, or rather, misquotes Thucydides on the siege of Plataea; and he lauds Athenian democracy when he hears that Pickle and Pallet have been haled off to the Bastille. He hopes that they 'will fall a sacrifice to lawless tyranny' that so, in vengeance, revolution may ensue and restore 'that liberty which is the birth-right of man'. He has begun an ode in their praise 'illustrated with quotations from the Greek writers' when, to his chagrin, they are released from imprisonment and the opportunity of martyrdom. Akenside's political opinions, which Smollett derided, Dr Johnson deplored; but they are representative of the neo-classical movement as we see it in the paintings of David. 'The ties of private affection were too weak to engage the heart of this republican, whose zeal for the community had entirely swallowed up his concern for individuals.' Such is Smollett's final comment on the doctor's character: it makes him sound very like a man of our own day. Yet, through some quirk of fashion, Smollett's novel, which was not a notable success when published, is available now in a cheap edition, while Akenside's poem, which was much admired in the eighteenth century, has not been reprinted in the twentieth.

Mark Akenside was born on 9 November 1721, some eight months after Smollett and seven weeks before William Collins. His father was a butcher in Newcastle-upon-Tyne and his mother also was of Northumberland: no doubt that disparagement of the Scots which irritated Smollett was bred into the son. When he was seven years old and was playing in his father's shop a cleaver fell on his foot and lamed him; in later life he resented this constant reminder of his father's trade no less than the physical inconvenience. For he very early showed those literary gifts which were to exalt him above a sirloin of beef when, in 1737, *The Gentleman's Magazine* published his Spenserian imitation *The Virtuoso* in April, a fable entitled *Ambition and Content* in May, and in July *The Poet, A Rhapsody*. These contributions from a fifteen year old schoolboy have more of interest in them than mere precocity, and the son of a North country butcher can have had no advantage other than literary merit with which to attract the attention of the editor of the leading journal of the time. In

August 1738 *The Gentleman's Magazine* printed an ardent piece of patriotism, *A British Philippic*, and in October of the next year it printed his *Hymn to Science*. These early verses already declared the chief preoccupations of his maturity, in poetry, science, politics, and taste.

By the age of eighteen therefore Akenside had established a reputation in Newcastle, and the Dissenters Society subscribed to send him to the University of Edinburgh, there to train for the ministry. This must have seemed the obvious career for a gifted youth, and both Akenside's parents were dissenters. But he soon discovered that he had no ambition that way, repaid the money which he had received, and turned to the study of medicine. His early success had clearly not spoilt him or hindered him from attaining the mature self-knowledge which led to this change of plan. The notice which his abilities as a speaker at the meetings of the Medical Society of Edinburgh soon attracted led him, for a time, to be ambitious of a political career, as other young men have been on the tenuous assurance of success in a university debating society. But Akenside was to make his living as a doctor, and, in spite of a reputation for being harsh and rough with his poorer patients at St Thomas's, where he became principal physician, he attained the distinctions of election to a Fellowship of the Royal Society in 1753 and to a Fellowship of the Royal College of Physicians in the following year, both before he had reached his thirty-third birthday. Before the Royal College he delivered the Gulstonian lectures in 1755 and next year the Croonian lectures. The former* were printed in the *Philosophical Transactions of the Royal Society for 1757*, but the latter have not been printed, perhaps because a physician chose to address an audience of medical men on so unprofessional a topic as *The Revival of Learning*. Yet the views of a poet who played a significant part in the revival of Greek learning in the eighteenth century would be of considerable interest. Besides, this choice of subject for the Croonian lectures asserts, with characteristic forthrightness, a preference for literature over science which derived not from ignorance of the one but from a comprehensive understanding of the aims and methods of both.

Akenside had the intellectual energy of a man of genius, which allowed him to continue his literary studies at the same time as he trained for, and pursued, a career in medicine. In addition to his Greek and Latin he was deeply interested in the philosophical thought of

---

* *Observations on the Origin and Use of the Lymphatic Vessels of Animals*

the time, especially in the field of aesthetics. Here Shaftesbury's *Characteristicks* was the primary influence, supplemented by the work of two of his followers, Addison's *Spectator* papers of 1712 on *Taste and the Pleasures of Imagination*, and Francis Hutcheson's *Inquiry into the Original of our Ideas of Beauty and Virtue*, 1725, and also his *Thoughts on Laughter*, 1725–27. These works developed suggestions originally made by Shaftesbury and together with the *Characteristicks* provided the source of the ideas explored in *The Pleasures of Imagination*. But Akenside was not, like Henry More of Cambridge, a philosopher who preferred the medium of verse; he was a poet whose principal interest was in the nature of aesthetic experience, both of creation and of appreciation. (Collins, Blake, and Shelley shared this interest, and wrote much about it.) Even in his earliest poems Akenside had shown a remarkable command of poetic form, in the Spenserian stanza (in which he preceded Thomson and Shenstone), in the heroic couplet, and in blank verse. Dr Johnson, indeed, was to observe, in his *Life of Akenside*, that 'in the general fabrication of his lines he is perhaps superior to any other writer of blank verse', and though he qualified this comment by remarking that 'the concatenation of his verses is commonly too long continued', this was, nonetheless, generous praise of a poet whose political opinions he detested. And when, late in 1743, Akenside took the manuscript of *The Pleasures of Imagination* to Dodsley, and asked £120 for it of the famous publisher, Pope advised Dodsley to accept the offer, 'for this is no everyday writer'.

Now one of the chief concerns of Shaftesbury had been to restore to poetry and the arts a freedom from the limitations imposed by empiricism. Like Sir Thomas Browne he saw nature as the Art of God; not as a mechanistic universe to be exploited for man's use, but as something worthy to be contemplated for its own sake. Man's artistic activity therefore was not mechanical construction but creation. And in a famous passage he distinguished the true poet from the false.

> I must confess there is hardly any where to be found a more insipid race of mortals, than those whom we moderns are contented to call *poets*, for having attain'd the chiming faculty of a language, with an injudicious random use of wit and fancy. But for the man, who truly and in a just sense deserves the name of *poet*, and who as a real master, or architect in the kind, can describe both *men* and *manners*, and give to an *action* its just body and proportions, he will be found,

if I mistake not, a very different creature. Such a *Poet* is indeed a second *maker*: a just PROMETHEUS under JOVE. Like that sovereign artist or universal plastick nature, he forms *a whole* coherent and proportion'd in it-self, with the subjection and subordinacy of constituent parts.

What was more likely to attract the attention of an aspiring poet at this time than the celebrated philosopher's *Advice to an Author*, from which this passage is taken? Besides, in his search for a philosophy which would counter the empiricists and provide a rational basis for aesthetic judgment, Shaftesbury had been driven to the Platonism of seventeenth century Cambridge, and beyond this to Plato himself, whom long before Sir Philip Sidney (also seeking to define the true poet) had described as 'of all philosophers the most poetical'. In this Shaftesbury was reacting against the teaching of his Oxford tutor, John Locke, whose intellectual power he could not match, but whose sensibility he called in question. Akenside, no less than Thomson, was conscious of a need to reconcile the philosophies of Locke and Shaftesbury, for both poets had a lively understanding of the scientific thought of the time. One of Akenside's earliest poems had been a *Hymn to Science*; and Thomson's *Seasons* constantly discloses an interest in science which his poem *To the Memory of Sir Isaac Newton* admirably confirms.

The philosophical relation of beauty and truth is the chief subject of the first book of *The Pleasures of Imagination*, in which Akenside's conclusion that

> truth and good are one
> And beauty dwells in them, and they in her,

may sound, at first, perilously close to Keats' sentimental identification of beauty and truth. But whereas Keats reached this judgment by rejecting the claim of science to truth, in order to assert that of imagination alone, Akenside would accept both. In his ode to Dr Caleb Harding this is the concluding stanza:

> Oh! reared in all the human frame,
> Lead thou where'er my labour lies,
> And English fancy's eager flame
> To Julian purity chastise:
> While hand in hand at Wisdom's shrine

Beauty with Truth I strive to join,
And grave assent with glad applause,
To paint the story of the soul,
And Plato's visions to control
By Verulamian Laws.

To Keats, as to Blake, Verulamian Laws, the empirical philosophy of
Bacon, Locke and Newton (Blake's infernal trinity), were destructive
of poetry. So indeed they had seemed in Locke's day when a
mechanistic view of Nature had deprived it of all possibilities for
poetry. And on a famous occasion in Haydon's studio Keats (who
may have been sober) and Lamb (who was not) agreed that Newton
'had destroyed all the poetry of the rainbow by reducing it to the
prismatic colours', and then drank the toast of 'Newton's health, and
confusion to mathematics'. But for Akenside,

Nor ever yet
The melting rainbow's vernal-tinctured hues
To me have shown so pleasing, as when first
The hand of Science pointed out the path
In which the sunbeams, gleaming from the West
Fall on the watery cloud, whose darksome veil
Involves the orient.
[*Pleasures of Imagination* II. 103–09.]

He goes on to expound Newton's hypothesis in a passage whose
excessive length must testify to his sincerity. Shelley, who was to
make far greater poetry out of precise meteorological observation,
would have agreed with Akenside, not with Keats and Lamb, for he
shared with Akenside a first-hand knowledge of Greek thought,
especially of Plato. Nor would he have spurned Akenside's wish to
control Plato's visions by the laws of Bacon's new philosophy, for to
him both Plato and Bacon deserved the name of poet.

In *The Pleasures of Imagination* Akenside is more concerned with
imagination as the faculty by which we appreciate beauty in the
natural world or in works of art than with the power of imagination
to create these works, as indeed the title of his poem suggests. He takes
the poet's creative power for granted: works of art clearly exist, and
the question that interests him is, how do we form a rational
judgment of them to which we may expect assent. Dryden had led
the way when he first defined criticism as 'a standard of judging well;

the chiefest part of which is to observe those excellences which should delight a reasonable reader'. In the prefatory essay on the design of his poem Akenside says that the powers of imagination 'like the external senses . . . relate to matter and motion, and, at the same time, give the mind ideas analogous to those of moral approbation and dislike'. Imagination occupies a middle ground between sense-perception and the understanding, and our appreciation of beauty is comparable to our recognition of moral excellence, especially in its immediacy. Francis Hutcheson stated this view succinctly, at the beginning of his *Inquiry*. 'This superior Power of Perception' he wrote,

> is justly called *a Sense*, because of its Affinity to the other Senses in this, that the Pleasure does not arise from any knowledge of Principle, Proportions, Causes, or of the Usefulness of the Object; but strikes us at first with the Idea of Beauty: nor does the most accurate knowledge increase this measure of Beauty, however it may superadd a distinct rational Pleasure from prospects of Advantage, or from the Increase of Knowledge.

This was an attempt to come to terms with the observed facts of aesthetic experience, in which our immediate delight in a beautiful painting or sculpture, or in a beautiful human face or figure, precedes, though it may be supplemented by, rational analysis into mathematical proportion or relationship of parts. Frequent attempts at such analysis had been made during the Renaissance, through discussion of the golden section, of Vitruvian man. But as Sir Henry Wotton had then observed, the power of proportion is secret: the visitor to Wilton House will respond to the beauty of the double cube room without being aware that Inigo Jones so designed it, for the eye cannot detect a double cube. Our awareness of its beauty is not suspended until we have measured it with a foot-rule; and the mathematical basis of the design is irrelevant to our aesthetic response. It seems therefore that we have an aesthetic sense analogous to Shaftesbury's 'moral sense', and, since a man who is blind and deaf from birth can have no appreciation of works of art, this 'sense' is properly so called.

Akenside concludes the first book of *The Pleasures of Imagination* with an invocation:

> Genius of ancient Greece! whose faithful steps,
> Well pleased, I follow through the sacred paths

> Of Nature and of Science; nurse divine
> Of all heroic deeds and fair desires!

And he asks for the guidance of the Genius of Greece throughout his ambitious poem,

> while far above the flight
> Of Fancy's plume aspiring, I unlock
> The springs of ancient wisdom: while I join
> Thy name, thrice honoured, with the immortal praise
> Of Nature; while, to my compatriot youth,
> I point the high example of thy sons,
> And tune to Attic themes the British lyre.

This conclusion develops logically from the rest of the first book, which had begun with the optimistic view of a harmonious Nature held by Shaftesbury. This in turn drew its philosophical authority from Plato's theory of functional form: the beauty of an object derives from its fitness for the purpose for which it was designed. The word used by Plato to designate this fitness, ἀρετή, was also the word for moral excellence or virtue, and it is part of Akenside's purpose to show that the imagination is the faculty by which we apprehend the good, as well as the beautiful and the true.

The original act of creation which gave material form to divine intent arose when God

> deep retired
> In his unfathomed essence, viewed at large
> The uncreated images of things,

that is, when he contemplated the Platonic ideas of sun and moon, of mountains, woods and streams,

> And all the fair variety of things.

But the imaginative power which is the privilege of a few enables them to perceive and appreciate beauty, which is

> The lovely ministress of Truth and Good.

In a long note to this passage Akenside quotes from Xenophon's *Memorabilia Socratis*.

'Do you imagine,' says Socrates to Aristippus, 'that what is good is not also beautiful? Have you not observed that these appearances always coincide? Virtue*, for instance, in the same respect as to which we call it good is ever acknowledged to be beautiful also. In the characters of men we always join the two denominations together,' in the words καλοκάγαθος and καλοκαγάθια.

And Akenside notes the elaboration of Xenophon's words by 'the noble restorer of ancient philosophy', Shaftesbury, and by 'his most ingenious disciple', Hutcheson.

He then describes with candour the current disputes about taste: whether our perception of beauty is entirely subjective, or whether it is reasonable, and objective; whether beauty lies only in the eye of the beholder or whether, when we say 'This is beautiful' we are entitled to the assent of reasonable men. Beauty alone is suspect as the instigator of a feeling of pleasure, but since it is truth 'whose dictates bind assenting reason', beauty must be shown to convey truth before we can describe it as reasonable. The subjective view Akenside associates with Gothic superstition; but the idea of beauty as a partner with truth he derives from Grecian wisdom.

One effect of this attempt to establish appreciation on a rational basis was the emphasis given to form and composition rather than to colour, even in the art of painting. In the paper entitled *A Notion of the Historical Draught of Hercules*, in which Shaftesbury instructed Paolo de Mattheis how to set about painting the Choice of Hercules—the choice which the youthful Hercules made between Virtue and Pleasure—he dismissed the sensuous pleasure which we derive from colour as secondary and unintellecutal.

For of this *imitative art* we may justly say; 'That tho it borrows help indeed from colours, and uses them, as means, to execute its designs; It has nothing, however, more wide of its real aim, or more remote from its intention, than to make a *shew* of colours, or from their mixture, to raise a separate and *flattering* pleasure to the SENSE.'

* ἀρετή.

This same point Akenside makes with even greater austerity.

> Of degree
> The least and lowliest, in the effusive warmth
> Of colours mingling with a random blaze,
> Doth Beauty dwell. Then higher in the line
> And variation of determined shape,
> Where Truth's eternal measures mark the bound
> Of circle, cube, or sphere.

The same rejection of colour is common to many of the theorists and artists of the next seventy or eighty years. Kant gave it the approval of his judgment; and Winckelmann insisted that form, not colour, was of the essence of beauty. The remarkable success of Flaxman's designs for Homer, Hesiod and Aeschylus shows how widespread was the preference for line and contour throughout Europe by the end of the century. By then the archaeological discoveries in southern Italy had made Greek vase-painting accessible, and Josiah Wedgwood and others had made it familiar, so that these designs seemed to give visual confirmation to preceding theory. The taste of Shaftesbury and Akenside, which derived from intellectual principle, prepared men's minds to receive with admiration an art of which Shaftesbury and Akenside themselves can have had no knowledge. For them Greek art meant, above all else, sculpture, and sculpture from which all traces of the original colour had long since vanished. In forming a judgment of Greek art, therefore, considerations of colour were irrelevant, and for those to whom the Genius of ancient Greece was the guide in matters of taste they must remain so.

Smollett, in his caricature of Akenside, had remarked his predilection for quotation from the dialogues of Plato, especially about τὸ καλόν. The Greek words were so well-known that they were often thus used, without gloss; but 'ideal beauty' was an accepted translation, and Shelley, in his version of the *Symposium*, was to use the phrase 'intellectual beauty'. In the first book Akenside had shown his interpretation of this concept in his description of divine creation; and at the end of the poem, in his discussion of taste, he returns to it again. He recognizes innate differences in response due to differences of temperament.

> Different minds
> Incline to different objects; one pursues

The vast alone, the wonderful, the wild;
Another sighs for harmony, and grace,
And gentlest beauty.

In illustration of this difference he names Shakespeare—the Shakespeare of *King Lear*—and Waller, the acknowledged ancestor of the Augustan poets. His own preference is for the grand effects in nature, and, to quote from Mrs Barbauld's elegant and perceptive *Essay* on the poem, he 'closes with the sublime idea, that in admiring the works of nature, we form our taste upon the conceptions of the Deity himself'. Such must be the logical conclusion to an argument that had begun from the premiss that Nature is the Art of God and worthy our contemplation.

In the course of his poem Akenside had divided the objects of aesthetic response into three categories: the sublime, the wonderful, and the fair. This derived from Addison whose terms were the great, the new or uncommon, and the beautiful; but when Akenside revised his poem fifteen years later he preferred to follow Burke in reducing the categories to the sublime and the beautiful, and perhaps did so the more willingly because Shaftesbury had not included novelty along with these.

The treatise *On the Sublime*, attributed to Longinus, was made famous by Boileau's translation of 1674 and by his later exposition of it in his *Réflexions sur Longin*. The earlier English translation by John Hall, published in 1652, seems to have been little regarded, perhaps because the date was unpropitious for any development of Longinus' thought beyond its original rhetorical context. To Shaftesbury more than to anyone else we owe the transformation of the idea of sublimity to an aesthetic context, where it denotes the feeling of awe with which we contemplate a thunder-storm or an earth-quake, a mountain, a waterfall, or the sea, the life-giving radiance of the sun, or the countless stars and unimaginable distances of the night sky. Longinus related our experience of these things to our experience of religion, and Shaftesbury followed this suggestion for, like Dr Johnson, he considered that the truths of religion were beyond the compass of poetry. But the more majestic aspects of Nature could the more readily be accepted as evidences of divine power because they seemed beyond the limitations of human understanding, even of human imagination. Hence the celestial hymn of Theocles in Shaftesbury's *The Moralists*, in which he addresses Nature.

Thy being is boundless, unsearchable, impenetrable. In thy immensity all thought is lost; fancy gives o'er its flight; and weary'd imagination spends it-self in vain; finding no coast nor limit of this ocean, nor, in the widest tract thro which it soars, one point yet nearer the circumference than the first center whence it parted—Thus having oft essay'd, thus sally'd forth into the wide *expanse*, when I return again within *my-self*, struck with the sense of this so narrow being, and of the fulness of that immense one; I dare no more behold the amazing depths, nor sound the abyss of DEITY.—

Yet since by thee (O *sovereign* MIND!) I have been form'd such as I am, intelligent and rational; since the peculiar dignity of my nature is to know and contemplate thee; permit that with due freedom I exert those facultys with which thou hast adorn'd me. Bear with my ventrous and bold approach. And since nor vain curiosity, nor fond conceit, nor love of ought save thee alone, inspires me with such thoughts as these, be thou my assistant, and guide me in this pursuit; whilst I venture thus to tread the labyrinth of wide nature, and endeavour to trace thee in thy works.

(It is easy to understand why Shaftesbury called his dialogue *A Rhapsody*, and why the sardonic Smollett thought it 'frothy'.) Akenside's verse is more restrained, less rhapsodical; but the conclusion is similar when, after the passage on the rainbow, he acclaims the power of Science to reveal the truths of Nature.

> Whether in the sky,
> The beauteous laws of light, the central powers
> That wheel the pensile planets round the year;
> Whether in wonders of the rolling deep,
> Or smiling fruits of pleasure-pregnant earth,
> Or fine-adjusted springs of life and sense,
> Ye scan the counsels of their Author's hand.

Throughout the poem, whatever modifications were suggested by Shaftesbury and his followers, Akenside's thought was prompted by the Greeks, by Plato and Xenophon, reporting or representing the thought of Socrates, and by Longinus.

Even the least satisfactory part of the poem, the allegorical episode in Book II, derived from the same sources. Here Akenside is considering the problem posed by elegy and tragedy, where we derive pleasure from experiencing the painful emotions of grief and pity and terror. 'To solve the problem, which has been one in all ages,' says Mrs Barbauld, 'a long allegory is introduced, which, though wrought up with a good deal of the decoration of Poetry, is nearly as difficult to comprehend as the problem itself.' There is a kind of infinite regress in his treatment, from the poet, to Harmodius, who introduces the Genius of Man, who introduces Euphrosyne, who. . . . There is, as Mrs Barbauld implies, more imagery than logic, but in a philosophical poem the mind demands logic. 'Upon the whole,' she concludes, 'this allegory . . . has the effect upon most readers which it seems to have had upon the author himself, who tells us that

> Awhile he stood
> Perplexed and giddy.'

But the substance of the allegory is the myth of the Choice of Hercules, told by Prodicus in Xenophon's *Memorabilia Socratis*. This had formed the subject of Shaftesbury's Seventh Treatise, where he gives instructions to a painter how to treat the subject, which was a favourite with painters and poets of the time. Pompeo Batoni, who painted the portraits of so many English grand tourists, made several versions of the subject, and it was parodied by Sir Joshua Reynolds in his painting, 'Garrick between Tragedy and Comedy'. William Shenstone had written a poem on the theme three years before Akenside's was published. Two scholars of some note, Robert Lowth and Joseph Spence, also attempted the subject in verse; but it cannot be claimed that Spence's poem adds to the value of *Polymetis*, in which it was included. They, no doubt, had read their Xenophon, but Shenstone had read only Shaftesbury: as if to acknowledge his debt for much the best of these poems Shenstone included in some editions an engraving of the painting which Paolo de Mattheis had also made in accordance with Shaftesbury's instructions.

Akenside derives from contemporary theories of the association of ideas his explanation of the fact that phenomena in the inanimate world seem to suggest human moods. He regards this as 'the foundation of almost all the ornaments of poetic diction', and certainly his own practice is to rely on what he calls

> The grateful charm
> That speechless Nature o'er the sense of man

Diffuses, to behold in lifeless things
The inexpressive semblance of himself,
Of thought and passion.

This is consistent with his view of Nature as the creation of a
benevolent God, who makes all Nature beauty to man's eye. In this
belief we see the origins of Romantic delight in scenery which earlier
generations had rejected as useless and horrid, as in Scott's commendation of the Trossachs or Wordsworth's of Helvellyn. Something of this feeling for wild country is shown by the Northumbrian
Akenside in the last poetry he ever wrote, the fragmentary fourth
book of *The Pleasures of the Imagination*, on which he was working at
the time of his final illness. 'Would I again were with you!' he cried,
perhaps aware that he would never again see the dales of Tyne, and, in
the nostalgia of sickness, recalling his boyhood there, when he first
knew the gift of poetry in him.

> O ye Northumbrian shades, which overlook
> The rocky pavement and the mossy falls
> Of solitary Wansbeck's limpid stream;
> How gladly I recall your well-known seats,
> Beloved of old, and that delightful time
> When, all alone, for many a summer's day,
> I wandered through your calm recesses, led
> In silence by some powerful hand unseen.

Even here he was but giving a local and personal context to a
suggestion made by Shaftesbury. 'The wildness pleases. We seem to
live alone with nature. We view her in her inmost recesses, and
contemplate her with more delight in these original wilds, than in the
artificial labyrinths and feign'd wildernesses of the palace.' So
enduring and so pervasive had been that early reading of the
Characteristicks.

Akenside began recasting *The Pleasures of the Imagination*—the
insertion of the definite article before 'Imagination' in the title of the
new version is suggestive—in 1757, and he worked at it in-
termittently till the end of his life. He had been but twenty-two when
it was first published and when he died he was forty-eight. The busy
life of an eminent London doctor must have reduced the time he
could spare for poetry, so that it may have seemed easier to rework
the poem which had so early established his fame rather than to

attempt something new on a comparable scale. Poetic inspiration had not failed him; he need not regret the flight of the visionary gleam. For over the years he had written and published a number of short poems called *Odes*, which range in date from 1740 to 1758, a few *Inscriptions*, and the *Hymn to the Naiads*.

Of the *Odes*, in Dr Johnson's judgment, 'nothing favourable can be said', a challenge which it would be pusillanimous to refuse. The first edition of these, *Odes on Several Subjects*, which contained ten poems, was published in March 1745, and preceded Collins' *Odes* by two years; indeed Akenside published the earliest of Collins' odes in 1746 in a journal called *The Museum* which he edited for Dodsley. This was the *Ode to a Lady on the Death of Colonel Ross in the Action of Fontenoy*, which Collins had written in the latter part of May of the previous year. But it will be more convenient to discuss whatever influence Akenside may have had on Collins in the next chapter. The earliest of Akenside's odes was written in December 1740, *For the Winter Solstice*, and is further evidence of his precocity; but wonder at the youth of a performer is no substitute for a critical judgment of the performance, and Akenside later considerably revised the poem. Among the best of these poems are the ode *To the Evening Star*, the *Ode to the Country Gentlemen of England*, which was published independently in 1758, the ode *On Recovering from a fit of sickness; in the country*, of the same year, and the *Ode to the Earl of Huntingdon*, also independently published, of 1748. Any of these (and others besides) may be called in evidence against Johnson.

The last named ode is one of several Pindarics, on the strict model advocated by Congreve, with strophe, antistrophe and epode—it precedes Gray's famous Pindarics by some nine years—but the others named are stanzaic. The prefatory ode, first published in 1745, was then entitled *Allusion to Horace*. But, although Horace (whose 'familiar epistolary way' Akenside had named along with the *Georgics* as one of his models for *The Pleasures of Imagination*) is sometimes recalled in the *Odes*, we are far more often reminded of Greek lyric poetry. In an ode *On Lyric Poetry* Akenside names Anacreon, Sappho, Alcaeus and Pindar, but not Catullus nor Horace. In the *Ode to Lord Huntingdon* he even disparages the poets of Augustan Rome for their subservience.

> Are there, approved of later times,
> Whose verse adorned a tyrant's crimes?
> Who saw majestic Rome betrayed,

> And lent the imperial ruffian aid?
> Alas! not one polluted bard,
> No, nor the strain that Mincius heard,
> Or Tibur's hills replied,
> Dare to the Muse's ear aspire;
> Save that, instructed by the Grecian lyre,
> With Freedom's ancient notes their shameful task they hide.

It requires little imagination to suggest the response of that belated Augustan Dr Johnson to such sentiments: 'the imperial ruffian' was not how men who were proud to call themselves 'Augustans' had thought of the founder of the Roman Empire. The influence of Greek poetry on the work of Virgil and Horace has also suffered some distortion from the political prejudice of Smollett's 'rank republican'. But Akenside was as consistent in his praise of Greek political liberty as of Greek poetry, and he was disposed to associate liberty with the Whigs, who had ended 'the mouldering Gothic reign' of James II in the Glorious Revolution. He was convinced, as he says in a note to this ode, 'that great poetical talents, and high sentiments of liberty, do reciprocally produce and assist each other, . . . Pindar is perhaps the most exemplary proof of this connection'. With this Milton would doubtless have agreed; and Akenside's admiration of Milton, whom he names more often than any other English poet, was, again, both of the poet and of the defender of liberty.

To Shakespeare Akenside's attitude was one of respectful, but critical, enthusiasm. In *The Pleasures of Imagination* he contrasted him with Waller. In the *Odes* the first of the second book is *The Remonstrance of Shakespeare: supposed to have been spoken at the Theatre Royal, while the French Comedians were acting by subscription 1749.* Shakespeare confesses to an unclassical manner:

> What, though the footsteps of my devious Muse
> The measured walks of Grecian art refuse?
> Or, though the frankness of my hardy style,
> Mock the nice touches of the critic's file?

But he claims other qualities, appropriate to the age of Elizabeth, and especially a patriotic power of portraying Englishmen, whether in tragedy, history or comedy.

What other bard in any clime appears
Alike the master of your smiles and tears?

Shakespeare is seen, like Milton, as the upholder of English liberty. And, in an ode *On the Use of Poetry*, Akenside proclaims the Horatian theme of the lasting fame conferred by poetry which no political achievement can rival.

Yet then shall Shakespeare's powerful art
O'er every passion, every heart,
Confirm his awful throne:
Tyrants shall bow before his laws;
And Freedom's, Glory's, Virtue's cause,
Their dread assertor own.

In spite of his ardent partisanship there can be no doubt that Akenside was convinced that this was the truth. Poetry gave him an influence far more lasting than any political office could have done.*

One other theme with which Akenside concerns himself is appropriate to his profession as a doctor: his certainty of the blessings of good health. He treated the theme in the second book of *The Pleasures of Imagination*, where health increases youthful beauty and enhances the pleasure of Spring time. He introduces Hygieia into his *Hymn to the Naiads*, and refers there to his dedication as a doctor. But his most moving poetry on this comes in a personal poem *On recovering from a fit of sickness* in 1758. He addressed the poem to his lifelong friend and benefactor Jeremiah Dyson, at that time Clerk to the House of Commons, who (though he was but recently married) had invited Akenside to come to his house at Hampstead to recuperate.

How gladly 'mid the dews of dawn,
By† weary lungs, thy healing gale,
The balmy west or the fresh north, inhale!
How gladly, while my musing footsteps rove
Round the cool orchard or the sunny lawn,
Awaked I stop and look to find
What shrub perfumes the pleasant wind,
Or what wild songster charms the Dryads of the grove!

* Cf. *Inscriptions*, IV, 'On a Statue of Shakespeare'.
† 'By', the reading of the original edition accepted by Dyce, should perhaps be emended to 'My'.

Now, ere the morning walk is done,
The distant voice of health I hear,
Welcome as beauty's to the lover's ear.
'Droop not, nor doubt of my return,' she cries;
'Here will I, 'mid the radiant calm of noon,
Meet thee beneath yon chestnut bower,
And lenient on thy bosom pour
That indolence divine which lulls the earth and skies.

How admirably Akenside here suggests both the languour and the relief of convalescence in congenial surroundings! It seems odd that he should not have been more sympathetic to his patients.

The *Ode to the Evening Star*, which is perhaps the best known of Akenside's *Odes*,* is not very well named, for in only the second stanza the poet invites Hesper to stoop his delighted ear to mortal sounds; and the substance of the poem is about the song of the nightingale. The poem begins with deceptive simplicity:

Tonight retired, the queen of heaven
With young Endymion stays.

Phoebe's seclusion admits no intruder. (We are reminded of Spenser's gay admonition to her in the *Epithalamion* not to intrude upon him and his bride.) We are immediately in the world of Greek myth: the evening star is Hesper; the poet's dead beloved is Olympia (the name Akenside always uses); the nightingale is Philomela, and so on. Nevertheless the bird is a real bird, and we never doubt that Akenside had listened to its song; it is simply that he brought to that experience a recollection of myth, but that, too, had been prompted by the song of a wild bird. He recalls listening to it with Olympia.

Oft by yon silver stream we walked,
Or fixed, while Philomela talked,
Beneath yon copses stood.

Nor seldom, where the beechen boughs
That roofless tower invade,
We came.

* Had Collins shown Akenside his *Ode to Evening*?

Now, hearing the song again, he follows the sound until he comes where the bird is singing.

> But hark! I hear her liquid tone.
> Now, Hesper, guide my feet
> Down the red marl with moss o'ergrown,
> Through yon wild thicket next the plain,
> Whose hawthorns choke the winding lane,
> > Which leads to her retreat . . .

> Hark, how through many a melting note
> > She now prolongs her lays:
> How sweetly down the void they float!
> The breeze their magic path attends;
> The stars shine out; the forest bends;
> > The wakeful heifers gaze.

Akenside achieves here a Grecian simplicity of manner entirely in keeping with the subject, but far removed from the sensuous richness of epithet which Keats supplies in his *Ode to a Nightingale*.

Now Akenside, who certainly had never heard the song of a nightingale in his boyhood in Northumberland or in Scotland, very probably listened to it in Jeremiah Dyson's garden on Golder's Hill, near where Keats heard the song. Joseph Severn said that Keats 'so hated Akenside that he would not look in him'. But he must have looked in him at some time in order to acquire this hatred. Besides, living at Hampstead at a time when Akenside's poetry was still widely read, Keats can hardly have been as ignorant of it as Severn supposed, even if he came to have a distaste for it: Akenside, like Shelley, does not 'load every rift with ore'. The *Ode to a Nightingale* in fact does have a number of reminiscences of the *Ode to the Evening Star*. The old word 'beechen' is in both poems; in both the song is 'plaintive'; in both the moon is called 'queen' and is attended by a 'starry throng' or by 'starry Fays'. So much might be coincidental, but Akenside's lines,

> Down the red marl with moss o'ergrown,
> Through yon wild thicket next the plain,
> Whose hawthorns choke the winding lane,

must surely have been echoing in Keats' brain when he wrote of 'winding mossy ways' and of

> The grass, the thicket, and the fruit-tree wild;
> White hawthorn, and the pastoral eglantine.

I would not claim that Akenside's ode suggested Keats', nor even that Keats consciously recalled it as he wrote his own; but it can hardly be doubted that Akenside's ode was one of the ingredients in the process of decomposition (to use Keats' phrase) that preceded the composition of one of the greatest odes in the language. That may seem but faintly favourable to Akenside's ode; but it is not dispraise.

The eight verse *Inscriptions*—there is a ninth, in Latin prose, on Akenside's hero, William III—are mostly Greek in inspiration and in manner. The first, *For a Grotto*, and the seventh, *The Wood-Nymph*, are reminiscent of Theocritus, and Akenside converts the grotto of rococo fashion into a Sicilian cave such as Amaryllis inhabits in the third Idyll. The eighth of these poems, which has no title, invokes the 'powers unseen, to whom the bards of Greece erected altars' to come to his aid, and recalls the invocation to the Genius of Greece in *The Pleasures of Imagination*. Two others are for statues of Chaucer at Woodstock and of Shakespeare: of the latter I have written above. The poem on Chaucer returns to the theme of the enduring fame of poetry. Chaucer, 'who first informed the language of our fathers', deserves to rival the fame of the Duke of Marlborough, commemorated in Blenheim Palace; and we remember Gibbon's similar claim for the poet who felt that Chaucer had been reborn in him: 'The nobility of the Spencers has been illustrated and enriched by the trophies of Marlborough; but I exhort them to consider the *Fairy Queen* as the most precious jewel of their coronet.' The brevity of these poems compels Akenside to write with a lapidary simplicity which we see also in the best of the *Odes*, but which, in the longer poems, too often gives way to a turgid diffuseness which is perplexing. Like Wordsworth, he was liable to suffer from the weight of too much liberty, which blank verse can so easily bring in a long poem. Wordsworth's *Inscriptions* are more personal and less public; he is not really thinking of the unknown passer-by who will read them, but of himself. Akenside better achieves the impersonal manner which an inscription demands, and is closer to Landor than to Wordsworth.

Of the *Hymn to the Naiads* Akenside's nineteenth century editor, Alexander Dyce, said, 'Throughout the range of English literature there is nothing more deeply imbued with the spirit of the ancient world,' a large, but no unconsidered claim. In this poem Akenside

achieved what Milton intended, a hymn in the manner of Callimachus. It is in blank verse and the longest of Akenside's poems after
The Pleasures of Imagination, and it suffers at times from the lack of
clarity which a more closely controlled form can prevent. Akenside
took Milton for his chief model and though he had independent
vigour enough to avoid the mischance of domination by his style,
which finer poets have not always escaped, he would have benefited
more from the Greek simplicity of manner which he sometimes
achieves in his shorter poems. It is of greater interest that he followed
Milton in his treatment of myth. In a note on Amalthea, the mother
of Bacchus, he quotes from the description of the Garden of Eden in
the fourth book of *Paradise Lost* and observes that Milton was 'the
only modern poet (unless perhaps it be necessary to except Spenser)
who, in these mysterious traditions of the poetic story, had a heart to
feel, and words to express, the simple and solitary genius of antiquity'.
His treatment of Greek myth therefore is far removed from that
given by Keats; he does not seek by the use of rich, sensuous imagery
to provide a static picture of a scene. His art is not pictorial, but
narrative, and he uses myth much as Shelley uses it. 'Other poets,' says
Bagehot in his essay on Shelley, 'have breathed into mythology a
modern life; have been attracted by those parts which seem to have a
religious meaning, and have enlarged that meaning while studying to
embody it. With Shelley it is otherwise; the parts of mythology by
which he is attracted are the bare parts.' We may substitute here
Akenside's name for Shelley's and acquire a pertinent criticism of his
treatment of myth in the *Hymn to the Naiads*. This quality in the poem
led Leigh Hunt to complain that he had as cold a recollection of it as of
a morning in November, or one of old Panope's washing days. But
this is the very quality which makes it come so close to 'the simple and
solitary genius of antiquity'; Akenside would have failed of his intent
if Leigh Hunt, or Keats, had enjoyed it. He is at pains, too, to get his
mythology correct, as Callimachus, 'who was very learned in the
school-divinity of those times', would have done. He quotes fifteen or
more Greek authors in his notes, and even sets out conflicting ancient
opinions there to account for his choice. His deference to the Greeks
was such that he not only scans Greek names correctly (unlike Keats)
but attempts to recount their myths as they would have done.

But the Naiads are, so to say, naturalized in England, as the 'blue-
eyed progeny of Thames', and the Thames invites praise of English
naval and commercial enterprise, a theme which Thomson also
exploited. Turner in his painting 'The Fall of the Clyde, Lanarkshire,

Noon', exhibited in 1802, added a reference to Akenside's *Hymn*. He introduced the nymphs because he wished his picture to celebrate the industrial and mercantile aspects of the river together with its more primitive powers of cleansing and fertilizing. The introduction of Hygieia, goddess of health, suggests a passage on English rural sports, but without Thomson's humanitarian sentiment. These English references are well accommodated to the overall classical tone of the *Hymn*, which is best seen in such passages as this, where, at the end of the poem, he addresses the Naiads, in contrast with the Bacchic rout, as the source of poetic inspiration.

> The immortal Muse
> To your calm habitations, to the cave
> Corycian, or the Delphic mount, will guide
> His footsteps; and with your unsullied streams
> His lips will bathe; whether the eternal lore
> Of Themis, or the majesty of Jove,
> To mortals he reveal; or teach his lyre
> The unenvied guerdon of the patriot's toils,
> In those unfading islands of the blessed,
> Where sacred bards abide. Hail, honoured Nymphs!
> Thrice hail! For you the Cyrenaic shell,
> Behold, I touch, revering. To my songs
> Be present ye, with favourable feet,
> And all profaner audience far remove.

The closing lines recall Milton's hope to reach fit audience, though few; there is no reason to suppose that Akenside sought popularity. And in a note on Cyrene, as the native country of Callimachus, he says that he had been induced, by the pleasure he derived from Callimachus' poetry, to attempt somewhat in the same manner. 'It was therefore thought proper to select some convenient part of the history of nature, and to employ these ancient divinities as it is probable they were first employed; to wit, in personifying natural causes, and in representing the mutual agreement or opposition of the corporal and moral powers of the world.' This seems an accurate account of the poem as we have it, and it sums up Akenside's poetic ambition.

Born into a family in which literary talent must have seemed extraordinary, Akenside very early recognized his own gifts and had the audacity to persuade others to do so when he was but fifteen years of age. He was well taught, he read widely in the classical languages as well as his own, and his judgment of English literature is perceptive and unprejudiced. He also had a taste, unusual in a poet, for contemporary philosophy. He became especially interested in the nature and validity of aesthetic experience, and he soon recognized that for him the poetry of Greece and the thought of Plato were far more rewarding than the poetry or philosophy of Augustan Rome. He wished to 'tune to Attic themes the British lyre' before others had conceived the same purpose; he was a pioneer, ahead of his time, and an impatient precocity led him to attempt the Attic themes before he had succeeded in tuning the instrument of language. His diction remains too often heavy, and clogged with inappropriate Augustan effects, and he seldom attains the Attic simplicity he needs. In some of the *Odes* and *Inscriptions*, in a few passages in his longer poems, he does come near the unstudied ease and grace of Goldsmith; but more often he is restricted and hampered by a Latinity derived ultimately from Milton, which precludes the expression he sought. He turned away from the Augustan heroic couplet, with its rhetorical antithesis, its compact parcelling out of meaning into two conclusive lines; and his preference for blank verse—for the hexameter rather than the elegiac couplet—was correct. But he did not achieve a style which could be described as resembling 'clear, pure water, which flows from the spring'. That was the style he required, and which would have made a great poem, instead of a good poem, out of the *Hymn to the Naiads*; but he had not the genius to fetch it straight from his beloved Greek sources, from Sophocles, or Plato, or Xenophon.

Because of this divergence between what he had to say and the means he found of saying it he was not a great poet. Yet, of the poets who were writing when the death of Pope brought the long Augustan age to its close, there was none who more clearly pointed towards the phase of taste that would follow. That, no doubt, was why his poetry appealed so much to the later eighteenth century, which, like every other age, was eager to welcome what was new without troubling overmuch about residual traces of earlier fashion. Akenside did not quite succeed in breaking free from the manner of the Augustans (and probably Shaftesbury's rhapsodical prose was a further hindrance), but the keen intelligence which he brought to his reading of Greek poetry and philosophy won him a reputation in his own time, and for long afterwards, which he altogether deserved and before which it would be impertinent in us to show surprise.

3 William Collins (1721 – 59)

> Return, sweet maid, at length
> In all thy ancient strength
> And bid our Britain hear thy Grecian song.
>
> *To Simplicity*

The literary career of William Collins shows some striking similarities to that of Mark Akenside, and some no less striking divergences.
Born in the same year as Akenside, Collins was the son of a
'respectable hatter' (in the terminology of the *Dictionary of National
Biography*) and Akenside was the son of a 'respectable butcher'. The
difference in social status of the two poets was therefore about as
inconsiderable as the seven weeks' difference in their ages, and the fact
that Collins was educated at Winchester is no evidence to the contrary.
He was born at Chichester and he went to Winchester because it was a
reputable school within a day's journey; and he was intelligent
enough to be elected scholar. While he was at school he, like
Akenside, contributed to the pages of *The Gentleman's Magazine*, but
whereas Akenside sent in five varied and ambitious poems amounting
to more than six hundred and fifty lines in all, Collins submitted two
modest quatrains entitled *Sonnet*. In December 1744, the year in
which Akenside published *The Pleasures of Imagination*, a notice
appeared in *A Literary Journal* of '*A Review of the Advancement of
Learning from 1300 to 1521*, by Wm. Collins, 4to.', of which nothing
has since been heard. Akenside chose a similar subject for his
Croonian Lectures, which, though never published, were apparently
read before the Royal College of Physicians in 1756. Most of Collins'
projects came to nothing, but there is no record of the vigorous and
capable Akenside failing to carry out any task which he had promised
to undertake. Akenside's talent may have lacked the refinement and
elegance of Collins'; it also lacked the fragility. It is not surprising
therefore that Akenside's poetry was much admired in his life-time,
and was translated into French, German and Italian, while Collins'
was ignored. Yet in the twentieth century, when there has been no

edition of Akenside, there have been seven or eight of Collins.

His poems have often been included in a single volume with those of Gray, perhaps for no better reason than the diminutive bulk of their output—a little over two thousand lines of English verse in forty-seven poems (including translations) by Gray, and a little under two thousand lines in thirty-four poems (including drafts and fragments) by Collins. There seems no other reason for associating two poets who have little else in common;* but the convenience of the arrangement may have fortuitously enhanced Collins' reputation by thus placing his poems alongside the *Elegy written in a Country Churchyard.* For this continues to draw in countless thousands to the churchyard at Stoke Poges American tourists who perhaps can quote from no other poem in the language. But Gray's *Elegy* belongs to the tradition of Young's *Night Thoughts,* which Mrs Barbauld contrasted with Akenside's *Pleasures of Imagination* (to which Collins was much indebted): 'the one resembles the Gothic, the other the Grecian architecture', she said; and certainly Collins' poetry is Grecian. Gray saw Collins' *Odes* as soon as they were published, and did not think very well of them: Collins had, he wrote, 'a fine Fancy model'd upon the Antique, a bad ear, great variety of Words, and Images with no Choice at all'. The association of their poems has nothing but practical convenience to recommend it.

Collins devised a different method from Akenside for breaking with the dominant Augustan tradition. In his first book, *Persian Eclogues,* published in January 1742, the pretence of translation allows him to write in a manner which was intended to be other than Augustan; and in the Preface he contrasts the 'rich and figurative style' of his poems with that of the English poetry of his day, whose 'strong and nervous'† qualities were to be exhibited again that year in the fourth book of *The Dunciad.* But the exotic setting and the pseudo-orientalism of the *Eclogues,* which had been prompted by reading the volume on Persia in Thomas Salmon's *Modern History* while still at Winchester, were insufficient to disguise their dependence on Pope's *Pastorals.* The four poems follow the same sequence of Morning, Noon, Evening and Night; they are in heroic couplets; and the

---

* Swinburne, in his essay on Collins, (*Miscellanies,* 1886) says, 'Even in his own age it was the fatally foolish and uncritical fashion to couple the name of Collins with that of Gray, as though they were poets of the same order or kind. As an elegiac poet, Gray holds for all ages to come his unassailable and sovereign station; as a lyric poet, he is simply unworthy to sit at the feet of Collins.'

† That is, sinewy, muscular.

diction, in spite of Collins' disclaimer, is derived from Pope. It was not, after all, likely that a gifted schoolboy could break free altogether from so powerful a tradition, but the fact that he failed to do so was, no doubt, the reason why the *Persian Eclogues* remained more popular during Collins' life-time than the more independent *Odes*. Collins, Joseph Warton said, 'was greatly mortified that they found more readers and admirers than his Odes'. The taste of English readers in the 1740s was not yet ready for the change of which Collins and Akenside were the pioneers. But Akenside argued for change in his poems, and was persuasive; while Collins expected his readers to accept his poems as evidence for an unstated argument.

The subterfuge of offering original poems as translations, preferably from some exotic and scarcely known language, or as discoveries in ancient manuscripts, was adopted by other poets of the mid-century who were not bold enough directly to assert their rejection of the Augustan tradition. Collins' pretence of Persian originals was not many years ahead of Macpherson's much more successful pretence of Gaelic originals for the poems he attributed to Ossian; and Chatterton's pretence of a medieval source for his Rowley poems is in the same class of deception.* It is significant that all these poets were precocious; Akenside was twenty-two when he published *The Pleasures of Imagination*, anonymously, but without deception; Collins was twenty when he published the *Persian Eclogues*; Macpherson was twenty-three when he published his *Fragments of Ancient Poetry*; Chatterton was seventeen when he died. Such precocity led them to establish a manner too early, and so to inhibit further development. By contrast Wordsworth and Coleridge began writing in a manner which they would soon reject, but Wordsworth was twenty-eight and Coleridge twenty-six at the time of the publication of *Lyrical Ballads*.

Collins was a poet of more individual genius than Akenside, Macpherson or Chatterton, and it would be generally agreed today that his *Odes* contain poems of finer quality than anything in the work of these others. We can see them in perspective, as eighteenth century readers could not, yet it need not impair our appreciation of them if we attempt to see them in the context of their time. The story of their publication is well known: Collins met Joseph Warton, who had been his contemporary and friend at Winchester and Oxford, at Guildford Races on the Tuesday of Whit-week 1746; and Joseph wrote to tell

---

* Landor's *Poems from the Arabic and Persian* followed two years after *Gebir*.

his younger brother Thomas about the meeting. (Thomas, who had also been at Winchester, had got to know Collins at Oxford.)

Dear Tom,
    You will wonder to see my name in an advertisement next week, so I thought I would apprize you of it. The case was this. Collins met me in Surrey, at Guildford Races, when I wrote out for him my Odes, and he likewise communicated some of his to me; and being both in very high spirits we took courage, resolved to join our forces, and to publish them immediately.

They had previously joined together, when at Winchester, in submitting their first poems to *The Gentleman's Magazine* in 1739, and in their enthusiasm for their new odes a few years later—Warton believed his to be (as he told his brother) 'infinitely the best things I ever wrote'—it was natural enough for the two young poets to think of a combined volume. Both were consciously seeking a new poetry, free of Augustan restrictions; both were turning away from Rome to Greece for fresh inspiration; both were following Akenside's lead in writing the first Pindarics since Congreve had argued for the regularity of the true Pindaric against the loose Pindaric of Cowley. By the end of the year Joseph Warton had written thirteen odes, and Collins had written twelve, so the projected book would not have been of excessive length, nor unevenly balanced. In the upshot two volumes of *Odes* appeared from different publishers at an interval of a few days in December 1746. Dodsley published Warton's, and Andrew Millar published Collins'. Within three weeks of the poets' meeting at Guildford Races Dodsley published Collins' *Ode to a Lady* in *The Museum*, the periodical which Akenside edited for him. However, he may have doubted the saleability of Collins' *Odes*, and he refused the ten guineas which Collins was asking: if so, his commercial judgment was sound, for Warton's *Odes* were reprinted within a few weeks but Collins' remained unsold. Andrew Millar was James Thomson's publisher, and had probably met Collins with Thomson at Richmond; in any event it is likely that Thomson would advise him to offer Collins his modest fee, which he did.
    Akenside had published his *Odes* in March 1745, a collection which Dyce properly described as 'the most valuable accession which the lyric poetry of England had received since Dryden's time'. Not unexpectedly, this set a pattern for succeeding volumes of odes, Joseph Warton's and Collins' in 1746, Gray's *Ode on a Distant Prospect*

of Eton College (which was independently published) in 1747, and his *Ode on the Death of a Favourite Cat* and the *Ode on Spring* in 1748. (The two great Pindaric odes, though not published till 1757, had been largely written some years before.) Dodsley published Gray's three earliest odes, two of them in his *Collection of Poems by Several Hands* of 1748, perhaps on Akenside's advice, for his contract with Akenside for the editorship of *The Museum* shows how highly he valued Akenside's critical judgment. When Collins met Warton at Guild-ford Races he must have known that Akenside had accepted his *Ode to a Lady* for *The Museum*, for it was published there within three weeks; no doubt he was encouraged by this approval of the most celebrated poet of the day, as any young poet would have been, and mentioned his success to Warton. Such encouragement was what he then needed, and he seems to have written most of his *Odes* in the summer or autumn of that year.

In the *Odes* Collins shows his indebtedness to Akenside's poetry, in addition to his criticism. In the first four he is concerned, as Akenside had been in *The Pleasures of Imagination*, with the nature of aesthetic experience, and the last of the group, the *Ode on the Poetical Character*, is pervaded by verbal reminiscence of Akenside's *Odes* as well as of his didactic poem. Collins begins his poem with the image of Florimell's girdle, from *The Faerie Queene*—the girdle that proved the fitness or unfitness of anyone who attempted to wear it; and he takes this as an allegory of genuine poetic power. Such power he calls 'godlike' since the poet's creative imagination ('Fancy' in Collins and in Akenside) is analogous to God's imaginative act of Creation, as Akenside describes it. In this Akenside had been following Shaftesbury, but verbal similarities show that Collins was dependent on Akenside. He is so again in his insistence on the power of imagination to perceive Truth, in his admission of Wonder as a source of the pleasures of imagination, and in his reference to 'the dangerous Passions'. To bring 'Passion's fierce illapse' within his intellectual scheme Akenside, with good Platonic precedent, invented an allegory in his second book. Both poets sought to break free from a tradition which, through its subservience to empiricism, degraded poetry to the status of mere pastime. Both looked for support to the acknowledged masters of English poetry, Spenser and Milton.

The *Ode on the Poetical Character* is one of Collins' adaptations of Greek choric form rather than of the Pindaric (to which it is usually referred), in which he places the metrically independent section between strophe and antistrophe, as a mesode, instead of at the end, as an epode. This central position provides some relaxation between the more highly stressed and matching stanzas, whereas a final position would require it to provide reconciliation between two opposed, or incomplete, descriptions. There are no precedents for such an arrangement in Pindar, though there are some in Greek tragedy, as in the *Trachiniae* of Sophocles. Collins, following Akenside's example, used as an epigraph on the title-page of his book a passage from Pindar,* but in the poems themselves there are many more references to the three tragedians than to Pindar, and it is likely that he was better acquainted with their work. He 'planned several tragedies', Dr Johnson said, and these would probably have been on the Greek model, like Thomson's *Agamemnon* and William Whitehead's *Creusa, Queen of Athens*, both of which were acted in London. Besides, he had recently been working on a translation, with commentary, of Aristotle's *Poetics*, for which he must often have been obliged to turn to Aeschylus, Sophocles, and Euripides, but not to Pindar, so that choric metrical patterns must have been present to his mind.

In the strophe he begins with Spenser, and converts to his own purpose a famous image in *The Faerie Queene*. In the antistrophe he exalts Milton, who had praised Spenser above all his English predecessors; and he draws a contrast with Waller whom, like Akenside, he takes as representative of the Augustan school, which is opposed to the school of Spenser and Milton. The mesode associates the creative imagination of the poet with divine Creation, and ends with the question: where shall we find a new poet of the stature of Spenser or Milton?

> Where is the bard, whose soul can now
> Its high presuming hopes avow?
> Where he who thinks, with rapture blind,
> This hallowed work for him designed?

Again, Collins was following Akenside, who, in his ode *On Lyric Poetry*, had put a similar question. There, after celebrating Anacreon, Alcaeus, and Sappho, Akenside asked who might succeed to these, and he gave as answer, Pindar,

---

* Akenside took his from the eighth Nemean Ode, Collins from the ninth Olympian. Gray's epigraph was from the second Olympian.

> For some there are, whose mighty frame
> The hand of Jove at birth endowed
> With hopes that mock the gazing crowd.

But Collins' poem was not, like Akenside's, a progress piece, and he could give no factual answer to the question, who should succeed Spenser and Milton; rather he was offering a challenge to the poets of the time, himself among them. Joseph Warton, in the preface to his *Odes*, said that 'as he looks upon Invention and Imagination to be the chief faculties of a Poet, so he will be happy if the following *Odes* may be look'd upon as an attempt to bring Poetry into its right channel.' If their first plan of publishing their *Odes* together had been carried out Collins could have accepted Warton's preface for them both.

The two odes which Collins placed first in his collection, *To Pity* and *To Fear*, by their very juxtaposition recall Aristotle's doctrine of catharsis, by which he accounted for the pleasure that we derive from theatrical presentation of tragic events which in themselves are not pleasurable. In the *Ode to Fear* Collins himself unites them in a theatrical context:

> Though gentle Pity claim her mingled part,
> Yet all the thunders of the scene are thine.

Dr Johnson, in his *Life*, tells how Collins came to accept the commission to translate the *Poetics*:

> One day I was admitted to him when he was immured by a bailiff that was prowling in the street. On this occasion recourse was had to the book-sellers, who, on the credit of a translation of Aristotle's *Poeticks*, which he engaged to write with a large commentary, advanced as much money as enabled him to escape into the country. He showed me the guineas safe in his hand.

John Ragsdale, who got to know Collins after his escape into the country (to Richmond), said that Collins showed him 'many sheets' of this translation. Probably these were the 'oft-turned scrolls' which Collins 'left behind' when he decided to complete his volume of *Odes*; like most of Collins' projects, the translation was never finished.

Yet Collins showed that the *Poetics* was present to his mind when he was writing these two odes, for, in a note to explain a reference to Euripides in the first of them, he quotes Aristotle's opinion that, in comparison with Sophocles, Euripides 'was the greater Master of the tender Passions, ἦν τραγικώτερος (was the more tragic)'.* The two emotions of pity and fear are considered in a dramatic, rather than in a social or personal context. Though he was writing immediately after the suppression of the Jacobite Rebellion, he does not think of pity or fear in that connexion and anticipate Wilfred Owen's claim that the poetry of war is in the pity. He is thinking of the drama—the word 'scene' occurs in the opening sentence of both poems—and is concerned solely with aesthetic experience. In the *Ode to Pity* he names Eúripides, and also Thomas Otway, who, like himself, was a native of Sussex and educated at Winchester and Oxford. (While they were still at Winchester Collins and Joseph Warton set up a marble memorial there to him.) Similarly, in the *Ode to Fear* Collins names Aeschylus and Sophocles, and also Shakespeare, and in his own notes he quotes from the *Electra*, the *Oedipus Tyrannus* and the *Oedipus Coloneus*, and there are allusions in the poem to *Hamlet*. Throughout the two odes Collins is describing the emotions of pity and fear as these are aroused by tragedy.

The association of these two odes with Greek tragedy, and with Aristotle's theory about the sources of the aesthetic pleasure we derive from watching it, is incontrovertible. They were followed by the *Ode to Simplicity*, which is linked to them by another mention of Sophocles' *Electra*. But the subject of this poem is not restricted to the drama: simplicity was an essential element in Grecian taste, and was as relevant to our appreciation of sculpture, which Collins introduces towards the end of the poem, as to tragedy or to poetry generally. An earlier draft of this ode survives in a fragment of some forty lines, but Collins discarded it presumably because it lacked the simplicity of structure which he needed to achieve. It was an obvious fault in a poem addressed to Simplicity if the reader was left in doubt whether the poet was invoking Fancy and bidding her return to an ancient strength ensured by Simplicity, or whether he was invoking Simplicity herself. In its final form there is no such ambivalence: the poet addresses Simplicity at once in words which recall Shaftesbury's linking of Simplicity with Nature, which 'began chiefly to be sought' during the great age of Greek civilization. Winckelmann, following where Shaftesbury had led, claimed Simplicity as one of the two outstanding qualities of Greek art. But it is a quality of the work of

---

* Joseph Warton, in his *Ode on Reading Mr. West's Translation of Pindar*, writes of 'Euripides, soft Pity's priest' in contrast with Sophocles.

art, not of our aesthetic appreciation of it, and it was therefore important for Collins to demonstrate this in his writing of the ode. It would have been absurd to write an *Ode to Simplicity* in the involved and complex manner of the *Ode on the Popular Superstitions of the Highlands of Scotland*, where a more Gothic manner was in keeping with the subject, or even in the 'rich and figurative style' which he had attempted in the *Persian Eclogues*. In the result, the *Ode to Simplicity* comes as near as any of Collins' poems to the Grecian ideal. In keeping with this Collins personifies Simplicity as

> a decent maid
> In Attic robe arrayed.

She disdains 'the wealth of art' and prefers the natural qualities of the song of the nightingale,

> whose love-lorn woe
> In evening musings slow
> Soothed sweetly sad Electra's poet's ear.

This reference to Sophocles, especially to passages on the nightingale in the *Electra* and in *Oedipus Coloneus*,* is apposite, both because (as Collins notes) Sophocles 'seems to have entertain'd a peculiar Fondness' for the song, and because (to quote Walter Bagehot) 'If we examine any of Sophocles' greater passages, a principal beauty is their reserved simplicity.' Collins also had in mind Akenside's invocation to the Genius of ancient Greece with which he concludes the first book of *The Pleasures of Imagination*. For Collins again, as for Akenside, the reign of Augustus terminates the true classicism of Greece, though his response is not ferocious scorn but a more composed regret. He concludes, as he had begun, by associating Simplicity with Nature (to which the nightingale passage had given substance), but now with the 'temperate vale' that is suited to pastoral poetry, in contrast to the 'mountains wild' of the opening stanza, the mountains of Helicon where the Muses endowed Hesiod with 'the powers of song'.

The Grecian simplicity of this ode Collins seldom repeated, but it is evident in the *Ode to Evening*, where he fulfils the pastoral hope there

---

* T. L. Peacock refers to this passage in *Rhododaphne*, canto v, and again in *Crotchet Castle*, ch. VIII.

expressed, and again in the *Ode Occasioned by the Death of Mr Thomson*, which also has pastoral connotations. The unrhymed stanza of the *Ode to Evening*, which derived through Thomas Warton from Milton's version of Horace's *Quis multa gracilis te puer in rosa**, was an English substitute for the Alcaic stanza, which does not transpose so easily into English as the Sapphic. Horace himself had modified the Greek metrical pattern in order to naturalize the stanza in Latin, and in the seventeenth century several attempts were made to naturalize it in English. Milton's version was the most strictly classical, in its rejection of the 'barbarous' ornament of rhyme; but Fanshawe, in his translations from Horace, devised the rhymed stanza which Marvell adopted for his *Horatian Ode upon Cromwell's Return from Ireland*. In the *Ode to Evening* Collins, as so often, makes use of Spenser's vocabulary, but without destroying the overall effect of classical taste. As Dryden said, 'Spenser, being master of our northern dialect, and skilled in Chaucer's English, has . . . exactly imitated the Doric of Theocritus', and Spenserian diction was therefore especially appropriate to a pastoral poem. There are echoes from Milton's poetry here too, and from Akenside's and from the Wartons', but all perfectly fused in the peculiar glow of Collins' inspiration. For, like Spenser's, Collins' imagination was vividly pictorial. Addison had given his authority to the view that it is the sense of sight 'which furnishes the imagination with its ideas; so that by the pleasures of the imagination . . . I here mean such as arise from visible objects, either when we have them actually in our view, or when we call up their ideas into our minds by paintings, statues, descriptions, or any the like occasion.' Collins' method is to exhibit and illustrate the allegorical figures which are central to his poems by surrounding them with symbolic properties, much in the manner of a baroque painter. Mario Praz has well compared passages in the *Ode to Evening* with Guercino's frescoes in the Villa Ludovisi, and a contemporary reviewer considered that the opening image of the *Ode to Mercy* afforded 'the finest subject for a picture that imagination can form'. But these comparisons imply that Collins' visual imagination was too full of colour, too 'rich and figurative' to meet the requirements of the more austere taste of the coming age. He would not, we may suppose, have accepted Blake's dictum, 'That the more distinct, sharp and wirey the bounding line, the more perfect the work of art.' Such epithets are irrelevant to a consideration of Collins' art, and a poet

---

* What slender youth bedew'd with liquid odours / Courts thee on roses. . . .

who can be illustrated from Guercino cannot be equally well illustrated by Flaxman. Yet, ironically, it was Flaxman who, long after Collins' death, designed the noble monument to the poet in Chichester Cathedral.

When Dr Johnson found a bookseller willing to facilitate Collins' escape from his London creditors to Richmond, he gave him the further benefit of friendship with James Thomson. And when, two or three years later, Thomson suddenly died, Collins was moved to write in his memory an ode which again achieves classical simplicity in a pastoral context. There are apt recollections from *The Seasons* and from *The Castle of Idolence*, and of Spenser's *Shepheardes Calendar*, and again, as in the *Ode to Evening*, Collins unites classical myth with elements derived from what Dryden called 'the fairy kind of writing'. In a poem whose 'scene . . . is supposed to lie on the Thames near Richmond' the 'sedge-crowned Sisters' recall the Naiads* whom Akenside had recently addressed in his *Hymn*:

> and o'er the lawns,
> And o'er the vale of Richmond, where with Thames
> Ye love to wander.

This *Ode, Occasioned by the Death of Mr Thomson* is not only one of Collins' best poems, it is one of the best elegies in the language. The lyrical movement is suggested and controlled by the imagined movement of the boat downstream past Thomson's grave at Richmond, and even the obscurities of the final stanza are redeemed by the last line of all, which repeats the first line of the poem. Collins knew and liked Thomson, and he admired his poetry, and though in the ode he mourns the poet rather than the friend, there is nothing frigid in his restraint.

Collins had earlier written two other elegiac odes, one ostensibly personal, the other ideal. He was not acquainted with 'Colonel' Ross—who was in fact a Captain when he was killed at Fontenoy— but he knew the lady to whom he addressed his consolatory poem; but the *Ode, Written in the Beginning of the Year 1746* is so much more successful that many have regarded it as a reworking of the other, which was certainly the earlier. However, this is an oversimplification. Collins would not have included an early and a late version of

---

* The Naiads of the Thames reappear in the first line of the *Ode on the Popular Superstitions of the Highlands of Scotland*.

the same poem in his book—he rejected the earlier form of the *Ode to Simplicity*—and there are signs that he went back to the *Ode to a Lady* after completing the other. 'How sleep the brave' has twelve lines; the *Ode to a Lady* has sixty, and this accounts for much of the superiority of the 1746 ode. 'The Greek Anthology', says Edmund Blunden, 'has taught him this brevity, and—if we may follow Matthew Arnold— the Celtic spirit creates these supernatural presences', of 'fairy hands' and 'forms unseen'. This perplexing combination is characteristic of Collins' poetry: like Horace Walpole, though he admired the Grecian temple, 'in the heretical corner of his heart' he adored the Gothic building. But he was most often at his best when the heresy was recognized for what it was, and kept in its place.

The *Ode, to a Lady* and the *Ode, Written in the Beginning of the Year 1746* were both political, in the sense that both were occasioned by political events, in fact, by military defeats. The battle of Fontenoy in Flanders was fought on 11 May 1745, and the battle of Falkirk on 17 January 1746. The latter was the last success of the Young Pretender against the English troops before his final defeat at Culloden three months later. Then Collins showed himself no fire-eating, vengeful non-combatant, and he shared the widespread public sympathy for the rebel Scottish peers, the Earls of Kilmarnock and Cromartie, and Lord Balmerino. They all pleaded guilty to the charge of high treason, 'which, you know,' so Die Vernon assures Frank Osbaldistone, 'has been in all ages accounted the crime of a gentleman,' and the two earls (but not Balmerino) appealed to the King to exercise his prerogative of mercy.*

The two other political odes, *To Liberty* and *To Peace*, had no particular occasion. Both were written in the autumn of 1746, when there seemed some prospect of ending the War of the Austrian Succession. The *Ode to Peace* is stanzaic, and the longer, more elaborate *Ode to Liberty* is another variant of the choric, or Pindaric, ode, with strophe and antistrophe and two epodes (to use Collins' term), one after the strophe and a second following the antistrophe and so differentiating the form from that of the *Ode on the Poetical Character*. As there, the metre of the epodes is the octosyllabic couplet. The theme of liberty inevitably suggested Greece, and Collins follows Thomson in tracing the progress of Liberty from Greece to Rome, then, after precarious survival when barbarian invasions

---

* The Earl of Cromartie was pardoned. The Earl of Kilmarnock and Lord Balmerino were executed on 18 August 1746.

destroyed the Roman Empire, to resurgence in Italian city-states, and finally to establishment in Britain. The last section of the poem ('second epode'), which reads very much as if it were an after-thought,* describes an ancient Temple of Liberty supposed once to have existed in Britain, but now imagined as a Platonic idea:

> Beyond yon braided clouds that lie
> Paving the light-embroidered sky,
> Amidst the bright pavilioned plains,
> The beauteous model still remains.

It is also a sort of Valhalla where British heroes, happier than the classical heroes in the Blessed Isles,

> Hear their consorted Druids sing
> Their triumphs to the immortal string.

As we should expect, the architecture of this temple is a mixture of the classical and the non-classical:

> In Gothic pride it seems to rise!
> Yet Graecia's graceful orders join
> Majestic through the mixed design.

If Collins ever thought of erecting his temple

> Midst the green navel of our isle,

he could have found a suitable architect in Batty Langley who, four years before, had published his *Gothic Architecture, improved by Rules and Proportions, in many Grand Designs of Columns, Doors, Windows, Chimney-Pieces, Arcades, Colonnades, Porticos, Umbrellos, Temples, and Pavilions etc.* Perhaps, indeed, Collins derived his temple from *Gothic Architecture Improved*.

    This ambivalence of taste, rejecting the Augustan but uncertain whether to choose Grecian or Gothic, and sometimes seeking an impossible compromise between the two, or diverging into chin-oiserie, is widespread in the 1740s, when Collins was writing. Horace

---

* The first epode is simply headed "Epode", which may indicate that originally Collins intended only the one.

Walpole's sophisticated and ironic intelligence could differentiate, and appraise both. Strawberry Hill and *The Castle of Otranto* were the work of playing hours, when he chose to indulge the heretical corner of his heart. The serious business of his life was the composition, in series of letters, of a history of his own times, 'to make posterity stare,' said Gray, 'and all good people cross themselves'.

Collins placed the odes in his book with some care, and a collection which began with Pity and Fear might be suitably concluded with *The Manners* and *The Passions*. These abstractions are not addressed in the final pair of odes, which are purely descriptive, as their titles indicate, and which are closely linked together. *The Manners* is an appropriately Wykehamical title for an ode by one who, as Gilbert White (who knew Collins at Oxford) remarked, had 'too high an opinion of his school acquisitions, and a sovereign contempt for all academic studies and discipline'. The poem celebrates his relief at turning from the academic task of translating Aristotle's *Poetics* (from which the Odes *To Pity* and *To Fear* derived) to the more congenial study of observing human character. 'Under this general head of manners,' Dryden had said, 'the passions are naturally included as belonging to the characters. I speak not of pity and of terror, which are to be moved in the audience by the plot; but of anger, hatred, love, ambition, jealousy, revenge, etc., as they are shown in this or that person of the play.' In the second of these poems Collins describes the passions of Fear, Anger, Despair, Hope, Revenge, Pity, Jealousy, Love, Hate, Melancholy, Cheerfulness, Joy, and Mirth, a longer list than Dryden's (which was admittedly incomplete) but including all those he named, if Hope may be taken to include Ambition. He apportions various metres to them, in the manner of Dryden's *Song for St Cecilia's Day*, and sets these in a frame of octosyllabic couplets addressed to Music, which he derives from Greece. The poem, and the book, conclude with yet another invocation:

> O bid our vain endeavors cease,
> Revive the just designs of Greece
> Return in all thy simple state!
> Confirm the tales her sons relate!

The Passions, in a setting by William Hayes, Professor of Music at Oxford, was performed at Encaenia 1750. Later that year Collins told Hayes that he had written an ode on *The Music of the Grecian Theatre*, of which eighteen lines, perhaps all that he ever wrote, have survived.

In this ode, he said (in words which imply that it was already finished),
'I have, I hope naturally, introduced the various characters with
which the chorus was concerned, as Oedipus, Medea, Electra, Orestes
etc. etc.' The poem was therefore intended to bring together in a
wholly Grecian context the ideas which formed the theme of *The
Manners* and *The Passions*, but, like so many of Collins' projects, it
seems never to have got beyond an imaginative construction in his
brain. But it is of interest that as late as the autumn of 1750, shortly
before madness clouded that brain, Collins was still returning to the
Grecian taste which, in the eyes of those who understood him best,
was his true felicity.

Dickens, in *Great Expectations*, tells us that Mr Wopsle, after
reciting Mark Antony's oration over the body of Caesar, always
followed it with Collins' *The Passions*, wherein, says Pip,

> I particularly venerated Mr Wopsle as Revenge, throwing his
> blood-stain'd sword in thunder down, and taking the War-
> denouncing trumpet with a withering look. It was not with me
> then, as it was in later life, when I fell into the society of the
> Passions, and compared them with Collins and Wopsle, rather to
> the disadvantage of both gentlemen.

However, Mr Wopsle had not much in the way of Grecian taste: for
him *The Passions* was a fine declamatory piece of verse—good ham
stuff. Neither need we suppose that Dickens was expressing any
opinion on Collins' poetry.

In 1751 one Chimaericus Oxoniensis, who was most probably
Thomas Warton, published an *Ode to Horror, in the Allegoric,
Descriptive,*Alliterative, Epithetical, Fantastic, Hyperbolic and Diaboli-
cal Style of our Modern Ode-Wrights, and Monody-Mongers*. The
obvious victims were Joseph Warton and William Collins, though
Akenside and Gray were also qualified as Ode-Wrights. Joseph
Warton's poem *The Enthusiast; or The Love of Nature*, published in
1744, invites fraternal mockery:

> O curfeu-loving goddess haste!
> O waft me to some Scythian waste,
> Where, in Gothic solitude,
> Mid prospects most sublimely rude,

---

* Collins' book was entitled *Odes on Several Descriptive and Allegoric Subjects.*

> Beneath a rough rock's gloomy chasm,
> Thy sister sits, Enthusiasm.

Collins is contrasted with Warton as Grecian with Gothic. After a reference to Spenser's Florimell, who provided the initial image for the *Ode on the Poetical Character*, Horror is again invoked:

> O haste thee, mild Miltonic maid,
> From yonder yew's sequester'd shade;
> More bright than all the fabled Nine,
> Teach us to breathe the solemn line!
> O bid my well-rang'd numbers rise
> Pervious to none but Attic eyes.

To Thomas Warton, whose own preferences were the Gothic, the dominant feature of Collins' poetry was Grecian.

Collins' letter to William Hayes describing his new ode *On the Music of the Grecian Theatre* was dated 8 November 1750, and is thus his last known reference to writing poetry. Some time during the previous winter Collins addressed to John Home, the Scottish playwright, *An Ode on the Popular Superstitions of the Highlands of Scotland, Considered as the Subject of Poetry* (to give it the editorial title, which was not Collins'). Towards the end of 1749 Home came to London in the hope of persuading Garrick to stage his play *Agis*. Collins, who knew Garrick and other members of the theatrical world of London, was introduced to Home by Thomas Barrow, the 'cordial youth' of the first stanza, who was also a native of Chichester. There Collins and Home later made an expedition to visit him for a week or two. Home and Barrow had participated in a romantic and daring exploit during the Jacobite Rebellion. Both fought as volunteers, on the Hanoverian side, in the battle of Falkirk—they were at the University of Edinburgh, where Barrow was studying medicine—and both were taken prisoner by Prince Charles Edward's troops and confined in the Castle of Doune. From there they escaped, under Home's leadership, by the time-honoured method of twisting a rope from sheets and blankets and descending from a window. Barrow, who was sixth out, had to follow a large man, whose weight broke the rope short. Sir Walter Scott met Home, who was a friend of his parents, while still a child, and his first-hand story of the escape appealed to Scott's imagination, as it would to that of most boys. Home lived on till 1808, when he was eighty-five, and in later years

Scott was a frequent visitor to his house near Edinburgh, eager (we may suppose) to hear everything Home could tell of the '45. (Barrow's widow, who, at the time of the ode, was his 'destined bride', died in London in 1814, wheh she was eighty-seven.) In a note to *Waverley* Scott recounted the escape from Doune:

> Determined to take the risk, even in such unfavourable circum-
> stances, Barrow committed himself to the broken rope, slid down
> on it as far as it could assist him, and then let himself drop. His
> friends beneath succeeded in breaking his fall. Nevertheless, he
> dislocated his ankle, and had several of his ribs broken. His
> companions, however, were able to bear him off in safety.

Collins, who responded to the Jacobite Rebellion with excitement, and who, when news of the battle of Falkirk came, wrote 'How sleep the brave', would have been eager to hear again from the lips of the man who led the adventure the story of the escape, though it was already familiar to him from Barrow. Few things please us more than accounts of our friends' courage, and Home would certainly have praised the fortitude shown by Barrow at Doune. Collins cast his mind back to his own feelings at the time of Falkirk, and later, when he had pleaded for mercy to the three rebel peers. The sympathy which he then felt with the Scots was enhanced now by listening to a gallant and gifted Scot, and he was fascinated by the information which he could give of the primitive society of the clansmen. Characteristically, Collins' imagination was stirred to consider this as a subject for poetry, and he gave to Home, on the eve of his return to Scotland in 1750, the longest poem he ever wrote.

The ode begins with a graceful recollection of the *Ode, Occasioned by the Death of Mr Thomson*, since a farewell to one Scottish poet might properly recall that more sombre farewell to another. Again, the pastoral tone prevails, appropriate to the condition of the Highlands; and the juxtaposition of Celtic and Greek is as effective as in 'How sleep the brave'. Collins follows Spenser in giving a Northern tinge to his vocabulary in order to 'imitate the Doric of Theocritus':

> There must thou wake perforce the Doric quill,
>   'Tis Fancy's land to which thou sett'st thy feet;
>   Where still, 'tis said, the fairy people meet
> Beneath each birken shade on mead or hill.

There each trim lass that skims the milky store
To the swart tribes their creamy bowl allots.

Near the end of the poem Collins writes of the witches in *Macbeth*,
and of

The shadowy kings of Banquo's fated line;

and he refers to the story of Tancred in the Enchanted Wood in canto
XIII of Tasso's *Gerusalemme Liberata*, which he read in Fairfax's
translation. (A new edition was published in October 1749, and early
in 1750 there was twice advertised *An Epistle to the Editor of Fairfax
his Translation of Tasso's Jerusalem Delivered. By Mr William Collins*.
But this too seems to have been one of Collins' good intentions.)
Collins' purpose in quoting these great precedents of Shakespeare and
Tasso was to recommend John Home to write on such supernatural
themes, which were amply provided in the folk-lore and traditions of
his native Scotland, in preference to a Greek subject such as he had
used in his rejected tragedy, *Agis*.

Home wisely took Collins' advice, and based his next tragedy,
Douglas, on the Scottish ballad *Childe Maurice*. Garrick refused this
also, but it was successfully performed in Edinburgh in December
1756, and a few months later the success was repeated at Covent
Garden. It remained very popular for sixty years or more, and Tom
Bertram in *Mansfield Park* remembered it at country house theatricals. These things show Collins' perspicacious understanding of the
way in which Home might best develop his natural gift; they also
show how sincerely he himself was attracted by the primitive and
remote. But these romantic inclinations were not likely, even if he
had been able to write poetry after this time, to have prevailed against
his own often stated preference for the poetry and the traditions of
Greece. He was not, after all, a Scot, but a southern Englishman; and
much as he delighted in the fairy way he was best suited to the
sophisticated simplicity of the Grecian way.

Hindsight permits, or compels, us to make judgments which are
never open to a contemporary, since the foresight which might
enable him to anticipate the judgment of posterity is, at best,
precarious. We may justifiably discover in Collins' poetry suggestions
of the later romanticism: one of Wordsworth's earliest poems was his
Remembrance of Collins composed upon the Thames near Richmond, with
its obvious remembrances of Collins on Thomson; Coleridge and

Keats were also early indebted to Collins, especially for his vivid power of description; and Shelley sometimes seems to recall Collins' manner. They all drew from his poetry, as any poet must, what met their own imaginative needs. But we are not to judge the excellence of his poetry by the benefits it conferred on later, and greater, poets; their borrowings were necessarily selective, and partial, and we are to try to judge it for all those particular qualities which differentiate it from any other. Coleridge, in *Biographia Literaria*, recollects that in 1791 he helped a friend with a paper which he had been invited to read to a literary society in Devon: they 'assigned', he says, 'sundry reasons, chiefly drawn from a comparison of passages in the Latin poets with the original Greek, from which they were borrowed, for the preference of Collins' odes to those of Gray.' Coleridge's critical judgment was right. So was Hazlitt's, who said of Collins, 'In his best works there is an Attic simplicity.' Gray knew Greek literature perhaps more thoroughly than Collins; but it had not affected his imagination nearly so intimately. Whatever premonitions of their own poetry the Romantics discovered in Collins' these must not obstruct our view of poetry which, at its individual best, in the *Ode to Simplicity* and the *Ode to Evening*, in 'How sleep the brave' and in the *Ode, Occasioned by the Death of Mr Thomson*, is always predominantly Grecian.

4 Oliver Goldsmith (?1730– 1774)

The Greeks . . . now exerted all their happy talents in the investigation of truth, and the production of beauty. Before this, the works of art were remarkable only for the vastness of design, and seemed the production of giants, not of ordinary men; learning was another name for magic, or to give it its real appellation, imposture. But these improvers saw there was more excellence in captivating the judgment, than in raising a momentary astonishment: in their art they imitated only such parts of nature, as might please in the representation.

An Enquiry into the Present State of Polite Learning in Europe, 1759, Ch. II

Oliver Goldsmith was born in Ireland about 1730—the place and date of his birth are both uncertain. He went to Trinity College, Dublin, where, in 1747, he was publicly reprimanded for taking part in a student riot, but he stayed to take his degree; he failed to be accepted for ordination; thought of emigrating to North America; considered studying law in London, and finally went to the University of Edinburgh in 1752 to study medicine. After eighteen months there he went to Leyden to continue his medical studies, but he spent most of 1755 wandering about Europe, and in the course of his travels he reached Italy. During this year he commenced poet, with *The Traveller*, though this was not published until 1764; and in 1756 he returned from the Continent and came to London, where he spent the rest of his life.

Impecunious, ill–organized, tactless, vain of conversational talents which he conspicuously lacked, in many ways absurd, Goldsmith was compelled to make a hazardous living by hack-work for a variety of publishers, and much of his enormous output is now of very little interest. But, as Dr Johnson, who got to know him not long after he settled in London, said, 'Let not his frailties be remembered. He was a very great man.' Dr Johnson, who composed the Latin epitaph on his monument in Westminster Abbey (in which his place of birth is given the suitably Grecian name of Pallas*), and another in Greek verse, in

* That is, Pallas, Co. Westmeath, or Pallasmore, Co. Longford.

both described him as 'poet, historian and naturalist'. It may be doubted whether 'naturalist' with its modern connotations correctly translates Dr Johnson's *physici* or φυσικόν, for he believed that Goldsmith's knowledge had not progressed beyond the ability to distinguish a horse from a cow. But Johnson defended his praise of Goldsmith as a historian to Sir Joshua Reynolds and Boswell, and when the latter incautiously demurred, Johnson insisted: Goldsmith, he said, 'has the art of compiling and of saying every thing he has to say in a pleasing manner'. If we should be more likely to praise Goldsmith as poet, playwright, novelist and essay-writer, Dr Johnson would not have denied these other claims. 'Is there a man, Sir, now,' he asked a critic, 'who can pen an essay with such ease and elegance as Goldsmith?' (The phrase, 'ease and elegance', was the same that Goldsmith himself used to commend the prose of Dryden.) And on another occasion Dr Johnson gave this comprehensive praise of Goldsmith, that he 'was a man, who, whatever he wrote, did it better than any other man could do'.

Now Goldsmith, unlike Akenside and Collins, was no precocious writer contributing verses to *The Gentleman's Magazine* while still a school-boy, and this was probably to his advantage: his style did not prematurely settle into a manner from which he found it difficult to break free. His earliest essays have a happy simplicity which we should expect to be the result of long practice, but which must be the result of attentive reading combined with natural talent. 'To copy nature,' he wrote, 'is a task the most bungling workman is able to execute; to select such parts as contribute only to delight is reserved for those whom accident has blessed with uncommon talents, or such as have read the Ancients with indefatigable industry.' He himself was doubly qualified. His earliest work, *The Traveller*, is in verse, and even if a man fails to become a poet the attempt to write poetry is likely to benefit his prose style. For *The Traveller* Goldsmith chose the heroic couplet although he realized that, since Akenside and Thomson, the form was going out of fashion except for satire. It had been the favourite form of many writers whose work he admired, but did not wish to imitate; and he probably avoided blank verse for the same reason that Shelley avoided it in *The Revolt of Islam*, because in it 'there is no shelter for mediocrity; you must either succeed or fail.' He lacked the bold self-confidence which enabled Akenside to make a success of blank verse in *The Pleasures of Imagination*, and he used the couplet as Wordsworth would use it in his early poems, *An Evening Walk*, and *Descriptive Sketches*; but we must not deduce from this that either Goldsmith or Wordsworth was a belated Augustan in his youth. Some of Goldsmith's less attentive readers thought so, and even suggested that Dr Johnson had written *The Traveller* out of sheer benevolence to his struggling friend. But Johnson, while admitting that he had contributed a few lines to the poem, denied that Goldsmith's style resembled his own; and Akenside, who was always a most perceptive critic, saw from the first that it could not be Johnson's and praised it highly.

Goldsmith himself, in his *Account of the Augustan Age of England*, treats the writers of Queen Anne's reign as quite distinct from himself and his own contemporaries. He regrets the present decline of interest in poetry, but is uncertain whether the readers or the writers are most at fault. The *Account*, published in *The Bee* late in 1759, often recalls his first independent work, *An Enquiry into the Present State of Polite Learning in Europe*, which was published in the spring of the same year. There he condemns 'the inflated style that has for some years been looked upon as fine writing . . . Let us, instead of writing finely, try to write naturally.' Whichever writers he had in mind—Gray, perhaps, whose *Odes* he reviewed without enthusiasm—he himself had both the good sense to take his own advice, and the gifts that enabled him to put it into practice.

Goldsmith established his reputation first as a poet, with the publication in December 1764 of *The Traveller*. He had been nine years in writing it, for, as he reminded his brother in the dedication, he had sent part of it to him from Switzerland, where he was in the summer of 1755. Whether he then laid it aside for some years until encouraged by Johnson to take it up again, or whether he returned to it as time allowed, is unknown; neither do we know whether the delay in publishing was by his own choice, or his publisher's. He had been busy during these years in desperate attempts to earn a living (in Boswell's words) as 'an usher to an academy, a corrector of the press, a reviewer, and a writer for a news-paper'. He had published a translation from the French, the *Enquiry into the Present State of Polite Learning in Europe*, periodical essays in *The Bee* and the *Chinese Letters* (collected as *The Citizen of the World* in 1762), a biography, an oratorio, and a *History of England*. He had written *The Vicar of Wakefield*, which was ready for the press by the autumn of 1762 when Dr Johnson got him sixty guineas for it; but his reputation was too slight to induce the book-sellers to think it worth hurrying into print. Publication of *The Traveller* changed all that: it was immediately successful and, as Dr Johnson said, 'brought him into high reputation'. In some respects it anticipates *The Deserted Village*, which is now, but was not then, much preferred.

Dr Johnson told Boswell that he contributed nine lines to the poem, all near the end of it, and he marked them in pencil in Boswell's copy, which survives. They are clearly different in style from the rest of the poem, and by their contrast show up the un-Augustan quality of Goldsmith's writing. The first of these lines,

> To stop too fearful, and too faint to go

replaces the line with which Goldsmith originally completed his couplet:

> The pensive exile, bending with his woe,
> And faintly fainter, fainter seems to go.

This repetition of a word is characteristic of Goldsmith's style. Hazlitt remarked it: Goldsmith had (he wrote) 'a peculiar felicity in his turns upon words, which he constantly repeated with delightful effect'. But to Johnson the deleted line must have seemed ridiculously mannered, and he replaced it with a good Augustan antithesis, complete with chiasmic arrangement and heavy caesura. His line makes no compromise with its context in ten lines which form a single sentence, which seldom end with a heavier pause than a comma, and which nowhere else have the strong caesura. Johnson also contributed eight of the final ten lines to the poem: the closed Augustan couplets read as if Goldsmith had lifted them from one of Johnson's poems and sought to make them his own by the interpolation of a couplet which breaks the Johnsonian form.

There is some evidence that in its first draft *The Traveller* was closer to the Augustan manner than Goldsmith chose to leave it. The draft, to which Goldsmith gave the title of *A Prospect of Society* (the sub-title of the revised text), is known from a unique and confused copy which contains about three quarters of the final text. In *A Prospect of Society* we have these lines:

> And yet, perhaps, if states with states we scan,
> Or estimate their bliss on Reason's plan,
> Though patriots flatter, and though fools contend,
> We still shall find the doubtful scale depend,
> Find that each good, by Art or Nature given,
> To these or those, but makes the balance even.

The Augustan quality of imagery, diction, syntax and verse is obvious, though the couplets are not so tightly closed as in the *Essay on Man*, whose fourth Epistle they recall. The revised text is noticeably looser and more fluent:

> And yet, perhaps, if countries we compare,
> And estimate the blessings which they share,
> Though patriots flatter, still shall wisdom find
> An equal portion dealt to all mankind,
> As different good, by Art or Nature given,
> To different nations makes their blessings even.

The image of the balance, which invites antithesis, has been discarded; the second line quoted is more relaxed, both in metrical form and in sense, than in the first version; and the repetition of 'different' in the last couplet is in Goldsmith's characteristic manner. Other passages show similar types of revision in addition to simple corrections, or substitutions of a more suitable word.

In a poem which Goldsmith included in one of his *Chinese Letters* in 1760, and republished two years later in *The Citizen of the World*, and which is now entitled *The Description of an Author's Bedchamber*, there is a burlesque description of Nature, put into the mouth of the poverty-stricken poet. The poem ends thus:

> The morn was cold, he views with keen desire
> The rusty grate unconscious of a fire;
> With beer and milk arrears the frieze was scored,
> And five cracked tea-cups dressed the chimney board.
> A nightcap decked his brows instead of bay,
> A cap by night—a stocking all the day!

In the text of the letter in which the poem is inserted Goldsmith comments ironically on this Hogarthian scene:

> There gentlemen! (his poet cries out,) there is a description for you. Rabelais's bed-chamber is but a fool to it:
> A cap by night—a stocking all the day! There is sound and sense, and truth, and nature in the trifling compass of ten little syllables!

And the irony is not the less pointed because Goldsmith was portraying himself. For this comment on 'sound and sense, and truth

and nature' is precisely in the terms of serious Augustan commendation, to show that he is here ridiculing their standards. The
heavy median caesura in the final line is characteristic of the Augustan
heroic couplet, but, as I have shown, quite uncharacteristic of his
own. He is here burlesquing the Augustan manner in order to
burlesque Augustan appreciation: obviously critical comment
phrased in recognizably Augustan terms must have an equally
recognizable point of reference.

Goldsmith re-used some of the details from this parody in *The
Deserted Village*, but seriously, and changed to details of domestic
comfort. The description is of the village inn. Here, instead of

> The sanded floor that grits beneath the tread;
> The humid wall with paltry pictures spread . . .

we have

> The white-washed wall, the nicely sanded floor,

and

> The pictures placed for ornament and use.

Instead of

> The rusty grate unconscious of a fire,

we have

> The hearth, except when winter chilled the day,
> With aspen boughs and flowers and fennel gay.

And, quite apart from the substitution of gaiety for gloom, comfort
for discomfort, the easy flow of the verse, with no caesura, contrasts
with the heavy caesura of the parody. Again, in the parody, we have

> And five cracked teacups dressed the chimney board;

but in *The Deserted Village*, though the china is in no better repair, it is
made to point a moral fully in accord with the tradition of sentiment:

While broken teacups, wisely kept for show,
Ranged o'er the chimney, glistened in a row.

They suggest the house-proud domesticity of the village inn-keeper,
with his pathetic economy in preserving broken china for *ornament*
even when it can no longer fulfil the *use* for which it was bought.
Lastly, though not now at the end of the description, instead of the
stocking night-cap of the impoverished poet, we have a piece of
furniture which, again with decent economy, fulfils two uses:

The chest contrived a double debt to pay,
A bed by night, a chest of drawers by day.

It would obviously be inadequate to apply to these lines in all
seriousness the Augustan commendation of 'sound and sense, and
truth and nature' of the *Chinese Letter*. For they suggest a different
sensibility—more sympathetic and less detached, upholding the
claims of sentiment rather than of intellect, more willing to praise
what is good than to castigate what is evil or to deride what is false.
Those broken teacups, for example: what place could they have had
in Pope's poetry but as symbols of squalor?

However, I must not seem to suggest that in *The Deserted Village*
Goldsmith was anticipating Wordsworth. For all his kindness and
readiness to note the praiseworthy efforts of the poor to make the best
of things—to polish, until it glistens, china that had been demoted
from use to ornament—there is still an amused condescension in his
attitude. The swain and the milk-maid are part of the country scene,
observed from outside, and catalogued with the rest of the fauna.

There, as I passed with careless steps and slow,
The mingling notes came softened from below,
The swain responsive to the milkmaid sung,
The sober herd that lowed to meet their young;
The noisy geese that gabbled o'er the pool,
The playful children just let loose from school;
The watchdog's voice that bayed the whispering wind,
And the loud laugh that spoke the vacant mind.

Each couplet unites a human and animal element in the scene, with no
ironic suggestion of disparity of interest such as Pope implies in a
similar juxtaposition:

> Not louder shrieks to pitying Heav'n are cast,
> When husbands or when lap-dogs breathe their last.

Besides, the rhythm of Goldsmith's verse, here in its fullest development, is very un-Augustan, ignoring the antithetical possibilities that
Pope exploited so brilliantly, and using the couplet more in the
Elizabethan manner, so that it moves easily forward without the
emphatic Augustan pauses at the end of each couplet. For Goldsmith
the unit was not the couplet but the paragraph; he regards the couplet
not as stanzaic, but as an alternative to blank verse—the blank verse of
Thomson or Akenside or Cowper. He was not attempting epigram-
matic wit, but elegant description.

Goldsmith alludes to his style in his dedication to Sir Joshua
Reynolds: 'How far you may be pleased with the versification and
mere mechanical parts of this attempt, I don't pretend to enquire'; but
the qualities that are characteristic of his writing are immediately
apparent. There is no full stop until we reach the fourteenth line; most
couplets run on with no more than a comma at the end; few lines have
a marked caesura, and even those that do—

> The sheltered cot, the cultivated farm—

make no syntactic use of it. These opening lines also show that
sentiment is to be of great importance in the poem, and that
Goldsmith will be more concerned to express his own response to an
observed situation than to express the response of its victims. We feel
with Goldsmith rather than with the dispersed inhabitants of Auburn
who, as a result of the Inclosure Acts, have been sucked into the new
urban industries or, worse, forced to emigrate to America, to

> The various terrors of that horrid shore,

and to

> Those matted woods where birds forget to sing.

Goldsmith, certainly, is sad that such things are happening; it is less
certain that the labourers of Auburn are sad; they may, for all we
know, consider that they have bettered themselves.

In 1771, the year after the publication of *The Deserted Village*,
Reynolds returned the compliment of Goldsmith's dedication with a
picture to which, when it was engraved next year, he gave the title

'Resignation'; he dedicated to Goldsmith 'This attempt to express a Character in *The Deserted Village*'. The character is that of an old man in unspoiled Auburn, who

> crowns in shades like these
> A youth of labour with an age of ease,

—a circumstance whose frequency we are at liberty to doubt—and who there

> Bends to the grave with unperceived decay,
> While resignation gently slopes the way.

Hence the title of Reynolds' picture. Such subjects were common enough with neo-classical artists: Gainsborough's 'The Harvest Wagon' and his 'Milkmaid and Farmer's Boy,' which are contemporary with *The Deserted Village*, and Edward Penny's 'The Generosity of Johnny Pearmain,' of a few years later, show the English country folk as the inhabitants of a pastoral Arcadia whose fragility may be implied or frankly stated. Such pictures demonstrate the predominantly literary inspiration of neo-classical painting scarcely less clearly than pictures of Philoctetes or Niobe, or Wright of Derby's 'The Dead Soldier'.

These paintings also suggest the method of composition from an ideal image, from an idea; and this, clearly, is Goldsmith's method. *The Deserted Village* does not portray any particular village, and attempts to identify it with Lissoy or any other can only be undertaken by persons wholly incapable of understanding the poem. (The 'country excursions of these four or five years past' to which Goldsmith refers did not include Ireland.) What Goldsmith is writing about is the situation in the countryside generally in his time, which he, and others, regretted: it is a poem about the idea of rural depopulation, not about its effects observed in one particular place. Therefore Auburn has no individual characteristics which allow its identification; neither have its inhabitants. Reynolds' painting 'Resignation' is not a portrait. He did not, instructed by Goldsmith, go down to some village in the country to seek out an old man to whose cottage Goldsmith had given him directions: it shows an elderly peasant calmly resigned to old age and the approach of death. Reynolds and Goldsmith provide a view of a peasantry idealized by

the intelligentsia. Goldsmith may quote from the opening of
Theocritus' first Idyll:

> Sweet was the sound, when oft at evening's close
> Up yonder hill the village murmur rose,

and the frequent repetition of the epithet 'sweet' is Theocritean. But
he has nothing of Theocritus' intimate knowledge of the life of
peasant and shepherd. He does not understand such lives from within,
as Thomas Hardy does. Sentiment and actuality make unlikely
partners.

The village schoolmaster and preacher are, again, ideal. 'I knew
him well,' says Goldsmith of the schoolmaster, but surely with no
expectation that anyone would be so naive as to take this literally.
And the village preacher is claimed to be a portrait of Goldsmith's
father, or perhaps of his brother. No doubt filial and fraternal
affection had a part in this, and in the dedication to his brother of *The
Traveller*, he had described him as one 'who despising fame and
fortune, had retired early to happiness and obscurity, with an income
of forty pounds a year'. But, again, the portrayal is of the ideal village
preacher who is endowed with the Christian virtues of charity,
humility, meekness and compassion, and therefore

> A man he was to all the country dear,
> And passing rich on forty pounds a year;

and in his selflessness

> More skilled to raise the wretched than to rise.

Whether Goldsmith had in mind his father or brother when he
composed these lines is not important: very probably he derived from
them some elements in the ideal he sought to delineate.

Dr Johnson, who had contributed nine lines to the last part of *The
Traveller*, also contributed the final two couplets to *The Deserted
Village*: perhaps Goldsmith's very fluency made it difficult to come to
an end that satisfied him. (He wrote three epilogues to *She Stoops to
Conquer*, and the unfinished state of *Retaliation* need not be due to the
intervention of death.) Johnsonian couplets are more obviously
conclusive than anything in Goldsmith's manner. But Dr Johnson
preferred *The Traveller*, nor are the reasons far to seek. In *The Deserted*

Village Goldsmith had moved further from the Augustan tradition which Johnson especially admired; and instead of general descriptions of the state of society in Italy and Switzerland, in France and Holland and Britain, he was now offering descriptions of a country village and its former boorish inhabitants. Such persons, in Dr Johnson's opinion, did not make fit subjects for poetry.

> The state of a man confined to the employments and pleasures of the country, is so little diversified, and exposed to so few of those accidents which produce perplexities, terrors, and surprises, in more complicated transactions, that he can be shown but seldom in such circumstances as attract curiosity.

Goldsmith would probably not have dissented. His purpose in *The Deserted Village* was to exhibit another contrasting prospect of society; not now 'to show that there may be equal happiness in states, that are differently governed from our own', but to compare the present destitution in the countryside with a supposed former state of contented innocence. Wordsworth's leech-gatherer and Michael, his Betty Foy and Alice Fell are still far from Goldsmith's concern. He is sad that the pirates have invaded the Arcadia of his nostalgic imagination; Wordsworth grew indignant and angry at the undeserved misfortunes of men and women, and even children, whom he knew.

Goldsmith finished *The Vicar of Wakefield* before he began work on *The Deserted Village*. It has obvious affinities with *Joseph Andrews*, published a quarter of a century before, but one can hardly imagine Fielding commending his hero in the terms in which Goldsmith commends Dr Primrose; who 'unites in himself the three greatest characters upon earth—he is a priest, a husbandman, and the father of a family. He is drawn as ready to teach, and ready to obey: as simple in affluence, and majestic in adversity.' Fielding wrote *Joseph Andrews* to mock Richardson's *Pamela*: to laugh at sentiment, not to extol it. Fielding's novel is a comedy, with some serious overtones; Goldsmith's a serious novel of sentiment, with some comic episodes.

The neo-classical quality of Goldsmith's writing is at once apparent. In the opening chapter the Vicar's daughter Olivia is described as being 'now about eighteen, [and she] had that luxuriancy of beauty with which painters generally draw Hebe.' The description of her in terms of a painting, the selection of Hebe (a favourite neo–classical subject*) for comparison, and the suggestion of ideal beauty thereby implied (for Hebe was goddess of youth), are all in keeping. Then of Sir William Thornhill we are told that 'The slightest distress, whether real or fictitious, touched him to the quick, and his soul laboured under a sickly sensibility of the miseries of others.' 'Whether real or fictitious' made no difference to Sir William, nor, we may suppose, to his inventor. But Sir William's 'sickly sensibility' reminds one of the similarly afflicted Sarah Fletcher who, as the inscription on her grave at Dorchester-on-Thames assures us, 'at the age of 27 sunk and died a martyr to excessive sensibility'.

In the eighth chapter there is a conversation about poetry in which Gay is compared, to his disadvantage, with Ovid. To this Mr Burchell remarks,

> Both the poets you mention have equally contributed to introduce a false taste into their respective countries, by loading all their lines with epithet . . . English poetry, like that in the latter empire of Rome, is nothing at present but a combination of luxuriant images, without plot or connection; a string of epithets, that improve the sound without carrying on the sense.

(Mr Burchell might be criticizing *Endymion* or *The Eve of St Agnes* by anticipation.) And he proves his point with the ballad of *Edwin and Angelina*.

Other characters in the novel show their concern with taste, and when the Primrose family decide to give a commission to a travelling portrait painter, who had already visited the Flamboroughs,

> Our next deliberation was to show the superiority of our taste in the attitudes. As for our neighbour's family, there were seven of them, and they were drawn with seven oranges—a thing quite out of taste, no variety in life, no composition in the world. We desired to have something in a brighter style, and, after many debates, at length came to an unanimous resolution of being drawn together in one large historical family piece. . . . For all families of any taste were now drawn in the same manner.

---

* For example, Gavin Hamilton's '*Lady Hamilton as Hebe*'. Canova carved four statues of Hebe; M. W. Peters painted a sister of the painter J. H. Mortimer as Hebe.

That is to say, they resolved to be portrayed as figures from classical myth or history, in poses ('attitudes') derived from classical sculpture.

> My wife desired to be represented as Venus. . . . Her two little ones were to be as Cupids by her side. . . . Olivia would be drawn as an Amazon, sitting upon a bank of flowers, dressed in a green Joseph, richly laced with gold, and a whip in her hand. Sophia was to be a shepherdess, with as many sheep as the painter could get in for nothing.

The Vicar himself 'in my gown and bands', and Moses 'with a hat and white feather', somewhat disrupted the classical ensemble; nevertheless, 'our taste so much pleased the Squire, that he insisted on being put in as one of the family, in the character of Alexander the Great, at Olivia's feet.' Goldsmith was familiar with this kind of composition from the painting of his friend Reynolds, whose 'Lady Sarah Bunbury sacrificing to the Graces' and 'Garrick between Tragedy and Comedy' were executed in this same decade of the 1760s. Novel and paintings are the product of the same phase in taste, whose Grecian rather than Augustan ancestry is apparent in the inclusion in the painting of the Primrose family of Venus with attendant Cupids, an Amazon, a shepherdess, and Alexander the Great.

Goldsmith's novel was admired by many of his successors: by Scott and Jane Austen, by Dickens and Thackeray, among others. Scott, who was the best critic of them all, may be quoted: 'The admirable ease and grace of the narrative, as well as the pleasing truth with which the principal characters are designed, make this one of the most delightful of all novels, and this because it so well reconciles us to human nature.' More significant still with regard to Goldsmith's affinities with the neo-classical movement is Goethe's praise of *The Vicar of Wakefield*, of which Herder had recently read him a German translation. On his first visit to Sesenheim, in the company of Weyland, they went to call on the parson, whom Weyland knew. On arriving at the parsonage,

> The whole place was quiet and deserted, just as the village had been. . . . During supper I was preoccupied with an idea that had struck me before, so much so that I sank into thoughtful silence, though I was often roused from my meditations by the liveliness of the elder sister and the charm of the younger. I was speechless with amazement at finding myself in the midst of the Vicar of

Wakefield's family, in the flesh. Admittedly the father could not
compare with that excellent man—but where, after all, could one
find the like of him?

For a time, as he tells us in *Dichtung und Wahrheit*, he conducted his life
as a series of improvisations on Goldsmith's themes in the novel,
falling in love with Friederike (Sophia) and using the name Olivia for
her elder sister; and when Weyland handed him a copy of the book,
reading it aloud to the family, who at once recognized themselves
there. We have all, Goethe says, an awareness that we play a double
part in our lives, a real one and an ideal one; and it is from this
awareness that we are led to try to reach after the ideal. One of the
most innocent ways of intensifying this is by comparing ourselves
with characters in novels. Of those who deplore such behaviour he
asks whether 'the demands of every-day life so absorb people that
they should deny themselves the demands of something more ideally
beautiful'?

Now Goethe's response to the novel seems very similar to Scott's:
it reconciled him to human nature. Of Goldsmith's style, since he read
the book in a German translation, he can have had little knowledge,
apart from the humorous hints which Goldsmith himself gives in the
autobiographical twentieth chapter. There, looking back on his early
struggles for recognition—which at the time when he wrote had not
yet been accorded him—he observes that 'The public were more
importantly employed than to observe the easy simplicity of my
style, or the harmony of my periods.' This 'easy simplicity' prevented
remark by any but the most discriminating of critics, such as Dr
Johnson. A later critic, A. C. Bradley, wrote of Goldsmith that 'his
style is so spontaneous and fluid that you read without regarding it,
and only when you put the book down become aware that your mind
has been moving with perpetual ease and grace.' Just so: there is
nothing assertive, nothing mannered or idiosyncratic about it. No
one, hearing a paragraph from one of Goldsmith's essays read out,
could say at once, 'That is by Goldsmith.' His style is not immediately
identifiable as is that of many other great writers of prose, Sir Thomas
Browne, or Dr Johnson, or Gibbon, or Lamb, or Pater, or Doughty.
Most of us, on hearing a passage by Goldsmith read aloud, would be
more likely to say, 'That is very good. Who wrote it?' But it is not at
all easy, perhaps not possible, to distinguish those qualities which
might identify it as Goldsmith's alone. Indeed, in the quotation I have
made from Bradley, he is there seeking to suggest certain qualities in

Shelley's style by comparing it with Goldsmith's.

Nevertheless, we can discover what Goldsmith prefers to avoid. In passages already quoted he objects to 'the inflated stile that has for some years been looked upon as fine writing', and to the 'false taste' of Gay in loading all his lines with epithet. The inflated style of which he was thinking can be seen also in Gray's *Odes*—in the dedication of *The Traveller* he names Pindaric odes among contemporary absurdities— but it is something of a surprise to find him raising a similar objection to the *Elegy*. He included this in his anthology, *The Beauties of English Poesy*, but with the introductory note, 'This is a very fine poem, but overloaded with epithet.' And he was prepared to demonstrate this to Joseph Cradock: 'I'll mend Gray's Elegy,' he said, 'by leaving out an idle word in every line!

> The curfew tolls the knell of day,
>   The lowing herd winds o'er the lea;
> The plowman homeward plods his way,
>   And——'

In his own writing, whether in verse or prose, he was true to this ideal of an easy simplicity, uncluttered with epithet, the ideal of trying 'to write naturally'.

The mock epitaph on David Garrick in *Retaliation* (the poem Garrick had provoked by his extempore epitaph on Goldsmith) may demonstrate this.

> On the stage he was natural, simple, affecting:
> 'Twas only that, when he was off, he was acting.
> With no reason on earth to go out of his way,
> He turned and he varied full ten times a day.
> Though secure of our hearts, yet confoundedly sick,
> If they were not his own by finessing and trick,
> He cast off his friends, as a huntsman his pack,
> For he knew when he pleased he could whistle them back.
> Of praise a mere glutton, he swallowed what came,
> And the puff of a dunce, he mistook it for fame;
> Till his relish grown callous, almost to disease,
> Who peppered the highest was surest to please.

Goldsmith, with more acerbity than in any of the other portraits of his friends, contrasts the natural and simple qualities of Garrick on stage with his vanity and duplicity off stage. He does so, not by piling up descriptive epithets, but by noting Garrick's behaviour among his friends in a series of simple sentences composed of pronoun, verb and object—a pattern continued even into simile:

> He cast off his friends, as a huntsman [casts off] his pack,
> For he knew when he pleased he could whistle them back.

The effect is that of dramatic narrative, perfectly suited to show that the great actor when off stage was still acting.

In one of the most celebrated of his essays, in *The Bee*, Goldsmith describes the approach of Dr Johnson (perhaps not yet personally known to him) to the Fame Machine, a sort of Charon's chariot to carry deserving authors to the Temple of Fame.

> This was a very grave personage, whom at some distance I took for one of the most reserved and disagreeable figures I had seen; but as he approached, his appearance improved, and when I could distinguish him thoroughly, I perceived, that, in spite of the severity of his brow, he had one of the most good natured countenances that could be imagined. Upon coming to open the stage door, he lifted a parcel of folios into the seat before him, but our inquisitorial coachman at once shoved them out again. 'What, not take in my dictionary!' exclaimed the other in a rage. 'Be patient, sir, (replyed the coachman) I have drove a coach, man and boy, these two thousand years; but I do not remember to have carried above one dictionary during the whole time. That little book which I perceive peeping from one of your pockets, may I presume to ask what it contains?' 'A mere trifle, (replied the author) it is called the Rambler.' 'The Rambler! (says the coachman) I beg, sir, you'll take your place; I have heard our ladies in the court of Apollo frequently mention it with rapture; and Clio, who happens to be a little grave, has been heard to prefer it to the Spectator; though others have observed, that the reflections, by being refined, sometimes become minute.'

Again, the method is the same; there is little reliance on epithet, except for persons at a distance (Johnson, at first, and Clio), but we are shown Dr Johnson and the coachman responding to a dramatic situation by action and by speech which narrates action; and for this verbs and substantives, not epithets, are required.

Even in a passage of static description, where there is no opportunity for narrative, the method is unchanged. Dr Primrose describes his house:

> My house consisted of but one storey, and was covered with thatch, which gave it an air of great snugness; the walls on the inside were nicely whitewashed, and my daughters undertook to adorn them with pictures of their own designing. Though the same room served us for parlour and kitchen, that only made it the warmer. Besides, as it was kept with the utmost neatness, the dishes, plates, and coppers being well scoured, and all disposed in bright rows on the shelves, the eye was agreeably relieved, and did not want richer furniture. There were three apartments—one for my wife and me, another for our two daughters within our own, and the third with two beds for the rest of our children.

And there, with but two or three epithets, the Vicarage is before our eyes.

How well suited to comedy was Goldsmith's style scarcely needs illustration from *She Stoops to Conquer* or *The Good-Natur'd Man*: the sketches of Garrick and Dr Johnson already quoted are evidence enough. It provides a brisk forward impulse, with none of the delays and interruptions which fine writing and a surfeit of adjectives are sure to bring about. By making full use of the active verb rather than of epithet Goldsmith achieves a vigour and clarity which keep the reader's mind perpetually alert. The method is that of the Greek writers of prose such as Xenophon, whose style was then especially admired. William Hayley, in his *Essay on History*, thus praises Xenophon:

> Thy simple diction, free from glaring art,
> With sweet allurement steals upon the heart;
> Pure, as the rill that Nature's hand refines,
> A cloudless mirror of the soul it shines.

Hayley uses the same image of spring water that Winckelmann had used to define the stylistic ideal. We may suppose that the qualities of Xenophon's style that Hayley remarks were as apparent to Goldsmith as was the 'sweet allurement' that it conveyed. 'What historian can render virtue so amiable as Xenophon?' he asked in his *History of*

England: to render virtue amiable is surely the purpose of much of Goldsmith's writing.

Simplicity is a characteristic of the best writers of Greece, whom more and more of Goldsmith's contemporaries were coming to prefer as models. Collins invoked it in one of his finest odes; Winckelmann proclaimed it as one of the defining characteristics of Greek literature, no less than of Greek sculpture; and it was the quality which Goldsmith thought most apparent in his own style. In an imaginative piece of reminiscence Goldsmith tells how he offered his services as professor of Greek in the University of Louvain, only to be rejected by the Philistine principal who, no doubt, would have been just as insensitive to the easy simplicity of Goldsmith's English prose. We are accustomed to writers who insist on our attention, who demand our applause for their originality and cleverness; Goldsmith wrote for an audience whose taste had been refined and instructed by a wide reading in the literature of Greece or which was at least capable of appreciating in modern writers the unobtrusive Grecian qualities of ease and grace.

5 William Blake (1757–1827)

> . . . the purpose for which alone I live . . . is, in conjunction with such men as
> my friend Cumberland, to renew the lost Art of the Greeks.

Letter to Rev. Dr John Trusler,
16 August 1799

The art of William Blake, as engraver, painter and poet has generally been regarded as anomalous and unclassifiable. It is too idiosyncratic for useful comparisons to be made with the work of his contemporaries, and the obscurities of his private mythology hinder an easy understanding. In his own day he had little reputation except as an engraver, and a century and a half after his death the fame of the 'great, eccentric genius' seems to owe most to the eccentricity. In so far as his work can be associated with the taste of the later eighteenth century it appears more Gothic, as in the designs he made for Young's *Night Thoughts* or Blair's *The Grave*, than Grecian: Ossian is more evident than Sophocles. And his own apophthegm, 'Grecian is mathematic form, Gothic is living form' (formulated late in life), is quoted to settle an argument which, for most, never had much substance. But such remarks are the product not of consistent reasoning but of momentary insight, and we need to consider more closely what were the primary influences on Blake's awakening genius. The young 'Romantic' who delighted in the medieval architecture and sculpture of Westminster Abbey is more familiar than the middle-aged man who learnt Greek from William Hayley (and soon claimed that he could 'read Greek as fluently as an Oxford scholar'), or than the elderly man who engraved the Laocoon. An attempt to segregate the neo–classical, Grecian Blake from the Gothic (or Swedenborgian, or Christian) Blake may result in slight distortion of the uniquely composite Blake; but at least it will draw attention to aspects of Blake's art that have been somewhat neglected.

Blake was ten years old when his father sent him to the school in the Strand run by Henry Pars, for his first drawing lessons, his first lessons of any kind away from home. His family was not poor, and the school to which he went was the most fashionable and probably the best at the time; Blake's father, 'a moderately prosperous hosier', had the perspicacity to detect in his son's childish drawings signs of a talent which should be encouraged and guided. Henry Pars had a younger brother, William Pars, whose water-colours and drawings, transposed to engravings, illustrated the third volume of Stuart and Revett's *Antiquities of Athens*, 1794, and the two volumes of Revett and Chandler's *Antiquities of Ionia* which were published in 1769 and 1797. These famous books, which had so great an influence on the Grecian taste of the late eighteenth century, were sponsored by the Society of Dilettanti. In the years 1764–66 William Pars had accompanied Nicholas Revett and Richard Chandler as artist on their expedition to the Ionian coast, and he there made a series of water colours of ancient sites, among them the temple of Apollo Didymaeus at Branchidae and the temple of Athene Polias at Priene. When Blake went to Henry Pars' school William Pars had but recently returned from Ionia, and the child's imagination must have been immediately stirred by hearing of the Greek architecture and sculpture which the expedition had discovered. It seems likely that he then saw some of the drawings which Pars had brought back, for when, in 1791, Willey Reveley at the suggestion of George Cumberland wrote to ask him to engrave drawings by William Pars for the third volume of the *Antiquities of Athens* Blake replied in terms which suggest that he had already seen some of them: he was glad, he said, 'to embrace the offer of engraving such beautiful things'. But it is of more importance that the first great works of art with which he became acquainted were Greek, in the reliefs and capitals of temples depicted by Pars. Soon his father bought him casts of favourite works of the Greek Revival: the Farnese 'Hercules', the 'Dying Gladiator' (as the 'Dying Gaul' was then called), and the Medicean 'Venus'. There can be no doubt that the earliest, formative influences on Blake's imagination were Grecian, and, however much they would be masked by later Gothic influences, they remained dominant. Besides, for Blake the impact of visual experience was always primary; his education was entirely that of a painter and engraver, and throughout his life he associated almost exclusively with artists.

Blake remained with Henry Pars for about four years before going as an apprentice to James Basire who, in 1759, had succeeded George Vertue as engraver to the Society of Antiquaries. With him Blake soon worked on Jacob Bryant's *New System of Mythology*, which extended his knowledge beyond Greece to Egypt and Persia, and also showed him an eclectic approach to myth, which must have been congenial. After about two years, when Blake was sixteen, Basire sent him to draw in London churches, including Westminster Abbey, and so introduced him to Gothic architecture and sculpture. This was some six years after he had first become acquainted with the work of classical Greece, and though in Blake's imaginative world Gothic ornament overlay, and often obscured, Grecian design, the Grecian ideal remained.

One day, quite soon after he had begun his apprenticeship, Goldsmith walked into Basire's shop. Blake remembered how he 'mightily admired the great author's finely marked head as he gazed up at it, and thought to himself how much *he* should like to have such a head when he grew to be a man'. This first glimpse of a man of genius clearly made a vivid and lasting impression on him; there is no reason to suppose that Blake had then read any of Goldsmith's work, but he knew who he was. A book which Blake purchased, and no doubt read, while he was with Basire was Henry Fuseli's translation of Winckelmann's celebrated essay *Reflections on the Painting and Sculpture of the Greeks*. (This was ten years or more before he met Fuseli himself.) Blake's observations on art, in his letters, in the marginalia to Sir Joshua Reynolds' *Discourses*, in the *Descriptive Catalogue* of 1809, all show how strongly he was influenced by the prophet of neo-classicism. Other friends of later years besides Fuseli, among them John Flaxman, James Barry and William Hayley, were among the first in England to refer to Winckelmann's ideas in their writings: in the circle of which Blake was a member discussion of the *Reflections* must have been frequent, and it was under Winckelmann's guidance that they approached the arts of Greece and derived from these an ideal for their own attempts.

'The great and golden rule of art, as well as of life,' Blake proclaimed in the *Descriptive Catalogue*, 'is this: That the more distinct, sharp, and wiry the bounding line, the more perfect the work of art.' So Winckelmann called 'precision of contour' the 'characteristic distinction of the ancients. . . . The Greek artist . . . adjusted his contour, in every figure, to the breadth of a single hair.' And Blake's extravagant contempt for the Venetian painters' preference for colour rather than drawing derived no less certainly from Winckelmann. But Winckelmann would not have accepted Blake's savage criticism of Rubens or of Titian.

Some time during his years of apprenticeship to Basire Blake began to write poetry, but he must have realized that these first rather crude juvenilia had little promise, and when they were privately printed in 1783 he made no effort to circulate them. At the age of twenty-six he was not thinking of himself as a poet, if indeed he ever did: in his own judgment he was painter and engraver. This first book, *Poetical Sketches*, which was never published, was printed at the expense of John Flaxman, whom Blake had met the previous year, and of Harriet Mathew, wife of the Rev. A. S. Mathew of Percy Chapel in Charlotte Street. She held literary *conversazioni* in her house, and at these Blake read, or sometimes sang, these early poems. Flaxman took more interest in them than Blake himself, for he not only subscribed to the cost of printing, which he probably suggested, but in April 1784 sent a copy of the book to William Hayley, to whom he had been introduced by George Romney the previous autumn and whose recently published poem *The Triumphs of Temper* was at the time enjoying a remarkable popularity. Hayley, doubtless with the hope of introducing Blake to more influential patronage, passed on his copy of *Poetical Sketches* to the Duchess of Devonshire. Flaxman, in his letter to Hayley accompanying Blake's poems, mentioned a subscription which John Hawkins was trying to raise to pay for Blake to travel to Rome for a period of study such as he himself was to undertake a few years later; but whether or not Hayley expressed himself willing to assist Hawkins, nothing came of the project, and it was not until 1800 that Blake benefited from his generous patronage.

Flaxman remained a life-long friend, and he was the most distinguished of the group of neo-classical artists with whom Blake became friendly in the 1780s. Among the others were Thomas Stothard, who introduced him to Fuseli, and who is best known now for his illustrations to books; James Barry, a quarrelsome Irish Catholic who was expelled from the Royal Academy, where he was Professor of Painting, in 1799, a polemical writer, but a fine painter of portraits and of Grecian subjects; and Henry Fuseli, the expatriate Swiss painter whose work Blake greatly admired and whose influence on Blake's manner is immediately obvious. Fuseli had come to London from Zurich in 1764 and in the following year he published his translation of Winckelmann's essay, which had originally appeared ten years before. His father was a portrait-painter and writer on painting, and a great admirer of Winckelmann: he had been responsible for raising a subscription on his behalf, and he commissioned the well-known portrait which Angelica Kauffmann painted in Rome in 1764. No doubt the young Fuseli spoke

1 Stuart, Revett, Dawkins and Wood at the Monument of Philopappus, Athens (J Stuart and N Revett, *Antiquities of Athens*, III, 1794, ch. v, pl. l.). Reproduced by courtesy of the Bodleian Library, Oxford

2 Engraving by William Blake after William Pars Battle of Greeks and Centaurs, from Parthenon frieze, south side (for Stuart and Revett, *Antiquities of Athens*, III, 1794, ch. i, pl. xxiv). Reproduced by courtesy of the Bodleian Library, Oxford

3 Engraving after Paolo de Mattheis, 'The Choice of Hercules' (William Shenstone, *Works,* 1764). Reproduced by courtesy of the Bodleian Library, Oxford

4 Engraving by N Watson after Sir Joshua Reynolds, 'Resignation',
1772. Reproduced by courtesy of the British Museum

5 Engraving by Domenico Cunego after Gavin Hamilton, 'Lady Hamilton as Hebe'. Reproduced by courtesy of the British Museum

IRON AGE

Then cursed steel & more accursed gold
Gave mischief birth & made that mischief bold.
Ovid. Iron Age.

6 Engraving by William Blake after George Cumberland, 'Iron Age' (G Cumberland, *Thoughts on Outline*, 1796, pl. 18).
Based on a sarcophagus, Radcliffe Library, Oxford.

7 John Flaxman, Monument to William Collins, in Chichester Cathedral. Print reproduced by courtesy of National Monuments Record (Crown copyright)

8 Engraving by Thomas Piroli after John Flaxman, 'Prometheus visited by the Oceanides'

enthusiastically of Winckelmann's work to his new friends in England, who invited him to make it accessible in English. This he was well qualified to do, both because German was his native language, and because his first intellectual interest had been in classical philology, and he had read much Greek poetry. Flaxman was introduced to the Greek writers by Mrs Mathew, and is said to have drawn illustrations while she was reading to him from Homer—the first attempts for those compositions which were to bring him European fame. James Barry had been brought to London by Edmund Burke in 1764, the same year in which Fuseli arrived, and had been introduced by him to Reynolds and to 'Athenian' Stuart; from 1766 until 1771 he was in Italy, at Burke's expense. While in Italy he painted the first of his Grecian paintings, 'Philoctetes on the Island of Lemnos', whose inspiration, he said, was an epigram on the painting by Parrhasius of this subject, which dervied from Sophocles' tragedy.

Another of Blake's early friends—they seem to have known each other before 1780—was George Cumberland, also a proponent of neo-classicism, and an amateur artist. In 1796 he published his *Thoughts on Outline, Sculpture and the system that guided the ancient artists in composing their figures and groups. . . . to which are annexed twenty-four designs of classical subjects invented on the principles recommended in the essay.* Blake engraved two of the designs, and he agreed wholeheartedly with Cumberland's thoughts, which were the quintessence of Grecian ideals, as Blake recognized. 'Do not throw aside for any long time,' he wrote to Cumberland, 'the honour intended you by Nature to revive the Greek workmanship. I study your outlines as usual, just as if they were antiques.' That was in 1799, when the two men had been friends for twenty years, and Blake regarded Cumberland as a partner in the purpose of renewing the lost art of the Greeks. Cumberland thought Blake 'a little cracked, but very honest', and they remained close friends until Blake died.

In about 1784–85 Blake wrote a light-hearted skit to amuse his friends, which he called *An Island in the Moon*. This would scarcely have been comprehensible outside their circle, and it remained unpublished until the modern revival of interest in his work. Flaxman is there as Steelyard the Lawgiver; Blake himself is Quid the Cynic; Dr Joseph Priestley, theologian and discoverer of oxygen, is represented by Inflammable Gass; and Sipsop the Pythagorean is to be identified with Thomas Taylor, Greek scholar and Platonist, who a few years later published a translation of the so-called Pythagoric

Sentences of Demophilus. His translations from Plotinus, on which he must already have started work, and from later neo-platonists such as Porphyry, were soon to be of cardinal importance to Blake. In *An Island in the Moon* Suction the Epicurean (perhaps Blake's younger brother Robert) quotes from Collins' *Ode to Evening*, and more imaginative critics have somehow discovered in the irregular blank verse of *Poetical Sketches* traces of Akenside; but the best evidence in Blake's early writings of his sympathy with the literary ideals of neo-classicism is to be found in the first of his Prophetic Books, *Tiriel*, which again remained unpublished until the twentieth century.

Tiriel is usually dated about 1789* and it can hardly be any later. It is a blend of Gothic fantasy with the theme of Sophocles' *Oedipus Coloneus*, and perhaps best understood as Blake's interpretation of the history of Oedipus, as he found it in the plays of Aeschylus and Sophocles, in terms of Nordic and Ossianic myth and of Sweden-borgian speculation. (This is no more recondite than a twentieth century interpretation in terms of Freudian psychology.) Blake owned a copy of the 1779 edition of Robert Potter's translation of Aeschylus, and his plays and Sophocles' were among the first Greek works of poetry with which he was acquainted. Blake's crowded imagination brought Greek tragedy into strange contexts where it is scarcely recognizable, and the chaotic triviality of *Tiriel* could not for a moment sustain the comparison with the grandeur of *Oedipus Coloneus*. But the Greek substrate in *Tiriel* shows that the priority of Grecian influence over Gothic affected his literary work no less than his work as painter and engraver.

The importance of the myth of Oedipus in Blake's conception of *Tiriel* may be questioned, but in the drawings which he made for it the Grecian elements are apparent. Blake's intense visual imagination normally precedes and controls the total imaginative effect of his work: he was an artist before he was a poet, not a poet who illustrated his own poems, and his illustrations often provide clues to an understanding of his poetry which the words alone are insufficient to convey. In the first of the drawings for *Tiriel* the aged Tiriel supports the dying Myratana while three of their sons confront them; in the background a pyramid is seen beyond a portico of columns, to suggest the ancient cultures of Egypt and of Greece. The three sons are shown with differing head-dress: Heuxos, the eldest, wears a crown;

---

* Blake's most recent editor, W. H. Stevenson, dates it 1798, without adducing evidence.

next to him a nude figure wears a wreath of laurel, to suggest Apollo; beyond him the third son wears a wreath of vine-tendrils, to suggest Bacchus. These figures derive from Thomas Taylor's *Dissertation on the Eleusinian and Bacchic Mysteries*, in which the second part concerns the Mysteries of Bacchus. 'By Bacchus . . . we must understand the intellect of the mundane soul,' Taylor wrote; 'by Apollo, the deity of the Sun, who has both a mundane and super-mundane establishment, and by whom the Universe is bound in symmetry and consent, through splendid reasons and harmonizing power.' The laurel-wreathed figure stands appropriately between the other two, to harmonize them. The feeble figures of Tiriel and Myratana are contrasted with the three youthful figures, and also with the symbols of ancient cultures in the background.

The second drawing, which shows Har and Heva face to face in a shallow stream before the reclining figure of Mnetha, is not, at first sight, obviously Grecian. But the pose of Har and Heva derives from the painting of 'Jupiter and Juno on Mount Ida' by Blake's friend James Barry, and Mnetha's costume, exposing her right breast, is Grecian. Further, Mnetha (whose name suggests, or was suggested by, Mnemosyne, the Mother of the Muses) is the mother of Har and Heva, who represent the arts of poetry and painting in the limited vision of the Augustans,for whom the arts were tied to the imitation of Nature. Blake in a marginal note castigated Sir Joshua Reynolds' opinion 'that genius may be taught and that all pretence to inspiration is a lie and deceit'. For Blake this was a degenerate classicism: 'This opinion originates in the Greeks' calling the Muses daughters of Memory,' an observation which Blake expounded elsewhere in the Prophetic Books, and which provided a mythical framework for his aesthetic theory.

In the fourth drawing—the third is not known—Mnetha is shown in a dress with a leaf and tendril pattern; her hair is bound in a net, and her feet are enclosed in slippers. She clasps Heva protectively while Har blesses the kneeling Tiriel. In the eleventh drawing Har and Heva sleep face to face, as in the second drawing, under a coverlet patterned like Mnetha's dress, while Mnetha, again as in the second drawing, looks on them. Har and Heva, the arts of poetry and painting, are asleep under the spell of Mnetha, the aesthetic theory which restricts creative activity to the world of Nature and of memory, and which allows no scope for imaginative vision. 'No Man of Sense,' wrote Blake in his Note-book, 'can think that an Imitation of the Objects of Nature is The Art of Painting.'

Of the remaining drawings, the seventh shows Tiriel and Heva in
Grecian garb, and the ninth, now lost, showed, according to W. M.
Rossetti, 'figures kneeling near some richly sculptured columns,
seemingly in awe at some impending catastrophe'. These columns
may have belonged to the lofty towers of Tiriel's sons; they were
probably Gothic, in contrast to the severe Grecian columns of the first
drawing; but of this we cannot now be certain.

Tiriel is Blake's protest against what he considered the degenerate
and outmoded classicism of the earlier eighteenth century, a Roman
or Augustan phase of taste from which 'the immense flood of Grecian
light and glory' was about to set men free. Of this rejected classicism
he regarded Sir Joshua Reynolds, without much justice, as the
champion. Occasionally he found something to approve in the
Discourses, but then concluded that it could not have been by
Reynolds: 'I think that Barry or Fuseli wrote it, or dictated it,' he
jotted down in the margin. In the Fifth Discourse he strongly
commended Reynolds' appreciation of Poussin's painting which in
some respects anticipated the neo-classicism of the later eighteenth
century. Throughout his copious annotations to the *Discourses* Blake
is consistent in revealing the Grecian taste of his circle of friends: in his
emphasis on the importance of line and his indifference to colour, in
his admiration for Raphael and his disparagement of Rubens and the
Baroque, and his concern with ideal, or intellectual, beauty.

In his next Prophetic Book, written shortly after *Tiriel* and entitled
The Book of Thel, Blake is still concerned with the nature of the artist's
experience. Between completing *Tiriel* and beginning *The Book of
Thel* he had read Thomas Taylor's translation of Porphyry's treatise
Concerning the Cave of the Nymphs, which provided an allegorical
interpretation of Homer's description in *Odyssey* XIII of the cave near
the place where Odysseus, at the end of his wanderings, was put
ashore on Ithaca. Taylor's translation was included in the second
volume of his *Commentaries of Proclus*, published in 1789; but it had
been published separately earlier. The treatise remained vividly
present to Blake's imagination for many years, and in the Arlington
Court picture, the 'Cave of the Nymphs', which he painted in 1821,
more than thirty years after he first made use of the source in *The Book
of Thel*, he gave it supreme expression.

Porphyry was the most eminent of the first generation of the
followers of Plotinus, and he edited the *Enneads* early in the fourth
century—he is believed to have died in AD 305. Proclus was a Neo-
Platonist of the Athenian school in the fifth century. Such late Greek

writers and thinkers are neglected by most Greek scholars of the present day, so that we are not disposed to take them into account among Grecian influences; but they were much more highly regarded in Blake's day, and were of especial interest to Thomas Taylor. In 1789 he published a long essay entitled *A History of the Restoration of the Platonic Theology, by the Latter Platonists*, and it was with this that he included his translation of Porphyry. Blake therefore approached Plato, and Greek philosophy generally, by what would now be considered a very unorthodox route: he came to Plato through the writings of Plotinus and the Neo-Platonists (Taylor's 'Latter Platonists', for the term 'Neo-Platonist' was not invented until after his death), and indeed when Blake read the less 'theological' dialogues he rejected the rationalism he found there. This seemed to approximate Plato to Bacon, Locke and Newton, whom he regarded as the infernal trinity of western materialism. Besides, Plato's refusal of admission to his ideal republic of poets and artists was clearly unacceptable to Blake.

Before he became aware of Plato's arguments that the work of the artist or poet is at two removes from reality, an imitation of an imitation, Blake had discovered the Neo-Platonic refutation of them. Proclus, in denying Plato's contention, claimed that the artist's concern is not with the physical beauty of the world of Nature, but with intellectual beauty. In his *Descriptive Catalogue*, 1809, Blake wrote, 'The beauty proper for sublime art is lineaments, or forms and features that are capable of being the receptacles of intellect; accordingly the Painter has given in his beautiful man his own idea of intellectual Beauty.' And a little before, in a marginal note to Reynolds' Third Discourse, he had written, 'Knowledge of Ideal Beauty is Not to be Acquired. It is Born with us.' For Blake's antipathy to Locke was due to Locke's rejection of the Platonic concept of innate ideas, which, in his view, led inevitably to materialism. In this he was a follower of Shaftesbury no less than earlier neo-classical writers had been. In the same Discourse to which Blake wrote this note Reynolds himself had quoted Proclus: 'He who takes for his model such forms as nature produces, and confines himself to an exact imitation of them, will never attain to what is perfectly beautiful. . . . So that Phidias, when he formed his Jupiter, did not copy any object ever presented to his sight; but contemplated only that image which he had conceived in his mind from Homer's description.'

Blake's art was clearly not representational: he spurned the Muses that were the daughters of Memory. Rather, he attempted to depict those ideas of the beautiful (τὸ καλόν) of which natural appearances serve only to remind us. The painter was inspired not by what he saw before his eyes but by the idea in his mind which he must interpret through what he saw. Late in his life Blake wrote, in a note on Wordsworth's *Poems*, 1815 (*Influence of Natural Objects in calling forth and strengthening the Imagination in Boyhood and early Youth*), 'Natural Objects always did and now do weaken, deaden and obliterate Imagination in Me.' And he refers there to a translation by Wordsworth himself of a famous sonnet by Michelangelo:

> Heaven-born, the Soul a heavenward course must hold;
> Beyond the visible world she soars to seek
> (For what delights the sense is false and weak)
> Ideal form, the universal mould.

The Platonism of Michelangelo and Raphael derived, as is well known, through the Neo-Platonists, just as Blake's did; and Blake's admiration for Raphael, while it conforms to the received opinion of the age of neo-classicism, reveals a deeper affinity than that of mere fashion. Blake shared with Raphael, he believed, a common ideal for the art of painting, and the passage just quoted from the *Descriptive Catalogue* is very close to Raphael's comment in a letter to Castiglione written three centuries before: when he wished to paint a beautiful woman he made use of an ideal image rather than studying a model.

As I have said, one of the earliest works of aesthetic criticism which Blake read—indeed, it may well have been the first of all—was Winckelmann's essay *On the Imitation of the Painting and Sculpture of the Greeks*. There he would have found Raphael's letter to Castiglione quoted; and he would also have read Winckelmann's comment on ideal beauty: 'It is not only nature which the votaries of the Greeks find in their works, but still more, something superior to nature; ideal beauty, brain-born images, as Proclus says.' And he certainly sympathized with, or was influenced by Winckelmann's rejection of the Augustan precept of following nature. Blake did not hesitate to compare himself to Raphael, his admiration for whom, as supreme among the world's painters, is a recurrent theme of the marginal notes in his copy of Reynolds' *Discourses*. He did so without arrogance because he believed that they were both intent on a vision of ideal beauty beyond the mutable world of appearances.

The *Book of Thel* is Blake's first expression of an aesthetic based in

Neo-Platonism. The 'northern bar' of the eternal gates, in the first line of the last section of the book, is that by which mortals enter the Cave of the Naiads in *Odyssey* XIII, and which Porphyry interpreted as the means by which souls enter the physical world at the moment of birth. Thel is a symbol of the visionary power of the true artist who refuses to accept the limitations of the senses, or of physical, mortal existence. She is youngest of the daughters of Mne Seraphim, about whom there has been much needless debate: her name was suggested by Bne Seraphim in the work of Cornelius Agrippa (from whom Blake also derived the name Tiriel), but Mne recalls Mnetha of the earlier book, and is also intended to suggest Mnemosyne, the mother of the Muses. Thel's name comes from a recollection of Thalia, the name of one of the Muses and also of one of the Graces. She 'in paleness sought the secret air' of true, visionary inspiration, away from the traditional haunts of the Muses. She is 'mistress of the vales of Har' (II. 1) through which she walks (III. 18) and to which, at the end, she returns (VI. 22). Har in *Tiriel* symbolized a false, earth-bound approach to art in the Augustan tradition of the imitation of Nature. So now Thel replies to the Cloud (Blake's recurrent symbol for the physical world):

> I fear that I am not like thee,
> For I walk through the vales of Har, and smell the
> sweetest flowers,
> But I feed not the little flowers; I hear the warbling
> birds,
> But I feed not the warbling birds; they fly and seek
> their food:
> But Thel delights in these no more.

At the end of the poem is a series of rhetorical questions relating to the five senses. (In two copies Blake removed the two lines which refer to the sense of touch which, in the Neo-Platonic scheme of Ficino, so often found in the work of Renaissance writers, is regarded as the most corporeal of the five.) Thel, dismayed by this insistence on the false Augustan aesthetic,

> with a shriek
> Fled back unhindered till she came into the vales of Har,

that is, to the visionary source of true inspiration, as Blake understood it. Thel may be a symbol for the soul enclosed within a mortal body, for which the only means of communication are the deluding senses. But this is the Platonic doctrine of σῶμα σῆμα,* which Blake must have known from Taylor. In 1793 Taylor published a translation of the *Cratylus* in which one of the passages which treats of this may be found. 'But this name [body] appears to me to deviate in a certain small degree from its original: for, according to some, it is the *sepulchre* of the soul, which they consider as buried at present; and because whatever the soul signifies, it signifies by the body; so that on this account it is properly called σῆμα, a sepulchre.'

Blake composed *The Book of Thel* in the year of the storming of the Bastille, and he allowed the revolutionary excitements of the ensuing years to divert him from his concern with the nature of artistic experience to contemporary politics. 'Bliss was it in that dawn to be alive,' no doubt, even if Blake could not, like Wordsworth, claim the excuse of youth for his subversive enthusiasm. *The Book of Thel* was succeeded by *The French Revolution, a Poem in Seven Books*, of which the first book, the only one to survive (perhaps the only one ever written), was published in 1791. Next came *The Marriage of Heaven and Hell*, in which Blake renounced his early attachment to the creed of Swedenborg: it concludes with *A Song of Liberty*, which has no more than a physical connexion with the rest of the book. *Visions of the Daughters of Albion*, 1793, is again political, or social, in content, and owes most to the *Vindication of the Rights of Woman* by Mary Wollstonecraft, published in the previous year. Blake knew Mary Wollstonecraft well, as did others of his circle, most notably James Barry (who befriended her and her two daughters), and in 1791 he engraved six designs for her *Original Stories from Real Life*. Two more Prophetic Books, *America*, 1793, and *Europe*, 1794, show Blake's continuing interest in the politics of revolution; but soon Napoleonic aggression brought disillusion to him as to Wordsworth, and in the next series of Prophetic Books he moved away from the world of political aspiration to the world of myth, whose figures he attempts to describe. But his visual imagination, as always, is dominant and these books are much more significant for their designs than as works of literature.

The first of these mythical works was *The Book of Urizen*, 1794; then came *The Song of Los*, *The Book of Ahania*, and *The Book of Los*,

---

* The body a sepulchre.

all in 1795. Urizen* symbolizes human rationality which attempts to impose upon life the limitations of sense-perception: he derives from the philosophies of the Age of Reason. Los, the poetic Genius, and his consort Enitharmon come next in the hierarchy: she is mother of those visionary, ideal forms which provide the true inspiration of the artist. Orc, the child of Los and Enitharmon, is destined to overthrow Urizen as Cronos, in Greek myth, overthrew Ouranos and was, in his turn, overthrown by his son, Zeus. Their mythical history is continued in *The Four Zoas*, 1795–1804, *Milton*, 1804, and *Jerusalem*, 1804–20, in the last plate of which, drawn about 1820, the mystical marriage of the soul of man with Jesus, the Imagination, is depicted. For Blake, once he had become disillusioned with political remedies for the state of the world, the only area of human experience which had ultimate value was the aesthetic. Orc, the spirit of revolution, becomes much more so. The distraction of politics held Blake for only a few years, before his self-knowledge reasserted itself: he was painter and poet, and his philosophical inquiries were based in personal experience of artistic vision far more than in experience of politics, or even of human, temporal relationships. Apart from a few satirical epigrams, his poetry is not personal: the poem *William Bond* may possibly refer to an estrangement from his wife caused by his affection for Mary Wollstonecraft, but the evidence is very tenuous. Blake lived so intensely in a world of imaginative vision that he was seldom distracted from it by the sensuous world. 'Man has no Body distinct from his Soul;' he wrote, 'for that Call'd Body is a portion of Soul discern'd by the five senses.' This is not a creed from which poems of personal passion are likely to derive.

The early books of Blake's mythical world are all short. Then followed *Vala* or *The Four Zoas*, which is the second longest of all his books. He began working on this not later than 1797, but since this is the date on the title-page it is reasonable to conclude that by that time it was well-advanced. Blake kept returning to it for many years, perhaps even as late as 1810. In its earliest form it may have been complete before he withdrew from London in 1800 to Felpham in Sussex, where he was invited by William Hayley. Flaxman, who had returned from his seven years' stay in Italy in 1794, introduced Blake to Hayley in 1799. Some fifteen years before, he had tried to interest Hayley in Blake, in the hope of providing funds to enable him to visit Italy. Now, conscious of the great benefit to his own work which the

---

* Urizen apparently from ὁρίζειν, to determine, set limits to something.

years in Italy had given, Flaxman perhaps again hoped that Hayley would assist Blake to go there. Instead Hayley asked Blake down to Felpham, where he provided him with a cottage, and gave him a number of commissions for illustrations of his *Life of William Cowper*, which he was writing at the time, and for a series of imaginary portraits of poets (including Cowper and Hayley) to decorate his library.

To Hayley, as to everyone else, Blake was first of all an accomplished engraver: Flaxman had introduced him as one who could provide the illustrations for the *Life of Cowper*. Hayley knew of his visionary paintings, no doubt, but for his poetry the author of so successful a work as *The Triumphs of Temper*, which ran through a dozen editions in twenty years, had little regard. (Blake himself would have forgiven his indifference to *Poetical Sketches*.) Hayley gave Blake the copy of *The Triumphs of Temper* which had belonged to his beloved illegitimate son, who had recently died, and in it he inscribed on 12 July 1800 a poem of dedication to 'my gentle visionary, Blake'. Ten days later, in a letter to Cowper's cousin, Lady Hesketh, he wrote of Blake, 'He has attach'd himself so much to me that he has taken a cottage in this little marine village to pursue his art in various branches under my auspices, and as he has infinite Genius with a most engaging simplicity of character, I hope he will execute many admirable things.' Hayley, clearly, was thinking of Blake as an engraver and as an original painter, not as a poet.

After a time Blake inevitably grew restive at Felpham, and wished to reassert his independence of Hayley, 'to be no longer Pester'd,' as he wrote, 'with his Genteel Ignorance and Polite Disapprobation'. Hayley's talents, compared with Blake's, were no doubt commonplace; but he was a generous and sympathetic patron when Blake needed the freedom from financial worry which he provided. In December 1805, more than two years after he returned to London, Blake wrote to thank him for all he had done for him: 'You, Dear Sir, are one who has my Particular Gratitude, having conducted me thro' Three that would have been the Darkest Years that ever Mortal Suffer'd, which were render'd thro' your means a Mild & Pleasant Slumber.' Neither should we forget those benefits of a less material kind which Hayley conferred on Blake. He taught Blake to read Greek by reading the *Odyssey* with him, using Cowper's translation for the purpose. He was a friend of other neo-classical artists besides Flaxman: he had addressed Romney in a *Poetical Essay* as long ago as 1778, which was later enlarged as *An Essay on Painting*, 1781; he addressed an *Ode* to Joseph Wright of Derby two years later; and his *Essay on Sculpture*, 1800, was addressed to Flaxman and illustrated by Blake, and included one of the earliest English tributes to the decisive influence of Winckelmann. To Hayley Blake was 'the new Grecian', an artist of the school of Romney and Flaxman, whose attempts at poetry were secondary. Only those who are confident that in the early years of the nineteenth century they would have comprehended *The Four Zoas* or *Milton* are justified in now deriding Hayley.

Blake returned to London in September 1803 after three years at Felpham, years during which he had freed his imagination from the political concerns which had distracted him during the previous decade, and had recovered the interest in the nature of the artist's experience which he had treated in *The Book of Thel*. Its interpretation in accordance with the ideals of neo-classicism is apparent in the marginalia to Sir Joshua Reynolds' *Discourses*, and in the *Descriptive Catalogue*. It is present also in the Prophetic Books of these years, *Milton* and *Jerusalem*. *Milton* was for the most part composed at Felpham, and was probably the principal cause of that perplexity in Hayley (who had written a *Life of Milton*, 1796, and who recommended to English painters subjects taken from *Paradise Lost*) by which Blake was so exasperated that he decided to leave Sussex. To Blake, Milton was the greatest of English poets, yet he had allowed himself to be distracted from his acknowledged task of justifying the ways of God to men, which he should have performed by showing to man the visionary world of ideal imagination. (Just so Blake himself had for a time abandoned the world of vision for the world of political polemic.) *Jerusalem*, though composition did not begin until some years later, was also first imagined at Felpham: it was to occupy Blake's mind for many years and was not completed until 1820. The plate which accompanies the final page of text shows Jesus the Imagination embracing the Soul of Man; this was the vision from which Milton, like Blake, had allowed himself to be diverted. Blake too, in those years of revolutionary enthusiasm, had known the temptations of the practical and mundane; now he returned to those visions which he had imperfectly described in *Tiriel* and *The Book of Thel*, and which owed so much to the speculation of the Neo-Platonists. Contemporary with the later Prophetic Books were paintings such as 'Philoctetes and Neoptolemos at Lemnos', and 'The Spiritual Form of Nelson guiding Leviathan'. The first owed something to Barry's painting of Philoctetes, behind which lay not only the painting of Parrhasius and the tragedy of Sophocles, but also the criticism of this by Lessing, and Winckelmann's praise of Parrhasius who 'was master of the correctest contour'. The 'Nelson' derives from the Hellenistic group of Laocoon and his sons, of which the Royal Academy had a cast. Later, Blake would go there to make a drawing to illustrate an article by Flaxman in Rees' *Cyclopedia*, and he returned finally to the same subject in the extraordinary annotated engraving of 1820.

However, it is the linear quality of Blake's art, his concern with contour rather than with volume, that best shows his kinship with such Grecian artists as Barry and Flaxman; it is a matter of style, rather than of choice of subject. This continued after the disastrous failure of his first (and only) public exhibition in 1809, for which he wrote his *Descriptive Catalogue*. There he castigated as enemies of art 'all who endeavour to raise up a style against Rafael, Mich. Angelo, and the Antique'. These he praised for keeping the golden rule of art; 'the want of this determinate and bounding form evidences the want of idea in the artist's mind.' The artist's conception of ideal beauty must be precise: he must be able to draw it, as Raphael had done. Colour was secondary, as we may see from Blake's own practice in his illuminated books, where colour may vary from one copy to another. In all this Blake was very much a man of his own time, a follower of the aesthetic theory propounded by Winckelmann in the *Reflections* and further developed in the *History of Ancient Art*. From this Hayley quoted frequently in the notes to his *Essay on Sculpture*, which Blake illustrated. Blake would certainly have agreed with Hayley in calling

pure Design the very Soul of Art,

for, as he himself said, 'All depends on Form or Outline.' And he would have read with pleasure Hayley's note in the *Essay on Painting* which recorded that Titian himself had said that he chose an entirely new way of painting because 'I fear I should never equal the extreme delicacy which distinguishes the pencils of Correggio, Parmegiano, and Raphael.' In a marginal note to Reynolds' *Discourses* Blake indignantly dismissed the Venetians: 'Such Idiots are not Artists.'

If a man is not on oath in the publicity of epitaph, neither is he in the privacy of a marginal note, and Blake was not so intolerant in the company of his friends as he may appear to the injudicious eyes of the twentieth century. But there is a consistent aesthetic underlying Blake's comments on art, and it is that of the Grecian taste which he had first learnt as an apprentice when he read Winckelmann's

Reflections. The artists who were his friends in his early days, Stothard, Flaxman, Barry, George Cumberland, shared his ideals, however diverse their expression of them. Then, in his old age, Blake became the respected master of a group of younger artists assembled to learn from him by John Linnell, who was introduced to him by George Cumberland in 1818: he was a man of practical ability as well as being a fine artist, and he took Blake's affairs in hand. He introduced Blake to his own former master, John Varley, and at his house in Titchfield Street, only a few minutes walk from Blake's house in South Molton Street, Blake met other water-colourists, John Holmes and Henry Richter and also, no doubt, Varley's younger brother Cornelius. In 1824 Linnell introduced Blake to Samuel Palmer, then nineteen years of age, and his friends, who ironically called themselves the Shoreham Ancients: the oldest of them, Edward Calvert, was born in 1799, George Richmond was ten years younger, and F. O. Finch was born in 1802. These painters were in reaction against contemporary Romantic taste, and shared Blake's enthusiasm for the Neo-Platonic doctrine of intellectual beauty: the Arlington Court painting of the 'Cave of the Nymphs' as well as the last plates for *Jerusalem* date from these years when Blake no longer felt isolated except from a few old and faithful friends. Even of these he saw little: George Cumberland was living in Bristol; Flaxman and Fuseli were busy with their work for the Royal Academy, and Fuseli, who was sixteen years older than Blake, was advanced in years. Besides, the visionary qualities in his painting, which derived from sexually obsessive nightmares, were far removed from Blake's apocalyptic innocence. He had introduced Winckelmann to English readers, but the influence on his own art was much less than on that of his English disciples.

Blake's imagination was that of a painter: no one would be likely to prefer the text of *Jerusalem* to the illustrations. These reveal the influence of the aesthetic of Neo-Platonism, and also the Grecian insistence on contour, on 'the bounding line' which, in Blake's judgment, was the surest evidence of intellectual content in the visual arts. Blake wrote much about painting, but nothing about poetry, yet we may suppose that he, like Flaxman, or like Shelley, was capable of recognizing an affinity between the style of one art and the other. Indeed this was a tenet of neo-classicism from its first formulation in Winckelmann's *Reflections*: he had approached the sculpture of Greece through the literature of Greece. The 'noble simplicity and calm grandeur' which he regarded as the chief characteristics of Greek sculpture were also 'the true characteristical mark of the best and

maturest Greek writings. . . . Possessed by these qualities Raphael
became eminently great, and he owed them to the ancients.'

Whatever our judgment of Blake's achievement as a poet, certainly
he thought his most important work was in the Prophetic Books,
which are far more extensive than the rest of his work, but which are
also those in which the visual element plays the larger part. In his
writing, as in his painting, the Grecian influence shows itself in his
manner, not in his matter; in the way he writes, not in what he writes
about. 'He who admires Rafael must admire Rafael's Execution,'
Blake wrote: 'He who does not admire Rafael's Execution cannot
admire Rafael.' But it is easier to observe Blake's execution in his
lyrical poems, for the obscurity of theme in the Prophetic Books so
much engages our attention that it is difficult to attain a detached
appreciation of the style; the reader's mind is preoccupied with the
effort to understand what Blake is writing about. The austere neo-
classical ideal for literary style, that it should resemble clear, pure
water drawn from the spring itself, is realized in the *Songs of Innocence
and of Experience*, and in the poems of the Pickering MS. To take for
an example *The Garden of Love*:

> I went to the Garden of Love,
> And saw what I never had seen:
> A Chapel was built in the midst,
> Where I used to play on the green.
>
> And the gates of this Chapel were shut,
> And 'Thou shalt not' writ over the door;
> So I turn'd to the Garden of Love
> That so many sweet flowers bore;
>
> And I saw it was filled with graves,
> And tomb-stones where flowers should be;
> And priests in black gowns were walking their rounds,
> And binding with briars my joys & desires.

In these twelve lines there are only two epithets: sweet flowers, black
gowns. Both are perfunctory: everyone knows that flowers may
smell sweet and that a cassock is black. These two words hardly give
any taste to the flow of language. 'Priests in black gowns' are no more
sinister than 'Priests in their gowns'. But in these twelve lines there are
no less than sixteen verbs, which impel the verse forward to the final

couplet where the internal rhyme suggests an imprisoning monotony. The same manner of style may be seen in *Nurse's Song* in the *Songs of Innocence*, with which *The Garden of Love* is linked: in the sixteen lines of this poem there are three epithets and twenty-six verbs. This preference for verbs is not, however, so characteristic of Blake as of Shelley, nor does he use verbs and verbal adjectives to such purpose as Shelley. The famous prefatory lines to *Milton*, for example, have more epithets than verbs, and Blake does not try to remove the sensuous, pictorial qualities in what he describes: he was, after all, a painter before he was a poet, and therefore concerned with appearance. Shelley was not. Blake used his observation of the physical semblance of things to exhibit his vision of imaginative reality, and in this he compared himself to Raphael, who sought also by this means to disclose ideal beauty, as Zeuxis had done. If Blake's construction of his own mythology had been matched by a construction of forms, the result would have been monstrous.* For him, as he said, 'Imagination is the Divine Vision not of The World, or of Man, nor from Man as he is a Natural Man, but only as he is a Spiritual Man.'

No one was ever more convinced of the Platonic theory of ἐνθουσιασμός, divine possession, as an explanation of poetic inspiration. That is why he could make such vast claims for his painting and poetry, because he did not regard them as personal achievements. Writing to Thomas Butts in the summer of 1803 he mentioned his Grand Poem (*Milton*): 'I may praise it,' he wrote, 'since I dare not pretend to be any other than the Secretary; the Authors are in Eternity.' Nevertheless, however Greek in origin Blake's aesthetic theories may have been, we may doubt whether the Grecian manner was in essence appropriate to any other than a rational view of the world, and its incongruity with the irrationality of his Prophetic Books gives to them a naive quality which is often disconcerting. Thus it is difficult for most of us to suppress a smile when in *Milton*, after a passage relating Blake's work on engravings for Hayley,

> Los took off his left sandal, placing it on his head,
> Signal of solemn mourning.

But alas! a smile is not how we should receive a signal of solemn mourning; and for most of us, the removal of the left sandal and the

---

* *The Ghost of a Flea* may be taken as an example.

placing of it—which way up?—on the head, is not such a signal. But in the *Songs of Innocence and of Experience* and in the poems of the Pickering MS the Grecian manner is most evident, and is least at variance with the subject matter.

One day in 1838 Walter Savage Landor startled the company at Crabb Robinson's by declaring that Blake was 'the greatest of poets'. Landor could never resist making assertions which he knew would provoke astonishment—'a great deal of rattling on the part of Landor,' Robinson noted, of which this judgment of Blake was an example; but Landor's assertions were always based in some belief in what he was saying. We do not know to which of Blake's poems he was referring, but it seems likely that so dedicated a Grecian had in mind the lyrics rather than the Prophetic Books: *Songs of Innocence and of Experience* was also more accessible. Even now Landor's remark seems surprising; and it was the first from a man of letters with an established reputation. It could only have been made if Landor, like Hayley, and like Blake himself, saw in Blake's poetry the dominant influence of the Grecian taste of his early years.

6 Walter Savage Landor (1775–1864)

Wearers of rings and chains!
Pray do not take the pains
 To set me right.
In vain my faults ye quote;
I write as others wrote
 On Sunium's height.

Last Fruit off an Old Tree, 1853

What I am will be known, in good time, by the volume of my Greeks and Romans: a century later by my Hellenics.

Letter to John Forster, 9 December 1852

In the brief preface to the new and enlarged edition of *The Hellenics*, published in 1859, Landor admitted that his poetic style was out of fashion. 'Little in these pages will gratify the generality of readers,' he wrote; 'Poetry in our day is oftener prismatic than diaphanous: this is not so: they who look into it may see through. If there be anywhere a few small air-bubbles, it yet leaves to the clear vision a wide expanse of varied scenery.' And the scenery in these poems, as in much of his finest prose, is the scenery of ancient Greece. Landor had begun his literary career more than sixty years before with a volume of poems which derived something from Pope and the Augustans and something from the tenuous Romanticism of Thomas Warton; a premature collection which he soon came to regret. 'So early in life, I had not discovered the error into which we were drawn by the Wartons. I was then in raptures with what I now despise.' But in July 1798, two months ahead of *Lyrical Ballads*, he published *Gebir*, a poem as distinct from current fashion as the poems of Wordsworth and Coleridge. He had found the Oriental tale in a book which Rose Aylmer lent him, Clara Reeve's *Progress of Romance*, but he treated it in the manner of Greek pastoral, which he well understood. Long

afterwards, in his most sustained piece of criticism, he examined the
work of Theocritus and with that unhesitating decisiveness which
was so characteristic of him, declared, 'of all poetry in all languages
that of Theocritus is the most fluent and easy.' The tones are those of
Lawrence Boythorn in *Bleak House*, and it is beside the point to ask
whether Landor had read 'all the poetry in all languages'; but the
epithets 'fluent and easy' are those of neo-classical appreciation.

Landor began as a poet, and a poet he remained to the end of his
long life. The prose writings came later, and the first of the *Imaginary
Conversations* were not published until 1824, when he was in his
fiftieth year. 'Poetry was always my amusement,' he wrote in 1853,
'prose my study and business,' and though Landor's judgments of his
own work, or of others', always need to be treated with caution, most
now would agree that in the best of the *Imaginary Conversations*, in
Pericles and Aspasia, and in *The Pentameron* he achieved more than he
ever did in verse. In part, no doubt, this is a matter of scale. He
admitted that he lacked 'the constructive faculty', the ability to
construct a narrative, or a dramatic plot, and he is often at his best in
the poems where he writes in the tradition of the epigrams of the
Greek Anthology, with an elegant and compendious simplicity. Of his
nine poems in the *New Oxford Book of English Verse* eight are of this
kind; of twenty-one in the *Oxford Book of Nineteenth Century Verse*
there are thirteen, but John Hayward, with one century to choose
from instead of seven, had more room for longer poems, and
included three from *The Hellenics*.* Even so, his preference is for the
epigrams.

Landor's epigrams are unmistakably Greek in tradition; they owe
nothing to Martial, and do not insist on a turn of wit. In English
Martial's imitators have sometimes succeeded in being obscene,
seldom in being witty, most often in being merely coarse. Landor
does not attempt wit, is seldom obscene, and never coarse. Charles
Lamb was perhaps the first man of letters to be captivated by the lines
to Rose Aylmer: fascinated by their restrained elegance he would
repeat them, drunk or sober, and, since his day, most anthologists
have included them, so that it is scarcely necessary to quote them here.
That poem dates from about 1797, when Landor was in his early
twenties. More than fifty years later, after Dickens and John Forster
had visited him on his seventy-fourth birthday (like his master,
Epicurus, he always enjoyed celebrating his birthday), he wrote

* *The Death of Artemidora* was first published in *Pericles and Aspasia*.

another much quoted epigram, which he entitled *Dying Speech of an Old Philosopher*; and, in the fifteen years of life that remained, there were others yet to come. Indeed, through more than sixty years he would write in the manner of the *Greek Anthology* whether on English, personal themes or on classical, and seemingly impersonal themes, as in *Dirce*, which was much admired by Swinburne.

> Stand close around, ye Stygian set
> With Dirce in one boat conveyed!
> Or Charon, seeing, may forget
> That he is old and she a shade.

Here the deft insertion into a scene from Greek myth of the colloquial phrase 'ye Stygian set' suggests that this cargo of souls which Charon is ferrying across the Styx had lately come from a fashionable drawing room—Lady Blessington's, it might be—in Regency London; but it does so without disrupting the classical vision.

Elsewhere, Landor derived poems directly from the Greek: from a fragment of Sappho, this:

> Mother, I cannot mind my wheel;
> My fingers ache, my lips are dry:
> Oh! if you felt the pain I feel!
> But oh, whoever felt as I!
> No longer could I doubt him true . . .
> All other men may use deceit;
> He always said my eyes were blue,
> And often swore my lips were sweet.

And he translated an epigram ascribed to Plato, which Shelley also translated:

> Soon as Ianthe's lips I prest,
> Thither my spirit wing'd its way:
> Ah, there the wanton would not rest!
> Ah, there the wanderer could not stay!

Ianthe, derived from the Greek word for the violet, was the poetic name* that Landor gave to the great love of his life, Jane Sophia

---

* Byron used the name Ianthe for the eleven year old Lady Charlotte Harley, to whom he dedicated *Childe Harold* in 1812; Shelley named his daughter by Harriet, born 1813, Ianthe, and used the name in *Queen Mab*, of the same year.

Swift, whom he met in Bath in the late 1790s. She was descended
from the family of Dean Swift, and about 1803 she married a cousin,
Godwin Swift. He died in 1814 and she married secondly, in 1818,
Comte Pelletier de Molandé. She died in Versailles in 1851. She was
gay and vivacious and a little irresponsible, but her affection for
Landor remained undimmed. She saw much of him during the years
of her first marriage, and after the death of her second husband she
visited him in Florence in the winter of 1829–30. She lived more
securely in his imagination as Ianthe than she could ever have lived as
wife to so uproarious and unpredictable a man; and as Ianthe she is the
subject of many of his best epigrams. Perhaps most moving of all is
this:

> Proud word you never spoke, but you will speak
> Four not exempt from pride some future day.
> Resting on one white hand a warm, wet cheek
> Over my open volume, you will say,
> 'This man loved *me!*' then rise and trip away.

The theme is Shakespearean but treated in a manner wholly remote
from that of the sonnets. Great as was Landor's admiration for
Shakespeare as a dramatist he had no liking for the Elizabethan
manner of writing. 'The thoughts of our poets in the Elizabethan age
often look the stronger because they are complicated and twisted. We
have the boldness to confess that we are no admirers of the
Elizabethan *style.*' And of the sonnets he wrote, 'They are hot and
pothery: there is much condensation but little delicacy; like raspberry
jam without cream, without crust, without bread, to break its
viscidity.' He found them distasteful, and he preferred to model his
writing on the Grecian virtues of clarity and simplicity, to strive for
what, in the same essay on Theocritus, he calls 'the unattainable
insipidity of fresh air'. This is that diaphanous quality of style which,
at his best, he achieved, and which contrasted strongly with the style
favoured by his younger contemporaries, who owed so much to the
Romantic rediscovery of the Elizabethans. The 'insipidity of fresh
air', 'the clear, pure water which has no taste': these are both excellent
images for the neo-classical conception of Greek style, the Grecian
ideal which Landor, no less than Goldsmith or Blake or Shelley,
sought to attain.

The bright visual image in this poem, of Ianthe

Resting on one white hand a warm wet cheek
  Over my open volume,

recalls funerary reliefs of the late eighteenth century which we may
see in so many churches throughout England. A figure with an open
book was a favourite subject with the greatest of English neo-classical
sculptors, John Flaxman. Of these, his monument in Chichester
Cathedral to William Collins is probably the best known, but that at
Bradford in Yorkshire to Edward Balme is more apposite: the elderly
figure of Balme with an open book on his knees is seated between a
youth and a girl, who look intently over the book from which he is
reading to them. Some such design may have been in Landor's
memory, for his rooms were always full of pictures and he greatly
admired Flaxman's work. In the final line of the poem the triviality of
the verb, 'trip away', emphasizes the natural modesty of the girl,
awed by the realization that she had been loved and commemorated
by a poet. The conflict of pride and modesty—Why should *he* love
me? And yet he *did* love me—could not be more succinctly expressed.
But those who expect poetry to arrest their attention with a Keatsian,
or Shakespearean, richness of epithet pass through such diaphaneity in
vain search for prismatic colour, and are oblivious of the bare, classical
perfection.

Landor published the earliest of his epigrams in *Simonidea*, 1806, a
collection named after the greatest of Greek epigrammatists. Among
the twenty-five English poems were *Rose Aylmer*, 'Mother I cannot
mind my wheel,' and several addressed to Ianthe, which show him
already a master of the form. There were also five poems in Latin,
among them *Pudoris Ara*, the earliest of his epyllia, or narrative poems
on subjects taken from Greek myth. 'Incomparably the best poetry I
have been able to write,' was Landor's characteristic comment on
Pudoris Ara a few years later; and the English version which he
included in *The Hellenics* is one of the finest poems in that collection.
Landor had won a reputation as an accomplished Latinist while still a
schoolboy at Rugby, and he continued to write Latin poetry with
great facility throughout his life. But he did not write his epigrams
first in Latin: to have done so might have deflected him from the
Greek tradition towards the manner of Martial, which would not
have suited him. He had a greater command of Latin than of Greek,
but a greater sympathy with Greek literature and civilization. He
wrote the poems on Greek subjects, which eventually formed the
nucleus of *The Hellenics*, in Latin because his facility in Latin was

greater than in Greek; but he wrote them in Latin rather than in English in order to come closer to the ancient world in which the poems were placed. Virgil had set the precedent, in modelling his eclogues on the idylls of Theocritus: his influence, unlike Martial's, was not distracting.

In 1815 Landor published *Idyllia Nova Quinque*, in which he reprinted *Pudoris Ara*, and five years later he published *Idyllia Heroica Decem*, which added to the previous collection five new poems of the same kind and fifty-three shorter Latin poems. That the poems were conceived in Latin, not translated from English drafts, is confirmed by a curious lapse of memory years afterwards. In the first separate edition of *The Hellenics* in 1847 Landor printed English versions of the ten *Idyllia*, but when he came to prepare for publication a new edition in 1859 he had apparently forgotten about these, and he made new translations of them all. He was then in his eighty-fifth year, certainly, and excusably forgetful; but the form in which these poems had been first imagined, forty or fifty years before, was dominant in his recollection of them.

In his old age Landor believed that his eventual reputation as a poet would be founded on *The Hellenics*. He never expected, or wished, to reach a large audience. 'I shall dine late;' he says, in his *Imaginary Conversation* with Archdeacon Hare, 'but the dining-room will be well lighted, the guests few and select.' Milton, whom Landor admired beyond all other English poets, and at times even beyond the poets of Greece, had said much the same, in less convivial fashion: he expected that *Paradise Lost* would 'fit audience find, though few'. Landor, like Milton, or like Akenside, was disdainful of popularity; he wrote for the erudite few, who could supply from their own reading the undisclosed context of his poems and his *Conversations*. He provides no notes on myth or history, no identification of persons, no explanation of relationships, not even any 'argument' such as Milton was persuaded to add to each book of *Paradise Lost* before the first edition was exhausted. Like Milton, Landor demands constant, unremitting attention to the selection and placing of words, so that the qualities of his style, too, can only be appreciated by the informed and attentive reader. The minute criticism of Milton's poetry in the *Imaginary Conversations* between *Southey and Landor* and of Thucydides in *Pericles and Aspasia* exemplify the kind of criticism to which he was prepared to submit his own work. Landor does not write for persons in a hurry, and ready to skip: they will very soon be lost, as they deserve. And, again like Milton, his writings cannot be well represented by excerpts; they are too closely wrought. Those who believe that every writer hopes for an extensive audience will claim that Landor's disdain followed his lack of popular success; that it was simply the response of 'sour grapes'. But as early as 1800 he wrote, 'I sometimes thought how a Grecian would have written, but never what methods he would take to compass popularity.' In this, as in so much of Landor's thought, we see the influence of Epicurus, who said, 'I was never anxious to please the mob. For what pleased them, I did not know, and what I did know, was far removed from their comprehension'. Besides, Landor would hardly have published poems in Latin if he had sought popularity; neither would he so often have published with obscure firms remote from London. The truth is that he cared very little for other men's judgments of his conduct, of his opinions, or of the works of his imagination: he was a man of fierce independence and self-sufficiency. He did not, like Shelley, wish his voice to be the trumpet of a prophecy; he was therefore not distressed by the deafness of the populace.

Now if Landor hoped that in these latter years of the twentieth century the worth of his poetry would be known most surely from *The Hellenics* rather than from the epigrams, these poems must be attentively considered. We do not have to accept a poet's judgment of his own work—few would now accept Yeats' judgment of his—but even its apparent eccentricity may assist our concentration. *The Hellenics* were more substantial poems than the epigrams; many were imaginary conversations in verse—some even derived from the prose; they did not, like so many of the prose conversations, allow the anachronistic intrusion of nineteenth century political controversy, but almost all remained in the cool, remote world of antiquity; and they were exclusively Grecian. But Landor's preference for these poems would certainly have derived also from an awareness that in them he had written in his most elegant manner, as, long before, he believed that he had done in *Pudoris Ara*. That was in Latin; now the quality of these English poems was what he called 'diaphanous'. The significance of this is not to be immediately understood, but since this was the quality he most valued, and which, he supposed, he had achieved most successfully in *The Hellenics*, it must be examined.

In the *Imaginary Conversation* between Epicurus, Leontion and Ternissa Epicurus says, 'The origin of Theophrastus' dislike to me, was my opinion that perspicuity is the prime excellence of composition.' 'Diaphanous' is a word of Greek origin, 'perspicuous' of Latin origin: both mean 'capable of being seen through'. In the

Preface to *The Hellenics* Landor contrasts 'diaphanous' with 'prismatic', a quality of mid-Victorian poetry. In the *Imaginary Conversation* Epicurus, after remarking a difference of opinion from Theophrastus on the importance of perspicuity, nevertheless praises him for 'one great merit in style; he is select and sparing in the use of metaphors: that man sees badly who sees everything double.' Landor's ideal, then, is a direct, simple style, with little use of metaphor, a style which will convey the author's meaning with the clarity of glass, or air, or water. It is very close to Goldsmith's ideal of easy simplicity, in contrast to the 'combination of luxuriant images' which Mr Burchell condemned in Gay. This is not to say that Landor's manner, in verse or prose, is close to Goldsmith's; it is always marked by his own vigorous, assertive personality. But the two men, separated as they were by half a century in time and by wider margins of social circumstance and temperament, would have found themselves in close agreement about the use of their own language. Early in life Landor had shocked Dr Samuel Parr by preferring Goldsmith to Johnson as a writer of prose; nearing the end of his life he told Forster, 'I must confess I turn more frequently to Goldsmith.'

The Grecians differed from the Augustans not in their purpose but in the means they chose to effect it. The opening couplet of Buckingham's *Essay upon Poetry*, published in 1682, was equally acceptable a century later:

> Of Things in which Mankind does most excell,
> Nature's chief Master-piece is writing well.

Goldsmith and Landor, no less than Dryden and Pope, would have assented; but they preferred to learn from the Greeks rather than from the Romans, and therefore Grecian taste differed from Augustan taste. Primacy of subject was a Romantic heresy, with no appeal to either Augustans or Grecians. Milton himself knew what kind of poem he intended to write long before he decided to write of the Fall of Man; and he recorded without surprise that 'Tasso gave to a prince of Italy his choice whether he would command him to write of Godfrey's expedition against the infidels, or Belisarius against the Goths, or Charlemagne against the Lombards.' Milton, like Tasso, wished to write a heroic poem in the ancient tradition but more suited to a Christian audience than the pagan epics of Homer or Virgil; he might find a suitable narrative base in the Arthurian cycle (as Tasso had suggested), or elsewhere.

Landor accepted the same priorities: he wished to write poetry that would be like Greek poetry as he understood it, simple, diaphanous, and clear, and what better subjects could he choose for such treatment than those that were available in Greek myth, and that could be treated as Theocritus had treated them in his idylls? For, as Landor said, the greater part of Theocritus' poems are not pastoral, but are heroic; 'and some passages of these rival Pindar, and are indeed unequalled outside of Homer.' In his early poem, *Gebir*, Landor had treated an Oriental tale in this manner, with some incongruity, for a Grecian manner was better fitted to matter derived from Greece. In *The Hellenics* (in which he included a passage from *Gebir*, thereby showing that his primary interest was in treatment, not in theme), Landor believed that he exhibited at its best the style which he had taken so much care to perfect. These are poems for the literary connoisseur, capable of appreciating aesthetic excellence without any impatient reaching after a 'message'. 'Landor,' a distinguished critic has written—he has the candour to confess that he is not of that select company who are to dine late with him—'was a man of enormous and delicate literary sensibility, a unique craftsman in words, who had little or nothing to say.' (Tennyson once said much the same about his own poetry to Carlyle; he too was wrong.) But from *The Hellenics* Landor extruded those quirky opinions on politics and religion and on individuals which elsewhere, so often incongruously, force themselves on our attention. Some regret this extrusion and find *The Hellenics* frigid; they are more interested in Landor the man than in Landor the artist. In an *Imaginary Conversation* between Dr Johnson and Horne Tooke the latter says, 'When I was younger I read Swift as often as perhaps any other may have done; not for the sake of his thoughts and opinions, but of his style.' No doubt Tooke is here speaking for Landor, since Dr Johnson says that he prefers the style of Addison, which Landor ridiculed.

The Hellenics would have provided admirable scope for Flaxman as illustrator; they appeal to the same taste as his compositions from Homer, Hesiod and Aeschylus. Flaxman is not to be adversely criticized for taking the subjects of his sculpture from Greek myth, the Fury of Athamas, Hercules and Hebe, Apollo and Marpessa, Cephalus and Aurora: these provided him, as they provided Canova, with the opportunity to exhibit the ideal qualities of an art that was Grecian in inspiration and in which the principal concern was with form. The work of Flaxman and Canova was universally, perhaps excessively, admired in the early years of the nineteenth century; but it has been absurdly underestimated since then, at least until very recently. The poetry which Landor judged to be his best belongs to the same phase of taste, and the earliest of the poems in *The Hellenics* were written when Flaxman and Canova were at the height of their fame. *Chrysaor*, published in 1802, *Pudoris Ara*, published in 1806, are two of the most successful in the collection. Landor's recognition that these poems were not likely to please in the middle of the nineteenth century, but must wait another hundred years and more for recognition, was perceptive. Those to whom Canova's art suggests an erotic refrigerator are no more likely to respond to Landor's *Hellenics*; misfortunes of that kind are bound to afflict persons whose sensibility has been enervated by Romanticism.

The volume of *The Hellenics*, according to the title-page of the edition of 1859, comprises 'Heroic Idylls etc.', and *Idyllia* was the word which Landor used for the Latin originals of some of them. This was the traditional title of the poems of Theocritus, though the three Theocritean poems which provide the closest models for Landor's poems are more properly called epyllia. These were short narrative poems on mythical subjects, which usually included passages in dialogue, and also accommodated digression. The form was well suited to Landor, who lacked the faculty to construct a lengthy narrative; and the conversational form, which allowed, or invited, digression, was obviously congenial. I have already quoted his high praise of Theocritus, and he would not have accepted later judgments that the Hellenistic poetry of Alexandria in the third century was inferior to the 'classical' poetry of earlier times. In this, again, he was at one with the pioneers of Grecian taste such as Akenside, whose *Hymn to the Naiads* is in the manner of Callimachus rather than of Pindar. Besides, most of the works on which Winckelmann had based his revolutionary discussion of Greek sculpture, and thereby brought about the change in aesthetic taste in the later eighteenth century, had been Hellenistic, as were the new discoveries at Herculaneum and Pompeii. Grecian taste always included Hellenistic poetry in its purview alongside the work of the tragedians and lyric poets of previous centuries. The *Garland of Meleager*, which comprises many of the finest epigrams in the *Greek Anthology*, was compiled only in the first century BC, but the *Anthology* includes poems from nearly a thousand years. Landor would certainly have agreed with Joseph Warton's assessment of the arts of the time of Ptolemy II.

Like the Alexandrian poets, Landor often treats of myths that are little known; but it may be preferable to consider first his treatment of one that is widely known, the story of Europa and the Bull. The strange, primitive story of Zeus, in the form of a bull, enticing Europa when she was playing on the seashore to climb on his back and then carrying her off to Crete, had been the subject of an elegant epyllion by Moschus, written early in the second century, which Landor no doubt knew. The subject had long been a favourite with painters: it had been treated by Baldassare Peruzzi in the Farnesina, by Titian, by Veronese on several occasions, and by later painters, especially the great Venetians, and by Rubens, Poussin, Watteau and Boucher;* like these, Landor confines his treatment of the myth to the enticement of Europa. He shapes it as a dialogue between the innocent girl and her mother. Europa is puzzled by the beast, which is so unlike her father's draught oxen, 'with the hair rubb'd off their necks';† and yet she cannot accept her mother's assurance that all she has seen is a cow. (In a footnote Landor says, 'Bulls are never at large in those countries; Europa could not have seen one.') With dramatic irony the mother says,

> Who knows
> But some one of these very Gods may deign
> To wooe thee?

Europa is sceptical of such an honour: the Gods, even Zeus himself, are not very constant; she would be afraid. Well, her mother says,

> Some royal, some heroic youth
> May ask thy father for thy dower and thee.

Then, suddenly, Europa catches sight of her great white bull, garlanded with flowers; she is at once jealous of whoever had dared to give him these: she would gather more and sweeter flowers, but along the shore can see none worth gathering. She asks her mother to help her to mount; she does so; the bull takes to the water, to the mother's alarm. But the inadequacy of her comprehension is shown in her concluding words:

---

* The subject was also treated by Paolo de Mattheis.

† ταῦρος/οὐχ οἷος σταθμοῖς ἐνιφέρβεται, οὐδὲ μὲν οἷος/ὦλκα διατμήγει σύρων εὐκαμπὲς ἄροτρον.

Moschus, II, 79–81.

(Not the kind of bull that feeds in a stall, or draws a well-curved plough to cleave a furrow.)

> Against his nostril fondly hangs her hand
> While his eye glistens over it, fondly too.
> It will be night, dark night, ere she returns.
> And that new scarf! the spray will ruin it!

The diaphanous quality of the writing is here apparent: we look into the words and if, in so doing, we recollect a painting by Giorgione or Veronese or Watteau, it is the design we recollect, not the colour. There is much reference to flowers in the poem, but none to their colours; they are carved in marble, as is the bull of whom alone is a colour adjective used, white.

Even in a poem which contains an extended passage of description of flowers, *Acon and Rhodope*, written as a sequel to *The Hamadryad*, there is only one colour epithet.

> Along a valley, where profusely grew
> The smaller lilies with their pendent bells,
> And, hiding under mint, chill drosera,
> The violet shy of butting cyclamen,
> The feathery fern, and, browser of moist banks,
> Her offspring round her, the soft strawberry;
> The quivering spray of ruddy tamarisk,
> The oleander's light-hair'd progeny
> Breathing bright freshness in each other's face,
> And graceful rose, bending her brow, with cup
> Of fragrance and of beauty.

What pleases Landor is form and shape and scent, rather than colour: pendent bells, butting cyclamen, feathery fern, quivering spray. These are qualities which can be illustrated by line, without colour, the qualities which attracted Flaxman and Blake. And there are the tactile qualities of chill drosera and soft strawberry; but colour is disregarded, for colour obstructs diaphaneity. This catalogue of flowers made the poem a great favourite with Swinburne, but Landor omitted it from the edition of 1859, perhaps because he considered that *The Hamadryad* needed no sequel.

A poem of a different kind from *Europa and her Mother*, and on a much less familiar theme, is *Coresus and Callirhoë*. This is a true epyllion (or heroic idyll) with some dialogue inserted, and was originally written in Latin. The two English versions, of 1847 and 1859, differ considerably; the earlier of the two, though elliptical, is much easier to follow. Coresus, a priest of Bacchus, falls in love with Callirhoë, who must be sacrificed by his own hand. To save her, he slays himself. The story seems to have had great appeal to eighteenth century taste: there was an opera on the theme by Destouches and Roy, first performed in 1712, but still drawing audiences sixty years later; and in 1765 Fragonard submitted to the Académie as his *morceau de reception* a large painting entitled 'Le Grand-Prêtre Corésus se sacrifie pour sauver Callirhoë'. This was the picture which made Fragonard's name; it was purchased by Louis XV. When we read *Coresus and Callirhoë* we do well to remember Dr Johnson's advice to the reader of Richardson: 'If you were to read Richardson for the story, your impatience would be so much fretted that you would hang yourself. But you must read him for the sentiment.'

The eighteenth century tradition of sentiment informs other poems in *The Hellenics*. The short elegiac poem, *The Death of Artemidora*, recalls many a classical funerary monument such as may be seen in churches throughout England. *The Hamadryad* is an epyllion with something of Thomson's humanitarian feeling, or of Shelley's in *The Woodman and the Nightingale*—comparisons which Landor would not have dismissed.* The dialogue in *The Hamadryad* is in keeping with the descriptive parts; and the pastoral charm remains. Rhaicos, who has been watching the assembly of processions of worshippers to the temple of Aphrodite, is sent off by his father to help prepare an oak for felling. But the Hamadryad which dwells in the tree begs them to spare it:

> I have no flock, (she says), I kill
> Nothing that breathes, that stirs, that feels the air,
> The sun, the dew.

If they will spare the tree, she will provide honey and beeswax in abundance every year. She will employ a bee as her messenger to Rhaicos:

> If ever thou art false,
> Drawn by another, own it not, but drive
> My bee away.

---

* 'Thomson, in the Seasons,' he wrote, 'has given us many beautiful descriptions of inanimate nature; but the moment any one speaks in them the charm is broken.'

In the winter she sends her bee for news of Rhaicos; it comes upon
him while he is playing draughts with his father.

> Triumphant was old Thallinos; the son
> Was puzzled, vext, discomfited, distraught.
> A buzz was at his ear: up went his hand,
> And it was heard no longer.

One of Landor's purposes, when he acquired the Llanthony estate,
was to plant a large acreage with trees, among them eight or
ten thousand cedars of Lebanon. But almost at once some of his own
men cut down about sixty fine trees, and lopped others, which caused
him so much distress that he could not bear to go out of doors for
days. His interest in trees was aesthetic, rather than commercial, and
this *The Hamadryad* shows, employing Greek myth to illustrate the
delight in trees which he shared with the Greeks. The poem has
something of what Bagehot calls 'the impulse by which the populace
. . . of the external world was first fancied into existence': his
imagination functions like that of a Greek, and, instead of imposing
literary myth on the observed world of Nature, Landor creates myth
out of it, though without the imaginative power of Shelley. Landor
hoped that the poem would 'be found of that order of simplicity
which is simple in the manner of Theocritus'. Such may we judge it.

Swinburne, who visited Landor in the last year of his life, and who
dedicated to him *Atalanta in Calydon*, much admired *The Hellenics*:
'All are good,' he said, 'and some great.' He preferred *The Hamadryad*
to all except *The Shades of Agamemnon and Iphigeneia*. This, one of
several Aeschylean dramatic idylls in the collection, had first been
included in *Pericles and Aspasia*, in a letter from Aspasia to Cleone:
'Tragedy is quite above me,' Aspasia says, 'I want the strength, the
pathos, the right language.' It is tempting to suppose that she is here
speaking for Landor himself, though lack of 'the right language' is not
normally one of his faults. But he might have argued that his language
was better suited to the heroic than to the dramatic, since even in his
Conversations the language is not colloquial; and the compressed,
elliptical manner in which his characters often speak derives from an
assumption that they are addressing persons of equal intelligence.
Landor knew that he lacked 'the strength', if by that is intended the
power to construct and support a dramatic plot: his one attempt at a
full scale tragedy, *Count Julian*, completed in January 1811, failed, as
Sidney Colvin said, because 'the scenes of the play succeed each other

by no process of organic sequence or evolution.' (Yet Swinburne found no poetic drama with which it could be compared but *Samson Agonistes* and *Prometheus Unbound*.) Landor himself cited as his models those masters of dramatic construction, Sophocles and Euripides; unfortunately, unlike them, he had no knowledge of, or even liking for, the theatre. 'I have not seen a play acted a dozen times in my life,' he told Southey at this very time. A quarter of a century later he recognized his inability to write drama: he could write scenes for plays, but not plays. He included three such scenes, of Aeschylean origin, in *Pericles and Aspasia* in 1836, and he reprinted two of these in the following year, in the *Pentalogia* added to the *Pentameron*. All three were again included in *The Hellenics* of 1847, together with two others, *Agamemnon and Iphigeneia* and *The Prayer of Orestes*, which had not been published before. These scenes are dramatic idylls (to borrow a term from the friend of his old age, Robert Browning), to match his own 'heroic idylls'; and in 1850 he wrote *Five Scenes* on the story of Beatrice Cenci. Compositions of this kind are certain to be regarded as fragmentary: they may fail to arouse the reader's interest, but, even if they do, he will be disappointed because the author has not supplied the dramatic context.

Similar criticisms might be made of the *Imaginary Conversations*, which could be plausibly described as scenes from historical novels. Landor knew that his literary reputation must, in the end, chiefly depend upon these, so that any dissatisfaction they might induce must be seriously damaging. When he was working on them, with a new edition in mind, early in 1838, he wrote to Lady Blessington, 'The revisal of my *Imaginary Conversations* has cost me more time than the composition. For this, after all, is my great work; the others are but boudoir-tables to lay it on.' In them he assumes that his reader is sufficiently well read to know who the characters are, and he offers no introduction to them. Neither does he directly inform us of the temporal context, though this is often easily deduced. People engaged in the height of action do not converse much; and Landor sets the conversations usually just before, or occasionally just after, some climactic moment in the life of the principal character or characters. This is, necessarily, the method of the sculptor or painter and, as Lessing pointed out, the artist 'cannot be too careful that the moment chosen shall be in the highest degree pregnant in its meaning—that is, shall yield the utmost range to the activities of the imagination'. This the climax cannot do, since nothing is there left to the imagination to construct for itself.

In *Leofric and Godiva* the moment chosen is that when they approach the city of Coventry, and Godiva meekly accepts Leofric's intemperate challenge to her. 'Will I pardon? yea, Godiva, by the holy rood, will I pardon the city, when thou ridest naked at noontide through the streets.' And the brief scene closes when, as they enter the city, Godiva, inaudibly to Leofric because of the noise of the people, murmurs to herself, 'God help them! good kind souls! I hope they will not crowd about me so to-morrow. O Leofric! could my name be forgotten! and yours alone remembered! But perhaps my innocence may save me from reproach! and how many as innocent are in fear and famine! No eye will open on me but fresh from tears.' In a few pages—the whole Conversation is less than two thousand words long—Landor has let us enter the heart and mind of Godiva, tender, loyal, modest and resolute. We understand what it has cost her to take up Leofric's challenge; we know that she will ride on the morrow, and that she will be unabashed. Here, the story of Godiva is well known, and may serve the purpose of myth. But the persons and circumstances of the even shorter Conversation, between *The Lady Lisle and Elizabeth Gaunt*, will be known to few. The two women were condemned to death by Judge Jeffreys for harbouring rebels who had supported Monmouth; but in fact they never met. Landor never tried to recreate history, but rather to understand what it felt like to be such or such a person involved in historical events, and to comprehend the motives which led them to act as they did. Lady Lisle and Elizabeth Gaunt, like Godiva, were women responding to historical situations with sympathy for their fellows, without too much questioning of right and wrong, and, finding that this required of them a heroic resolution, did not flinch. That this resolution was, in all three, based in a steadfast Christian faith may seem surprising in the work of a man who could not share it. The dispute between Conyers Middleton and Magliabechi about the efficacy of prayer in another Conversation alarmed the publisher, John Taylor, whose objections prompted Landor to reply, in a letter to Southey of 2 July 1823.

In regard to prayer, if I ever prayed at all, I would not transgress or exceed the order of Jesus Christ. In my opinion all Christianity (as priests call their inventions) is to be rejected excepting His own commands. There is quite enough in these for any man to perform; which he will be best induced to do by reading His life and reflecting on His sufferings.

Landor's anticlericalism is strongly Puritan; it is not agnostic.

Landor considered that the finest of the *Imaginary Conversations* were those of the Greeks and the Romans, which he collected together in one volume in 1853, the only selection among them which he ever made. (Elsewhere he seems to have printed them more or less in the order of composition.) Landor dedicated this book to Charles Dickens, who, in thanking Landor for the honour said, 'The Queen could give me none in exchange that I wouldn't laughingly snap my figners at.' This dedication was published four months after the first number of *Bleak House*: clearly Landor was as amused by Dickens' caricature of him in Boythorn, as Shelley had been by Peacock's portrayal of Scythrop. We may think Dickens' praise of the *Imaginary Conversations of Greeks and Romans* not impartial; but Wordsworth years before and Swinburne later were also among those who shared Landor's opinion that these were his best.

However, his old friend Archdeacon Hare, in the last letter he ever wrote to Landor, made a suggestion which is of some critical interest. He wrote,

> The Greek and Roman dialogues you have printed separately, but I have always had a strong wish to see a selection made of the more purely poetical and dramatic dialogues, including almost all in which there are female speakers. It would be one of the most beautiful books in the language.

Hare's implication that Landor was at his best in portraying feminine character may seem to conflict with the more usual preference for the Greek and Roman *Conversations*, for there are female speakers in only four of these: *Achilles and Helena*; *Aesop and Rhodope*; *Epicurus, Leontion and Ternissa*; and *Tiberius and Vipsania*. These include almost the longest of all the *Imaginary Conversations—Epicurus, Leontion and Ternissa*—which was also Landor's favourite among them; and *Aesop and Rhodope* and *Tiberius and Vipsania* have perhaps been more admired than any of the others except that between *Marcus Tullius Cicero and his brother Quintus*. But another work should also be considered with the classical Conversations, the epistolary *Pericles and Aspasia*, since this was first conceived as an *Imaginary Conversation*.

Now Archdeacon Hare's preference for Conversations in which women speak might be no more than a personal preference for mixed company; or it might point to some quality of Landor's genius which was given more opportunity when he was portraying women. He was a man robust both in physique and in opinion, given to overemphasis and to dogmatic assertion; careless, at times, of other people's feelings; not invariably a good listener. His marriage was a failure, and he had to spend the last years of his life in exile in Florence because of a libel action brought against him by a woman. On the other side, he was attractively masculine; his manners were naturally courteous; he was fond of animals, and flowers, and trees, and gardens; he delighted in the company of children; and his incapacity for coping with the practical problems of life was more likely to elicit sympathy from women than from men. Then he had a disarming habit of roaring with laughter at his own outbursts of anger. Seymour Kirkup recorded one such occasion when Landor was living in a house belonging to the Marchese Medici-Tornaquinci in Florence. Landor had written to accuse the Marchese of enticing his coachman away from his service.

> Mrs Landor was sitting in the drawing-room the day after, where I and some others were, when the marquis came strutting in without removing his hat. But he had scarcely advanced three steps from the door when Landor walked up to him quickly and knocked his hat off, then took him by the arm and turned him out. You should have heard Landor's shout of laughter at his own anger when it was all over, inextinguishable laughter which none of us could resist.

Landor, after all, was not much like anybody else one ever met.

The paradoxes in Landor's character are repeated in his literary manner. The delicate sensitivity to feminine response, which led Archdeacon Hare to suggest a collection of the Conversations which include female speakers, to match the classical Conversations, is anything but Hellenic, though Apollonius Rhodius' sympathetic account of Medea's love for Jason may be cited as an exception of Landorian tenderness. But Landor's passionate, emotional nature was also un-Hellenic. The truth is that he found in Greek culture an antidote to the extravagance of his own temperament; he recognized the need, and he knew how to supply it. No man has ever found it more difficult to act in accord with the Greek ideal of μηδὲν ἄγαν, nothing to excess; yet Landor had the intelligence to keep this ideal constantly before him. If it was beyond him to eschew, in his daily life, every excess of pride and indignation and anger and scorn, he knew that these excesses were much to be deplored. But in his imaginative life he could provide the requisite intellectual discipline more easily. Lawrence Boythorn is a caricature of all the least Hellenic qualities of Landor: πᾶν ἄγαν, everything to excess. On that unwilling temperament his intelligence strove to impose a neo-classical, Grecian ideal of noble simplicity and calm grandeur. At his best, Landor achieves this: temperament provides the initial, personal impetus, and intellect controls the expression, so that his writing does not lose vitality in an academic concern with perfection, but the vitality is prevented from disrupting the elegance of it. Like every other writer, Landor is not always at his best: sometimes political passion makes his work 'too Tom Paine-ish', as de Quincey said; or personal scorn may involve him in a libel action; or there may be other mishaps more appropriate to Boythorn than to a follower of Theocritus. On the other side, the imposition of classical control may require such concentrated effort that obscurity, rather than clarity, results: the syntax becomes too compressed and elliptical, the vocabulary too self-conscious, and what was intended to be simple and brief becomes offensively abrupt. But no more than any other writer is Landor to be judged by his failures, which occur when the fine equilibrium between temperament and intellect has been disturbed.

Epicurus participates in three of Landor's *Imaginary Conversations*: with the comic poet Menander; with Metrodorus, who was his most eminent pupil and follower; and with the two girls, Leontion and Ternissa, who were also his pupils. (Epicurus was the first of the Greek philosophers to admit women to his school.) Leontion was a historical character and, according to Seneca, she married Metrodorus. Ternissa is a fiction of Landor's imagination, based on 'that pretty little Themisto, whom Leontion used to call *Terenissa*, and she herself and you *Ternissa*', in Menander's words to Epicurus. She is some three years younger than Leontion. The setting of the Conversation is a day in the country outside Athens, where Epicurus has recently purchased a plot of land for a garden; he established his school in a famous garden at Athens. There is, exceptionally, no dramatic context: the Conversation does not take place on the eve, or on the morrow, of some climactic event, but during a pleasant day in the country, in which Epicurus can share his delight in his new acquisition with two young disciples. It is an idealization of the sort of experience Landor had once looked forward to enjoying at Llanthony; it is also a statement of Epicureanism. They talk of the garden which Epicurus is constructing, of the art of writing, of death. This may seem a strange topic for two young girls, but it was one of the principal purposes of

Epicurus' teaching to free man from the fear of death; in this too Landor was a convinced disciple. The passage echoed, or suggested, the epigram *Dirce* already quoted: both were probably written at about the same time. Perhaps the summary epigram was prompted by Ternissa, whose youthful charm Landor so vividly suggests.

The Conversation ranges widely, to Theophrastus as a critic of Epicurus, and to his literary style; to other writers of prose; to the argument whether epic or tragedy is the higher form of poetry. There is an Epicurean insistence on clarity as the chief excellence in writing, and an assured conviction that 'all the imitative arts have delight for the principal object.' The first version of this Conversation was marred by two passages of political satire whose object was Landor's *bête noire*, George Canning. These were not only anachronistic but wholly out of keeping with the teaching of Epicurus, who advised man to take no part in public life but to live in the idyllic serenity which the Conversation depicts. 'Some are fitted for conviviality,' Epicurus says to Metrodorus, 'others for public life, others for discussion, others (much the fewer) for retirement. They are no philosophers who lay down strictly one rule and regulation for all.' Political satire sorts ill with Epicurus' famous precept: λάθε βιώσας, live a hidden life, untroubled by the concerns of the great world. Landor tried to follow the teaching of Epicurus, however much his own temperament urged him into conflict, and from later editions of *Epicurus, Leontion and Ternissa* he wisely expunged the attack on Canning. The often quoted phrase of Carlyle about Landor, 'that redoubtable old Roman', suggests a Stoicism which was far from Landor's ideal: he sought to follow Epicurus, not Zeno, and if the life of retirement which he led in England and in Italy seems to result more from infelicities of temperament than from purposeful choice, this is an illusion. His continuing struggle to impose a Grecian ideal on a temperament that was not, like Winckelmann's, naturally Hellenic, was given authority by the teaching of Epicurus. The republicanism which was a political product of neo-classicism might prompt him to attack, from time to time, those who did not accept it, but it did not tempt him to abandon a life of retirement for active politics. The simple manner of life which he led at Bath and in Florence may have been inescapable after the financial disasters of the Llanthony experiment; but he had always lived simply in the true Epicurean tradition. 'We aim at self-sufficiency not that we may always lead a simple and frugal life, but that we may not be afraid of leading it.' The words are those of

Epicurus; they might well be taken for Landor's.

Now if the Grecian ideal of Landor's imagination can be more precisely defined as Epicureanism, it is also true to say that his search for tranquillity, ἀταραξία, was anything but tranquil. His first attempt to retire from the world, in the remote Llanthony valley, involved him in litigation and bankruptcy; his marriage (an undertaking against the advice of Epicurus) involved him in long and bitter dispute; and even when he left his wife to return to England in 1835, the most tranquil period of his life which then ensued came to an abrupt end because of his inability to keep out of a trivial squabble with a vindictive woman. The immediate sequel to his departure from his wife was the composition of what many would regard as his greatest work, *Pericles and Aspasia*, most of it written after he left Fiesole but before he returned to England. Landor at first intended to treat the subject as an *Imaginary Conversation*, but soon decided that the epistolary form was more appropriate. He described his purpose in a letter to Southey, written before the separation.

I began a conversation between Pericles and Aspasia, and thought I could do better by a series of letters between them, not uninterrupted; for the letters should begin with their first friendship, should give place to their conversations afterwards, and recommence on their supposed separation during the plague of Athens. Few materials are extant: Bayle, Menage, Thucydides, Plutarch, and hardly anything more. So much the better.

For the imaginative liberty allowed by the lack of historical evidence was very much to his liking: in the *Imaginary Conversations* he always refused to be restricted by historical circumstance or chronology. His intention was to imagine the characters of his speakers, which they would reveal in conversation with their known friends, or with persons they never could have met. He was sceptical of the validity of history. 'All history is fabulous,' Epicurus says to Metrodorus, who demurs. 'Point out to me,' Epicurus rejoins, 'the historian who can explain all the motives to all the actions performed by Pericles, the wisest ruler that ever ruled any portion of mankind.' Landor's interest was in the motives to action, rather than in the actions themselves: these, no doubt, might be accurately recorded, but what did they matter?

The epistolary novel of the eighteenth century provided the model for Landor, whether we choose to classify *Pericles and Aspasia* with the work of Richardson and Fanny Burney or not. The bulk of the correspondence* passes between Aspasia and Cleone, the friend whom she has left behind in Miletus. Aspasia, but not Cleone, has other correspondents, Pericles, Alcibiades, Anaxagoras (the philosopher who was a friend and teacher of Pericles), Herodotus, and Xeniades, sick with love for the girl whom he had known in Miletus. The fictitious correspondence provides an admirable means for describing what it was like to be an intelligent woman in the brilliant, masculine society of Periclean Athens, concerned especially in its more private affairs. Shelley translated the *Symposium* of Plato 'to give Mary some idea of the manners and feelings of the Athenians'. Landor's work gives the neo-classical interpretation of that society, in which the human spirit attained its greatest eminence, and, better than any other book in English, shows what life in the Athens of Pericles may have been like. The principal characters are, as Landor acknowledged, a little idealized. 'Pericles was somewhat less amiable, Aspasia somewhat less virtuous, Alcibiades somewhat less sensitive; but here I could represent him so, being young, and before his character was displayed.' Besides, how should one not idealize the members of that society to which, at least in Landor's day, every intelligent man in Western Europe looked for an ideal of political liberty and of artistic achievement?

Throughout, Landor's prose is worthy of his subject: 'they who look into it may see through.' Nor could he have chosen a subject more suited to his style. Aspasia describes being present, immediately after her arrival in Athens, at a performance of the *Prometheus Bound*, by which she was so moved that she fainted.

Everything appeared to me an illusion but the tragedy. What was divine seemed human, and what was human seemed divine.

An apparition of resplendent and unearthly beauty threw aside, with his slender arms, the youths, philosophers, magistrates, and generals, that surrounded me, with a countenance as confident, a motion as rapid, and a command as unresisted as a god.

'Stranger!' said he, 'I come from Pericles, to offer you my assistance,'

I looked in his face; it was a child's.

'We have attendants here who shall conduct you from the

---

* In all there are two hundred and thirty-seven letters; of these the correspondence between Aspasia and Cleone occupies one hundred and fifty-nine. Twenty-five more letters are from Aspasia.

crowd,' said he.

'Venus and Cupid!' cried one.

'We are dogs,' growled another.

'Worse!' rejoined a third, 'we are slaves.'

'Happy man! happy man! if thou art theirs,' whispered the next in his ear, and followed us close behind.

I have since been informed that Pericles, who sate below us on the first seat, was the only man who did not rise.

So does Aspasia meet Alcibiades, who will ensure that she meets Pericles. Fittingly, the correspondence closes with two letters from Alcibiades to Aspasia, telling her of the death of Pericles and of the death of Cleone.

Aspasia! she will gladden your memory no more; never more will she heave your bosom with fond expectancy. There is none to whom, in the pride of your soul, you will run with her letters in your hand. He, upon whose shoulder you have read them in my presence, lies also in the grave. The last of them is written.

Landor, like Homer and Pindar and the Greek tragedians, like Shakespeare and Milton, was always most deeply moved when he pondered on man's capacity for greatness; most of all, therefore, in his evocation of the characters of the noble Grecians and Romans. The neo-classical painter David advised his pupil Jean-Antoine Gros not to waste his time on frivolous subjects: 'Vite, vite, mon ami, feuilletez votre Plutarque.' The most serious subjects must be sought in the world of Grecian antiquity; most of all, in Periclean Athens, when Phidias was building the Parthenon, and when Sophocles was competing against Aeschylus for the prize for tragedy. To his portrayal of that splendid society Landor brought also his own especial gift of tenderness, in his understanding of the apprehension and excitement with which Aspasia entered it, and of the sadness with which she heard from Alcibiades of the two deaths which, for her, brought it to a close. Because he describes Athens through the words of a woman and of one who was not by birth an Athenian, writing to a friend in distant Miletus, he can give his account at once an intimacy and an objectivity which is both moving and convincing. Many books tell us of events which he disregards and of facts which he ignores; no other so vividly conveys what it was like to live in Athens at the height of her fame.

7 Thomas Love Peacock (1785–1866)

Mr Chainmail. I am for truth and simplicity. *The Rev.Dr Folliott.* Let him who loves them read Greek; Greek, Greek, Greek.

Crotchet Castle, 1831, Chapter VII

The Greek taste was so exquisite in all matters in which we can bring it to the test, as to justify a strong presumption that in matters in which we cannot test it, it was equally correct.

Gryll Grange, 1860, Chapter XIV

On the evening of Tuesday, 10 March 1818, Shelley and Mary took a party of friends to the opera and afterwards entertained them to dinner at 119 Great Russell Street, where they had been staying since they came up to London from Marlow a month before. It was the Shelleys' last evening in London before setting out for Italy, and therefore something of an occasion, though none of them could have foreseen that Shelley would never return to England. He delighted in opera and ballet—at that time there was often a double bill, with an opera followed by a ballet—and he took it as a matter of course to have a box at the theatre when he was in town. There his tall, slim, aristocratic figure, dressed in a blue coat and white waistcoat, was regularly to be seen beside the handsome Mary, 'with her great tablet of a forehead, and her white shoulders unconscious of a crimson gown', as Leigh Hunt remembered her. The Hunts were with the Shelleys on this evening of 10 March, and so was another close friend, who was also an enthusiast for the opera, T. L. Peacock. He had accompanied them to a performance of *Don Giovanni* as soon as they arrived in London in February. 'There is nothing perfect in this world except Mozart's music', he wrote later, with *Don Giovanni* especially in mind; but the opera which they saw on 10 March was Rossini's *The Barber of Seville*. 'The evening was a remarkable one,' Peacock recalled nearly forty years later, 'as being that of the first performance of an opera of Rossini in England, and of the first appearance here of Malibran's father, Garcia. He performed Count Almaviva in the *Barbiere di Siviglia*. Fodor was Rosina; Naldi, Figaro; Ambrogetti, Bartolo; and Anguisani, Basilio.'

By the middle of April Peacock had begun to write *Nightmare Abbey*, which he finished before the end of July. Shelley, who, no doubt, had his suspicions, was very eager to know what it might contain, and he sent Peacock the passage from Ben Jonson's *Every Man in his Humour* for use as an epigraph. *Nightmare Abbey* was published in November, but Shelley's copy did not reach him until the following June, when he was at Leghorn. 'I am delighted with Nightmare Abbey,' he wrote at once to Peacock; 'I think Scythrop a character admirably conceived and executed, and I know not how to praise sufficiently the lightness, chastity and strength of the language of the whole. It perhaps exceeds all your works in this.'

Shortly before leaving England Shelley had sent Leigh Hunt a review of Peacock's poem *Rhododaphne* for *The Examiner*; but Hunt never printed this. Peacock wrote the poem while staying with Shelley at Marlow the previous autumn, and Mary transcribed it to a fair copy for him. Shelley will have followed the progress of this thoroughly Grecian poem with lively interest, for Peacock had been responsible for turning his own mind to the serious study of Greek literature and thought some years before.

The two men first met in November 1812, probably on the introduction of the publisher Thomas Hookham, but they did not meet more than three or four times until July 1813. Then the friendship rapidly developed and on 5 October Peacock accompanied Shelley and Harriet and her sister Eliza on their travels to the Lake District and on to Edinburgh. Peacock was then twenty-eight; Shelley was twenty-one.

Peacock's father, a London glass-merchant, died when he was only two or three years old, and he was brought up by his mother, who, on her husband's death, went to live with her father in a cottage at Chertsey named Gogmoor Hall—a most appropriate nursery for the future creator of Headlong Hall, Nightmare Abbey, and Crotchet Castle. Peacock's grandfather, Thomas Love (after whom the child was named), came from a seafaring Devon family, and had been a master in the Royal Navy, from which he retired to the Chertsey cottage in 1782. (He had lost a leg that year in Rodney's victory over

De Grasse in the West Indies.) Captain Hawltaught of *Melincourt* is based on him; and the bluff common sense which marks Peacock's response to the more extravagant Romantic enthusiasms of the time owes much to his naval grandfather. But his greatest debt was to his mother, a vigorous, intelligent woman, who encouraged her son's literary gifts, which first showed themselves in a verse epistle which he addressed to her at the age of nine. She was no sentimental lady, arranging herself in a disconsolate pose over a classical urn in which her husband's ashes lay; she was a devoted reader of Gibbon, and no doubt introduced her son to that master of irony at an early age. Peacock read to her all his books as he wrote them, and must have profited by her criticism. When she died in 1833, in her eightieth year, he said the heart had gone out of his writing, and the truth of this lament is shown by the fact that he published six of his seven novels between 1816 and 1831, but the seventh did not appear until 1860, twenty-seven years after his mother's death.

Peacock and his mother had enough money from his father's estate to live on, and, apart from brief experience as a clerk in 1800, and as Secretary on *H.M.S. Venerable* in 1809, Peacock had no paid employment until 1819 when, at the age of thirty-four, he was appointed to a post with the East India Company. There he remained for thirty-seven years, a capable and efficient but by no means over-worked servant of the same company that Charles Lamb served. The year after his appointment he married Jane Gryffydh, the 'milk-white Snowdonian antelope' of Shelley's *Letter to Maria Gisborne*. He had met her on a visit to North Wales in 1809, but presumably decided that he had not enough money to marry on at that time, and that the pleasures of marriage would not sufficiently recompense the pains of employment. They corresponded for a time, but this lapsed in 1811 until in November 1819, Peacock wrote to propose marriage in a letter dated from East India House and no doubt written during office hours. It must be one of the most extraordinary proposals of marriage ever sent; but the lady accepted, and the marriage was entirely happy. 'It is altogether extremely like the *dénouement* of one of your own novels,' Shelley wrote to him. Jane's health broke down before long, but Peacock remained devoted to her until she died in 1851. Their daughter Mary made a brief and disastrous marriage with George Meredith, from which she escaped by a no less rash elopement with a painter.

Peacock left the only school he ever attended, at Englefield Green, when he was about thirteen, but the headmaster, John Wickes, had seen enough of his ability to prophesy that 'he would prove one of the most remarkable men of his day.' At school he began to study Greek and Latin and he continued his interest after he left, so that by the time he met Shelley he was a widely read and discrimintating classical scholar. He also acquired a good knowledge of French and Italian, and later, through his wife, became interested in Welsh poetry and legend; presumably it was from her that he derived his knowledge of the language. But Greek always provided 'the strongest chord in his sympathies' (as it did for Mr Falconer of *Gryll Grange*), and the range of his reading extended far beyond what was normal for an amateur Greek scholar in his day, or in ours, as the quotations and references in the novels reveal. Homer and the Greek tragedians are there; Aristophanes and Menander; Pindar, but also Bacchylides (of whose work there was not much known until the discoveries at Al-Kussiyah in 1896); Callimachus, Theocritus, and the Anacreontea; the historians, including Arrian and Philostratus. Other favourite works were the *Deipnosophistae* of Athenaeus, of the second century of the Christian era, and the *Dionysiaca* of Nonnus, of the fifth century. Most unusual too, in the early years of the nineteenth century, was Peacock's knowledge of Plato, for it was not until long after his time that a scholar could be defined as 'a man who reads Plato with his feet on the fender'.

When Shelley was at Oxford the famous school of Literae Humaniores, soon to be more popularly known as 'Greats', had just been instituted; but Greats philosophy was still dominated by Aristotle, and little regard was paid to Plato. The Rev. Dr Folliott reminds his host in *Crotchet Castle* that 'in our universities Plato is held to be little better than a ringleader of youth; and they have shown their contempt for him, not only by never reading him (a mode of contempt in which they deal very largely), but even by never printing a complete edition of him.' This neglect of a favourite author perhaps caused Peacock to think ill of university education, and of the academic life: to so detached and unenvious a personality the cry of 'sour grapes' would not have come easily. Besides, there is no reason to believe that Peacock had ever wished to go to the university, or that, if he had, he might not have gone there. Thomas Taylor, the eccentric Platonic and Neo-Platonic scholar, who for a time influenced Blake and whom Peacock knew well, shared his antipathy to academic persons: he it was who gave to his young friend the nickname 'Greeky-Peaky'.

When Peacock and Shelley became friends in 1813 Peacock would not have taken long to discover both that Shelley had an exceptional linguistic gift and also that he had not yet exploited the knowledge of Greek acquired at Eton. He therefore encouraged Shelley in his reading of Greek literature, and especially of Plato, in the original. He could hardly have conferred a greater benefit on the young man who was to become the greatest poet of the neo-classical movement in England.

Friendship with a poet of genius must also have revealed to Peacock the limitations of his own poetic gifts. Before he met Shelley he had published only verse. The two long poems, *Palmyra*, 1806, and *The Genius of the Thames*, 1812, are composed in a run down Augustan manner from which Peacock's comedy and wit are wholly absent; and *The Philosophy of Melancholy*, 1812, allowed even less opportunity for the exhibition of his true gifts. Shortly before meeting Shelley Peacock had written a farce in verse, called *The Dilettanti*, and in 1813 he wrote another, *The Three Doctors*: he was at least beginning to feel his way, however uncertainly, towards comedy. Somehow Shelley must have brought him to realize that there, for him, future development would lie rather than in the assumed Romantic sentiment which contrasted with Shelley's more genuine feeling. In the same way Shelley was later to redirect Byron's far more powerful genius from the sentiment of *Childe Harold* and the associated *Tales* to the mature comedy of *Don Juan* and *The Vision of Judgment*. Shelley's critical insight into the literary abilities of his friends helped them to understand what these were, and to discriminate between the genuine and the assumed. Very soon Peacock turned to prose, and the first of his novels, *Headlong Hall*, was published late in 1815. During the summer of the following year, while Shelley was in Switzerland, Peacock wrote much of his second, and longest, novel, *Melincourt*, which was published in March 1817. Throughout the summer and early autumn of that year Peacock and Shelley were constantly in each other's company at Marlow: while Shelley was writing *Laon and Cythna* (afterwards called *The Revolt of Islam*) Peacock returned to poetry and wrote by far the best of his long poems, *Rhododaphne, or the Thessalian Spell*. This is thoroughly Grecian both in conception and in treatment. For once Peacock manages to conduct the narrative coherently, which he seldom succeeds in doing in his novels. Anthemion, an Arcadian youth, in order to find a cure for his beloved Callirhoë, who is mortally sick, goes to Thespiae to make an offering there in the Temple of Love. Rhododaphne, a beautiful Circe-like enchantress, falls in love with him, casts a spell upon him with a kiss, and tells him that henceforth his kiss will bring death to any other woman. He returns to Callirhoë, and kisses her, with (apparently) fatal effect. He wanders disconsolate by the sea-shore, and, like Daphnis, is kidnapped by pirates. Soon they also kidnap a beautiful maiden, who proves to be Rhododaphne. She bewitches both crew and ship, and when the ship is wrecked rescues Anthemion. They come to a cottage, which Rhododaphne enters. Anthemion wanders off once more, but circles back to the same place, only to find the cottage transformed into a palace, which he enters. Anthemion submits to Rhododaphne's love, but before long she is killed by Urania, because hers was not the spirit of true love. Anthemion returns to Arcadia; Rhododaphne's spell is broken by her death; Callirhoë is restored from her enchanted sleep, and forgives Anthemion. This charming idyll is told in the spirit of the Greek romances, and is, as it were, a transposing into myth of the situation which provides the basic comedy of *Nightmare Abbey*.

Narrative poetry does not, at the present time, have the widespread appeal that it enjoyed early in the nineteenth century as in other periods of great literary achievement. This is our loss. Then Scott delighted thousands of readers with *The Lay of the Last Minstrel*, *Marmion*, and *The Lady of the Lake* until, as he himself said, he found that 'a mighty and unexpected rival was advancing upon the stage' in the person of Lord Byron. The immediate and extraordinary success of *Childe Harold*, which Byron exploited in the *Tales*, forced Scott to move from narrative in verse to narrative in prose—something he had considered as early as 1805 but put aside so long as his poems found their public. When *Rokeby* in 1813 proved a failure he took up *Waverley* again and published it in July 1814; three more editions were called for before the end of the year. But if Scott chose to leave narrative verse to a greater poet than himself, and to start on a new, and almost equally successful, career as a novelist, many writers who were, perhaps, less concerned with what Scott called 'the art of attracting popularity', continued with the form. While Shelley himself was writing the longest of his narrative poems Peacock wrote this 'story of classical mystery and magic' which was the longest of his. In the same year Keats was writing *Endymion*.

For *Rhododaphne* Peacock used the octosyllabic couplet, which both Scott and Byron had used. 'Scott alone of the present generation,' Byron wrote, 'has hitherto completely triumphed over the fatal facility of the octosyllabic verse.' That was in his letter of dedication to Tom Moore of *The Corsair* in 1814. Peacock manages to overcome this 'fatal facility' by a number of devices. He uses both couplets and alternatively rhyming lines, and other variations in the rhyme-scheme; the lines are by no means always end-stopped; they do not keep to the easy monotony of eight syllables but may vary from four to twelve, on the principle enunciated by Coleridge in his preface to *Christabel*; the accentual stress is skilfully varied to bring out the sense. In the spell which the enchantress casts upon Anthemion the sinister power of her words is emphasized by the shifting of stress on to the first syllable in the final line:

> She clapped him to her throbbing breast,
> And on his lips her lips she prest,
> And cried the while
> With joyous smile:
> —'These lips are mine; the spells have won them,
> Which round and round thy soul I twine;
> And be the kiss I print upon them
> Poison to all lips but mine!'

When Anthemion sees again his beloved Callirhoë, and kisses her, and she falls as if dead, the spell recurs to his memory

> Distinct in every fatal word.

And though this is precisely what such a spell should do it requires the authority of a poet to ensure that it will. Elsewhere Peacock achieves an incantatory effect by shifting the iambic rhythm to trochaic:

> Flowers may fall from many a stem;
> Fruits may fall from many a tree;
> Not the more for loss of them
> Shall this fair world a desert be.

Again, by associating enjambement with strong medial pauses in the lines (a device which Marvell uses with dramatic effect in *The Nymph Complaining for the Death of her Fawn*) Peacock gets rid of the facile monotony of regular enclosed couplets.

> A night and day had passed away;
> A second night. A second day
> Had risen. The noon on vale and hill

Was glowing, and the pensive herds
In rocky pool and sylvan rill
The shadowy coolness sought. The birds
Among their leafy bowers were still,
Save where the red-breast on the pine,
In thickest ivy's sheltering nest,
Attuned a lonely song divine,
To soothe old Pan's meridian rest.

Such writing persuades the reader that the poet is attentive to what he is saying, and not merely humming a tune.

Characteristically, in this passage Peacock appends a note to the last line quoted: 'It was the custom of Pan to repose from the chase at noon. *Theocritus*, Id. I.' In a note to the next canto he quotes from Sophocles' *Oedipus Coloneus*, and refers to the poet's 'loved nightingale', as Collins had done in his *Ode to Simplicity*. Peacock refers in his notes to *Rhododaphne* to a generous selection of Greek authors: Homer and the Homeric Hymns and Hesiod, Apollonius Rhodius (whose Medea provided an obvious source for Rhododaphne), Pindar, Sophocles and Euripides, Aristophanes, Plato and Plutarch, Pausanias, Lucian, and several more. He also names the sculptors Lysippus of Sicyon and Praxiteles, whose statues at Thespiae Pausanias mentions. (Thomas Taylor had recently published his translation of Pausanias.) The poem had in it, Shelley said, 'the transfused essence of Lucian, Petronius, and Apuleius', and indeed of much more.

The Grecian affinities of Peacock's best poetry are not far to seek, but the novels have little in common with the surviving Greek romances. These have more or less elaborate plots and a coherent narrative line where character is revealed more by what the persons do than by what they say. Peacock's novels have only so much plot as is necessary to ensure that the various characters meet together in some sequestered country house, there to enjoy the pleasures of dining and of conversation. It is true that the hero of *Melincourt*, Sir Oran Haut-ton, never utters a human syllable and must therefore reveal his character in action; but he is present at, and responds (if not in words) to the conversation of others, to such effect that he is elected to the House of Commons. Peacock had early been introduced to the delights of country house hospitality. A childhood friend, Charles Barwell, lived in the Abbey House at Chertsey, and in an essay entitled *The Abbey House: Recollections of Childhood*, written in middle life, Peacock wrote an idealized account of the life he had observed there. Charles Dickens was the editor who accepted it for publication, in *Bentley's Miscellany*.

The country house setting is important, but even more so is the gathering together of the guests for dinner, and for a good dinner with excellent wine to stimulate the flow of their conversation. For Peacock was a gourmet, and a well instructed one, who not only gave recipes to his cook but wrote much of a book which was to be called *The Science of Cookery*. (It was never published.) In 1851 he contributed to *Fraser's Magazine* an elaborate essay entitled *Gastronomy and Civilization*, in which the first of the running titles is 'Social Habits of the Greeks'. In his novels he portrays a series of clergymen who much enjoy dining out—they remind us of Sydney Smith, whose idea of heaven was 'eating *pâtés de foie gras* to the sound of trumpets'—and of these the last, and best, is Dr Opimian of Gryll Grange. Dr Opimian derives his name from the most famous of Roman wines, but his sympathies were Greek.

'Consider,' he advises his fellow-guests, 'consider how much instruction has been conveyed to us in the form of conversations at banquets, by Plato and Xenophon and Plutarch. I read nothing with more pleasure than their *Symposia*: to say nothing of Athenaeus, whose work is one long banquet.'

This, the *Deipnosophistae*, Peacock often returned to, delighting in the large fund of miscellaneous learning which it contained; but it is scarcely comparable with the work of Plato.

In his *Symposium* Plato records the gay and varied conversation on a serious subject of a group of friends, whose differing manner and style his prose is subtle and precise enough to suggest. They had gathered together one day in January 416 BC for a dinner party in celebration of the victory of one of them, Agathon, in the contest for tragedy. Peacock's abstemious friend Shelley translated the dialogue in July 1818, to introduce Mary to the life of the Athenians. In essence, then, Peacock's novels are an adaptation of the Symposiac form to a comic, and at times satiric, purpose, an urbane and skilful device which, surprisingly, no one had thought of before and which only W. H. Mallock has successfully adopted since. They have a superficial affinity to Landor's *Imaginary Conversations*, but those are neither convivial nor humorous; and Landor's dislike of Plato would have inhibited him from following the tradition of the *Symposium*.

No doubt Peacock took suggestions from elsewhere, as from those French comic romances which he discussed in an essay in *The London Review* in 1836, and also from Italian opera in which he found so much pleasure. His novels, which include a number of his best lyrics (arias), often provide situations which seem to have been imagined in operatic terms. Marionetta, in *Nightmare Abbey*, 'could not debar herself from the pleasure of tormenting' Scythrop.

Sometimes she would sit by the piano, and listen with becoming attention to Scythrop's pathetic remonstrances; but, in the most impassioned part of his oratory, she would convert all his ideas into a chaos, by striking up some Rondo Allegro, and saying, 'Is it not pretty?' Scythrop would begin to storm; and she would answer him with,

> Zitti, zitti, piano, piano,
> Non facciamo confusione.

from *Il Barbiere di Siviglia* which Peacock had heard with Shelley and Mary a month or two before. And the hilarious scene in which Mr Glowry demands to know whose is the female voice he has heard in Scythrop's tower, and into which the owner of the voice obtrudes from behind a sliding book-case, to be joined shortly afterwards by her father and the rest of the house-party, seems designed for Rossini. *Maid Marian*, Peacock's next novel, was immediately made into an opera, with libretto by J. R. Planché and music by Henry Rowley Bishop.* It was produced at Covent Garden on 3 December 1822, in the same year that the novel was published. Indeed, Peacock's publisher threatened to bring an injunction against Planché, but Peacock was delighted that a work of his should have an operatic performance, and intervened. Charles Kemble took the part of the friar, and Thackeray records that his song,

> The bramble, the bramble,
> The jolly, jolly bramble,

was 'one of his famous songs in *Maid Marian*'.

Peacock's preference for opera to instrumental music—he even

---

* Bishop is perhaps best remembered now as the composer of 'Home, sweet home', and 'Lo! hear the gentle lark!'

preferred *Fidelio* to the rest of Beethoven's music—arose from his recognition that it represented something of the practice of the Greek theatre. Of Bellini's *La Sonnambula* he wrote, 'It came upon us as a shadow of the Athenian stage.' And in *Crotchet Castle* Mr Trillo's choice for the regeneration of society is 'Revive the Athenian theatre: regenerate the lyrical drama.' Indeed, though Peacock may not have known this, opera had originated in Florence at the end of the sixteenth century in the attempts of the Camerata, a group of aristocratic friends, to produce drama in the Greek tradition, in which choric odes had been sung to the accompaniment of music and dance. For some years he wrote reviews of opera for Leigh Hunt's *Examiner*, informed, generous and urbane; at their best, not unlike Bernard Shaw's half a century later. His love of music, especially of the music of Mozart, pervades his novels, in which many a scene seems to invite operatic performance.

I have suggested that *Rhododaphne* and *Nightmare Abbey* are different treatments, mythical and comic, of the same basic situation. In *Rhododaphne* Anthemion's love for the innocent Callirhoë is distracted by the enchantments of Rhododaphne; in *Nightmare Abbey* Scythrop's love for the innocent and frivolous Marionetta is distracted by the more sophisticated powers of Stella, under which name Celinda introduces herself to him. These plots originated in Shelley's relations with Harriet and Mary, both of whom Peacock knew. He preferred Harriet, whose naivety came nearer to his choice, and he was always a staunch defender of her character; he seems to have mistrusted the more intellectual Mary. (Her love might not have been approved by Urania.) For her part, Mary was inclined to disapprove of Peacock, especially in his role of *bon viveur*, which was no more to her taste than to Shelley's. 'Peacock dines here every day, *uninvited*, to drink his bottle,' she wrote to Shelley, 25 September 1817; 'he morally disgusts me.' Peacock and Mary each regarded the other as a bad influence on Shelley. Peacock's common sense allowed him to dismiss these suspicions, and to laugh at his friend's unworldly attitude to love and marriage. 'You have formed to yourself, as you acknowledge,' says Mr Fax to Mr Forester in *Melincourt*, 'a visionary model of female perfection, which has rendered you utterly insensible to the real attractions of every woman you have seen.' Shelley, whose opinions Mr Forester represents, eventually admitted the charge: 'I think one is always in love with something or other; the error, and I confess it is not easy for spirits cased in flesh and blood to avoid it, consists in seeking in a mortal image the likeness of what is perhaps eternal.' And so, when Marionetta interrupts a scene of self-dramatization in Scythrop's tower, and, to soothe him, says,

> 'What would you have, Scythrop?' Scythrop replies: 'What would I have? What but you, Marionetta? You, for the companion of my studies, the partner of my thoughts, the auxiliary of my great designs for the emancipation of mankind.'*

And to this Marionetta can respond only by saying as Harriet would have done, 'I am afraid I should be but a poor auxiliary.' But Mary, the daughter of two such formidable liberal intellectuals as William Godwin and Mary Wollstonecraft, accepted the challenge. To Peacock that seemed pretentious, and silly.

To circumstances such as these in the domestic life of an intimate friend Peacock must make an imaginative response. But his comedy is attracted to people's opinions, not to their personalities: to writers such as Shelley, Byron, and Coleridge as public figures, not as private individuals. Shelley made the same distinction. In a letter to Leigh Hunt of December 1818 he wrote,

> I never will be a party in making my private affairs or those of others topics of general discussion; who can know them but the actors? . . . My public character, as a writer of verses, as a speculator on politics or morals, or religion, as the adherent of any party or cause, is public property, and my good faith or ill faith in conducting these, my talent, my penetration or my stupidity are all subjects of criticism.'

In *Crotchet Castle* the Rev. Dr Folliott rounds on Mr Eavesdrop (Leigh Hunt) for publishing a character of him: 'You have dished me up like a savory omelette, to gratify the appetite of the reading rabble for gossip. . . . What business have the public with my nose and wig?' In *Nightmare Abbey* therefore Peacock makes the physical appearance of Celinda very unlike Mary's, and Scythrop he describes not at all. He was not deriding Mary or Shelley; he was deriding their opinions, especially insofar as these were accepted as a guide to conduct, and he was deriding them because they were representative of the age. On their private lives he was making no comment: his charity was not confined to Harriet. Besides, his own personal reticence, which

---

* Cf. The dedication of *The Revolt of Islam*.

prevented any intimate self-revelation in his writings, inclined him to respect the privacy of others. Only once, when his three year old daughter Margaret died, in 1826, did he express deep personal emotion in a poem. In his *Memoirs of Shelley*, published more than thirty years after the poet's death, he regretted the gossip that had made correction necessary. 'I could have wished,' he wrote, 'that he had been allowed to remain a voice and a mystery . . . and that he had been only heard in the splendour of his song.' Peacock's view of human nature was genial and tolerant. He did not wish to destroy the wicked but to laugh at the foolish. He was a Platonist, not a Presbyterian, and believed that men did wrong through ignorance or folly, not because they were sinful.

In his novels he quotes Aristophanes a number of times and for the country house theatricals in *Gryll Grange*, to which, in the tradition of the Christmas house-party, 'the beauty and fashion of the surrounding country' were invited, he devised a play entitled *Aristophanes in London*. In this, though the main target is the evils of industrialism, he introduces such favourite butts of Aristophanes' wit as the demagogue and the sophist; but the result is not much like Aristophanes. Peacock, a man of radical opinions but of conservative temperament, had no inclination towards the partisanship of Aristophanes: he enjoyed making fun of his friends' opinions, but did not care if they persisted in them. If he converted all the world to his own practical good sense, where would he find something to laugh at?

Scythrop and Mr Flosky are not studies in the personalities of Shelley and Coleridge; they are not even caricatures. Certainly Mr Flosky, in his conversation with Marionetta, exhibits Coleridgean traits, and Scythrop's talk is made authentic with quotations from Shelley's letters and conversation; but these things are not the objects of Peacock's satire—they are simply used to give some solidity to characters whose primary function is to deliver ridiculous opinions. Their names, in an ancient tradition of comedy, indicate their character. Scythrop derives from σκύθρωπος, 'of a sullen countenance' (which does not at all describe the vivacious Shelley); Flosky is from φιλόσκιος, 'a lover of shadows'. This is Peacock's normal method of naming his male characters, and we are not invited to regard them as persons, any more than we regard Mr Anyside Antijack as a portrait of Canning, or Mr Wilful Wontsee as a portrait of Wordsworth. His women, whatever their patronymics, have only slightly exotic Christian names: in the 1820s and 1830s we should not have been much surprised to be introduced to a Marionetta, a

Celinda, an Anthelia, a Clarinda. They are, as Raleigh said, 'pleasant and sensible', and everyone in the books likes them. They are not mouthpieces for opinions; they just behave in a normal, natural way (at least when the men do not prevent this), and so provide the basis of common sense to which the reader relates the opinions expressed by their fathers, brothers and lovers. In a fictional world that might otherwise be free-floating fantasy such anchorage is very important, as are the similar frequent reminders of the world in which we live to readers of the *Orlando Furioso* or *The Faerie Queene*. At their best Peacock's heroines remind us of Jane Austen's, especially, perhaps, of Elizabeth Bennett: quick-witted, charming and marriageable, they follow the pattern established by Caprioletta on her first appearance in the first of the novels. She arrived at Headlong Hall 'beaming like light on chaos, to arrange disorder and harmonise discord', which are assumed to be the inevitable products of masculine intervention in a practical world.

Peacock's mirth was provoked, as was Jane Austen's, by such fashionable foibles as the cult of the picturesque or the affectation of excessive sensibility. To both of them the application of theory to the natural world seemed absurd; and the Honourable Mr Listless must surely be some connexion of Miss Marianne Dashwood. The opening sentences of *Melincourt* recall those of *Pride and Prejudice*, which preceded it by some four years; if the similarity is accidental (and there is no evidence that Peacock had read *Pride and Prejudice*), then the affinity between the two comic visions is the more remarkable.

Peacock knew the *Lysistrata* of Aristophanes, from which he quotes in *Crotchet Castle*; Jane Austen, we may be sure, did not. Aristophanes was there devising a plot to exhibit a practical feminine response to man-made chaos of a kind which delighted Peacock. (He would also have enjoyed the Rabelaisian humour of the play.) Much more significant than this, or than the surfeit of Greek quotations which are to be found in all the novels except, strangely, *Nightmare Abbey*, and whose footnote identifications by Peacock savour of pedantry, are the Grecian elements in Peacock's, or in Jane Austen's, style. Shelley commended the language of *Nightmare Abbey* for its 'lightness, chastity, and strength', and if these qualities are not easily defined at least their opposites are open to discovery. Goldsmith, whose style, like Shelley's is the quintessence of neo-classicism, objected to such things as 'a combination of luxuriant images . . . a string of epithets'; from these defects his own writing is always free. 'Easy simplicity' was what he sought, and attained, in a style which never draws attention to itself by conscious striving after effect: it is a style well suited to comedy, as is Jane Austen's.

In his essay *The Four Ages of Poetry* Peacock gives the name of 'silver age' to the poetry of civilised life. 'This poetry,' he adds, 'is of two kinds, imitative and original.' Of the first, Virgil is the outstanding example. 'The original is chiefly comic, didactic, or satiric. . . . The poetry of this age is characterized by an exquisite and fastidious selection of words, and a laboured and somewhat monotonous harmony of expression.' When this silver age recurs in the poetry of modern vernaculars, in England it begins with Dryden, comes to perfection with Pope, and ends with Goldsmith, Collins, and Gray. It is with these writers, not with his own contemporaries, whom he derides in the essay, that Peacock felt most sympathy, no doubt because, by the time when he wrote *The Four Ages of Poetry* (1820) he was aware that his own natural gifts led him away from verse to prose, and away from melancholy to comedy. Peacock's comedy was addressed to persons of learning and information, capable both of appreciating an apt quotation from Greek or Latin and also of comprehending references to the views of Humphry Repton and Sir Uvedale Price on landscape gardening, of Dr Gall and Dr Spurzheim in phrenology, to the speculations of Lord Monboddo and Dr Malthus, and to the political opinions of George Canning or Lord Brougham, whose Society for the Diffusion of Useful Knowledge is transformed to the Steam Intellect Society* of *Crotchet Castle*. But Peacock not only expected his readers to have their eyes and ears open to the society in which they lived, he expected them to be alert to detect subtler ironies. For the ironist 'an exquisite and fastidious selection of words' is always necessary: if he is to convey two meanings rather than one and to hold them in delicate equilibrium he cannot risk imprecision. The requirements of irony Peacock learnt at his mother's knee from *The Decline and Fall of the Roman Empire*; if his comic irony is far removed from what he called 'the solemn irony' of Gibbon, yet the demands upon vocabulary were not less.

In the first of his novels, when Mr Milestone and Sir Patrick O'Prism are disputing about improvements to the grounds of Headlong Hall, and Mr Milestone invites Sir Patrick 'to make a distinction between the picturesque and the beautiful', Mr Gall, with the insensitivity of a journalist,† interrupts. 'Allow me,' he says. 'I

---

* Cf. Shelley, *Letter to Maria Gisborne*, 108–9.
† He is modelled on Francis Jeffrey, of the *Edinburgh Review*.

distinguish the picturesque and the beautiful, and I add to them, in the laying out of grounds, a third and distinct character which I call *unexpectedness*,' a comment which, to those of us who are nowadays often assured of the importance of some element of surprise in a garden, may seem plausible. But, 'Pray, sir,' said Mr Milestone, 'by what name do you distinguish this character, when a person walks round the grounds for the second time?' This mockery of an inexact use of words extends further. In *Crotchet Castle* the fashionable phrase 'The March of Mind' provides the heading for a chapter in which the Rev. Dr Folliott chastises the Scots political economist, Mr MacQuedy, 'whom he considered a ring-leader of the march of mind' (he derives from J. R. McCulloch, whom Peacock knew at East India House), both for his theories and for his claim that Edinburgh merited its contemporary title of 'the Athens of the North'. Dr Folliott will concede nothing to the Scots but their skill in 'the art and science of fish for breakfast', at which this conversation takes place. 'Modern Athens, sir! the assumption is a personal affront to every man who has a Sophocles in his library. I will thank you for an anchovy.' This brusque return from theory to fact is as characteristic of the Rev. Dr Folliott as of Dr Johnson. In the evening, after the ladies have withdrawn, young Mr Crotchet, the son of their host, offers to provide the company with a large fund to be used for the regeneration of society, a purpose as ill-considered as the march of mind. After making his offer Mr Crotchet says, 'Now let us see how to dispose of it.'

Mr MacQuedy. We will begin by taking a committee-room in London, where we will dine together once a week, to deliberate.

The Rev. Dr Folliott. If the money is to go in deliberative dinners, you may set me down for a committee man and honorary caterer.

Mr MacQuedy. Next, you must all learn political economy, which I will teach you, very compendiously, in lectures over the bottle.

The Rev. Dr Folliott. I hate lectures over the bottle. But pray, sir, what is political economy?

Mr MacQuedy. Political economy is to the state what domestic economy is to the family.

The Rev. Dr Folliott. No such thing, sir. In the family there is a *paterfamilias*, who regulates the distribution, and takes care that there shall be no such thing in the household as one dying of hunger, while another dies of surfeit. In the state it is all hunger at

one end, and all surfeit at the other. Matchless claret, Mr
Crotchet.

Mr Crotchet. Vintage of fifteen, doctor.

As his East India House examiners had said, 'Nothing superfluous,
and nothing wanting.' And Mr MacQuedy's initial proposal for the
administration of a charitable trust might have been made yesterday,
and will be made tomorrow.

The qualities of Peacock's prose, so apt to convey the tempo of
after-dinner conversation, are also apparent in passages of description.
The country houses where his convivial company meets together are
almost always in remote parts of England or Wales: Headlong Hall is
in the vale of Llanberis, Melincourt in 'one of the wildest valleys of
Westmorland', Nightmare Abbey 'pleasantly situated on a strip of
dry land between the sea and the fens, at the verge of the county of
Lincoln', and even if Crotchet Castle is in the valley of the Thames it
is somewhere near the unpolluted reaches of the Chilterns. Mr
Priestley has pointed to an advantage which Peacock derived from
thus placing his characters temporarily far away from the urban
society to which most of them belong, and where, if his purpose had
been primarily satirical, he would have been wise to leave them. 'If
the foreground in his fiction is mostly filled in with a caricature of
what actually goes on in the world, its background gives us a sketch of
what ought to go on in the world, of the author's ideal realm.' This
contrast is parallel to the contrast already noted between the sensible,
practical behaviour of the ladies in the novels and the foolish,
unpractical theorizing of the men. These two contrasting themes are
linked together in the person of the lady of the house: Squire
Headlong's sister Caprioletta, Anthelia Melincourt (whose father was
recently dead), Miss Gryll the adopted orphan niece of Gregory Gryll
Esq., and Marionetta O'Carroll, the orphan niece of Mr Glowry. The
ladies, with their feet firmly planted on the earth, are creatures not of
the city but of the English countryside.

Peacock himself enjoyed walking in the country, and met his wife
during a lengthy visit to North Wales in 1810 when he lived in a
cottage near Tan-y-Bwlch. He shared the Romantic appreciation of
wild country, but deplored the resulting growth of tourism which
was already affecting the Lake District, 'where every wonder of
nature is made an article of trade, where the cataracts are locked up,
and the echoes are sold'. When he describes a scene, he does so with
visual clarity and without an excess of epithet.

Miss Susannah often wandered among the mountains alone, even to some distance from the farm-house. Sometimes she descended into the bottom of the dingles, to the black rocky beds of the torrents, and dreamed away hours at the feet of the cataracts. One spot in particular, from which she had first shrunk with terror, became by degrees her favourite haunt. A path turning and returning at acute angles, led down a steep wood covered slope to the edge of a chasm, where a pool, or resting-place of a torrent, lay far below. A cataract fell in a single sheet into the pool; the pool boiled and bubbled at the base of the fall, but through the greater part of its extent lay calm, deep, and black, as if the cataract had plunged through it to an unimaginable depth without disturbing its eternal repose. At the opposite extremity of the pool, the rocks almost met at their summits, the trees of the opposite banks intermingled their leaves, and another cataract plunged from the pool into a chasm on which the sunbeams never gleamed. High above, on both sides, the steep woody slopes of the dingle soared into the sky; and from a fissure in the rock, on which the little path terminated, a single gnarled and twisted oak stretched itself over the pool, forming a fork with its boughs at a short distance from the rock.

In a letter written thirty years after he wrote *Crotchet Castle* Peacock told a friend that this description derived from a conflation of two scenes, on the rivers Velenrhyd and Cynfael, in Merionethshire; 'that on the Velenrhyd is called Llyn-y-Gygfraen.' This precision is typical of him, as is his plea of poetical licence for diverging from topographical fact.

The method by which he makes this description effective is worth remarking: he contrasts the lively torrent with its resting-place in a pool by contrasting the active verbs—fell, boiled, bubbled, plunged (twice)—with the static epithets—calm, deep, black. He repeats the Greek word 'cataract' three times, not because it is Greek, but because it is more precise than the usual English 'waterfall'. In a note to *Headlong Hall* he says, 'Pistyll, in Welsh, signifies a cataract, and Rhaiadr a cascade': not for him then the general word when what he had in his mind's eye was a cataract, where the falling water is broken in its descent by protruding rocks, rather than the unbroken fall of a cascade. 'Lightness, chastity, and strength'—these are the qualities which make Peacock's descriptive passages accurate and visual or, as Landor would have said, diaphanous; they are also the qualities which enable him to give coherence and progression to the conversations.

There are other, more idiosyncratic elements in Peacock's prose. He will delight in stringing together synonyms: 'the τουτεστι, the *id est*, the *cioè*, the *c'est à dire*, the *that is*, my dear Miss O' Carroll, is not applicable in this case.' Or he will list, 'the inexhaustible varieties of *ennui*: spleen, chagrin, vapours, blue devils, time-killing, discontent, misanthropy, and all their interminable train of fretfulness, querulousness, suspicions, jealousies, and fear', till we feel the full impact of *ennui*. He takes pleasure in inventing ludicrous polysyllables: 'the poeticopolitical, rhapsodicoprosaical, deisidaemoniacoparadoxographical, pseudolatreiological, transcendental meteorosophist, Moley Mystic, Esquire, of Cimmerian Lodge,' and the interpolation of the word 'transcendental' among the rest derides the philosophy of Coleridge and his German masters. These *jeux d'esprit* are reminiscent of writers of an earlier time, Nashe, or Sir Thomas Urquhart, or Urquhart's original, Rabelais, whom Peacock sometimes quotes. They are the burlesque by-products of his love of words, as if, grown weary of the concentration needed to make that 'exquisite and fastidious selection' in the immense resources of English vocabulary, he decides for a moment to give up the process and fling in everything. To a man who shared the chaste ideal of Goldsmith or Shelley it was tempting, now and then, to abandon himself to Rabelaisian riot.

In the end the most just estimate of Peacock's achievement is that of the friend who was himself often the butt of his humour, and whose perceptive genius had led him to recognize that his natural gift was for comedy. In the *Letter to Maria Gisborne* Shelley calls him

> A strain too learned for a shallow age,
> Too wise for selfish bigots; let his page,
> Which charms the chosen spirits of the time,
> Fold itself up for the serener clime
> Of years to come, and find its recompense
> In that just expectation.

Such was also Landor's expectation for his own writing. We may find it difficult to recognize in the late twentieth century 'the serener clime of years to come', but it would be salutary to hear Peacock's urbane comments on our age. What opportunities we could provide!

8 Percy Bysshe Shelley (1792–1822)

> Athens, diviner yet,
> Gleamed with its crest of columns, on the will
> Of man, as on a mount of diamond, set;
> For thou wert, and thine all-creative skill
> Peopled, with forms that mock the eternal dead
> In marble immortality, that hill
> Which was thine earliest throne and latest oracle.

Ode to Liberty, V

'We are all Greeks,' Shelley wrote, 'our laws, our literature, our religion, our arts have their root in Greece. But for Greece—Rome, the instructor, the conqueror, or the metropolis of our ancestors, would have spread no illumination with her arms, and we might still have been savages or idolaters.' To such opinions we are by now grown so accustomed that we scarcely pause to consider whether they might once have been new. Greece, we know, was where our civilization began, and the opening sentences of any *History of Europe* cannot differ much from those of H. A. L. Fisher's: 'We Europeans are the children of Hellas. Our civilization, which has its roots in the brilliant city life of the eastern Aegean, has never lost traces of its origin, and stamps us with a character by which we are distinguished from the other great civilizations of the human family.' When we read such words they remind us of something we never doubted, of the bright, attractive dawn of our European day,

> where in her Mediterranean mirror gazing
> old Asia's dreamy face wrinkleth to a westward smile.

But it has not always been so. Shakespeare, reading in North's translation of Plutarch's *Lives of the Noble Grecians and Romans*, preferred the Romans as subjects for his drama; and Ben Jonson wrote of Sejanus and Catiline. Dryden and Pope, a century later, were the Augustans, the children not of Hellas but of Imperial Rome. For them, as still for Gibbon, Rome provided the solid fabric of human greatness. The classicism of their architecture was Roman and Vitruvian; their sculpture portrayed their famous men in Roman armour, or in the Roman *toga*; they erected triumphal arches in the Roman tradition to celebrate their victories; their satirists adapted Horace and Juvenal to current purposes; their most applauded tragedy was on the theme of Cato; the rhythms of their prose derived from Cicero.

By the middle years of the eighteenth century Augustan taste had come to seem old-fashioned to sophisticated young men like Horace Walpole. He had been to Italy, and had the good fortune to visit Herculaneum within a year of its discovery. Pompeii and Paestum became known not long afterwards. Then Winckelmann published his famous essay and turned men's minds away from Augustan Rome to Periclean Athens. The society into which Shelley was born was strongly influenced by the Grecian taste of the Age of Neo-Classicism, of which Winckelmann was the prophet. About the very year of his birth Shelley's grandfather, Sir Bysshe, building at Castle Goring in Sussex a fashionable mansion to be a monument to his wealth and position, was one of the first to introduce into an English country house the Doric order, and the most austere and majestic of Greek architectural forms was thus imprinted on Shelley's imagination in childhood. Perhaps it was this which enabled him, when he visited Paestum in 1819, to respond to the architecture of the temples more immediately than Goethe thirty years before, who had first to dismiss from his visual memory the 'more slender style of architecture' to which he was accustomed.

Shelley learnt Greek at Eton, and though he seems not to have exploited his knowledge until Peacock insisted that he should do so, his facility in languages was such that thereafter he read widely and attentively in Greek. From time to time, when his own poetic inspiration lapsed, he would translate from other languages, from Greek and Latin, from Italian, Spanish and German. By far the most of these translations are from Greek, for Shelley never doubted that 'Grecian literature [was] the finest the world had ever produced.' He translated the Homeric Hymns, the *Cyclops* of Euripides, a few epigrams, some scraps of pastoral, and also two of Plato's dialogues, the *Symposium* and the *Ion*. The *Symposium* took him eight or nine days, with three more for revision, which is evidence enough of his fluency. The concentrated attention which he brought to the language and style of what he read is shown by a passage which Mary Shelley transcribed from one of his note-books in her own note to *Prometheus Unbound*. 'In the Greek Shakespeare, Sophocles,' Shelley had written,

we find the image,

$$\pi o \lambda \lambda \grave{a} \varsigma \; \delta' \grave{o} \delta o \grave{v} \varsigma \; \H{\epsilon} \lambda \theta o \nu \tau a \; \phi \rho o \nu \tau \acute{\iota} \delta o \varsigma \; \pi \lambda \acute{a} \nu o \iota \varsigma,$$

a line of almost unfathomable depth of poetry; yet how simple are the images in which it is arrayed!

Coming to many ways in the wanderings of careful thought.

If the words $\grave{o} \delta o \acute{v} \varsigma$ and $\pi \lambda \acute{a} \nu o \iota \varsigma$ had not been used, the line might have been explained in a metaphorical instead of an absolute sense, as we say '*ways* and means', and 'wanderings' for error and confusion. But they meant literally paths or roads, such as we tread with our feet; and wanderings, such as a man makes when he loses himself in a desert, or roams from city to city—as Oedipus, the speaker of this verse, was destined to wander, blind and asking charity. What a picture does the line suggest of the mind as a wilderness of intricate paths, wide as the universe, which is here made its symbol.

A poet who read Sophocles with such ease and with such insight into his technical mastery would be likely to reveal its influence in his own manner of writing. Shelley was, indeed, much closer to Sophocles than to Shakespeare, as Mary Shelley understood. That was why she quoted his criticism of a line in the *Oedipus Tyrannus* in her note to *Prometheus Unbound*. 'Shelley,' she says, 'tried to idealize the real—to gift the mechanism of the material universe with a soul and a voice, and to bestow such also on the most delicate and abstract emotions and thoughts of the mind. Sophocles was his great master in this species of imagery.'

There is a more pervasive influence still. Walter Bagehot, in his essay on Shelley, observes that 'the growth of civilization, at least in Greece, rather increased than diminished the imaginative bareness of the poetical art. It seems to attain its height in Sophocles.' In illustration he quotes from the *Oedipus Coloneus* the speech in which Oedipus contrasts the conduct of his sons with that of his daughters. The 'imaginative bareness' of which Bagehot writes is at its extreme in this last play, where Sophocles had discarded the Aeschylean $\H{o} \gamma \kappa o \varsigma$

(loftiness*) still evident in his earliest surviving plays, and has attained the mature perfection of style which, as Plutarch reports, he considered ἠθικώτατον καὶ βέλτιστον, his best manner and most expressive of character. A cursory examination of the sixteen lines quoted will show the total absence of ponderous, compound epithets, and indeed a paucity of epithet altogether. The two unusual words in the passage are by no means associated with tragedy: one is used by Plato, the other by Aristophanes. Sophocles at the end of his long career as a tragic dramatist does not need to rely on the vocabulary of tragedy: he can even use a word whose associations are with comedy. So it is with Shelley: he does not rely on connotative richness of epithet, nor on an obviously 'poetic' vocabulary. His classicism is of the Sophoclean kind. As Bagehot says, Shelley's 'verse runs quick and chill, like a pure crystal stream'.

The image invites further consideration, for Bagehot seems to have been recalling, whether consciously or not, a passage in Winckelmann's *History of Ancient Art*. In G. H. Lodge's then recently published translation of the section on Greek art, in a chapter entitled 'The Essential of Art', the words are these: 'Beauty should be like the best kind of water, drawn from the spring itself; the less taste it has, the more healthful it is considered, because free from all foreign admixture.'† This quality in Shelley's poetry, its 'thinness', its supposed tenuity, has led to all the insensitive criticism to which it has been subjected, from Keats' advice to him to 'load every rift of his subject with ore' down to the more recent ineptitudes of Eliot and Leavis. But it was this very quality which showed how well Shelley's verse approximated to the neo-classical ideal. Only when we consider his poetry in that context, in the context of Winckelmann's reappraisal of the art and literature of Greece, can we come to any balanced judgment of it.

In the passage where Bagehot compares Shelley's verse to spring water he is contrasting it with Keats', whose sensibility he rightly considered to be the exact opposite of Shelley's. And in the passage where he quotes from the *Oedipus Coloneus* he is again contrasting Keats (from whose *Ode on a Grecian Urn* he has just transcribed the

---

* Dr Johnson said of Milton, 'his natural port was gigantic loftiness.' 'Loftiness' is the definition of ὄγκος in a critical context in Liddell and Scott.

† Winckelmann in his turn was surely remembering a passage in P. Bouhours' *Les Entretiens d'Ariste et d'Eugène*, II ('La Langue Françoise'): 'Le beau langage resemble à une eau pure et nette qui n'a point de goût, qui coule de source, qui va où sa pente naturelle la porte.'

first stanza) with the Greek poets: 'no ancient poet,' he says, 'would have dreamed of writing thus.' But Shelley did write like a Greek poet; he was closer to Sophocles than to Keats, or to Shakespeare, and his poetry ought to be judged by Sophoclean standards, not by theirs, for its 'imaginative bareness', not for its abundance. The quality for which his verse has been ignorantly condemned is that for which it most deserves praise.

Shelley himself, in the preface to *Prometheus Unbound*, invited the comparison with Greek poetry. 'The imagery which I have employed,' he there says, 'will be found in many instances to have been drawn from the operations of the human mind, or from those external actions by which they are expressed. . . . The Greek poets . . . were in the habitual use of this power; and it is the study of their work (since a higher merit would probably be denied me) to which I am willing that my readers should impute this singularity.' He was aware both of the Greek antecedents of his style, and of the effect they had in differentiating it from the work of other English poets. But his response to Greek poetry was not that of the twentieth century, or of the Renaissance; it was that of his own time, of the Age of Neo-Classicism.

There is nothing obviously distinctive in Shelley's manner of writing; his style carries no signature. Probably no one could assign a passage from one of his poems to Shelley on grounds of style alone, without evidence from content. The same may be said of Goldsmith; the same has been said of Sophocles. The qualities of their style are elusive. To test this elusiveness in Shelley we need to examine some lines from a poem which is not widely known.

> So Gherardi's hall
> Laughed in the mirth of its lord's festival,
> Till someone asked—'Where is the Bride?' And then
> A bridesmaid went,—and ere she came again
> A silence fell upon the guests—a pause
> Of expectation, as when beauty awes
> All hearts with its approach, though unbeheld,
> Then wonder, and then fear that wonder quelled;—
> For whispers passed from mouth to ear which drew
> The colour from the hearer's cheeks, and flew
> Louder and swifter round the company;
> And then Gherardi entered with an eye

Of ostentatious trouble, and a crowd
Surrounded him, and some were weeping loud.

This is a vivid and dramatic telling of a story with sinister overtones,
such as Browning managed so well: someone who did not know it
might be forgiven for attributing it to Browning. There is nothing
idiosyncratic in the style, nothing of the qualities which make
attribution of even a few lines from Spenser or Milton or Sir Thomas
Browne or Gibbon certain on stylistic grounds. Nevertheless, there
are analogies with the passage from *Oedipus Coloneus* already
discussed: there is no ὄγκος; there are even fewer epithets; there are no
words which we should be surprised to find in prose except, perhaps,
'unbeheld'. (That word is itself very characteristic of Shelley: it is
participial—an adjective, but a verbal adjective—and it is negative.)
But especially the passage is remarkable for the preponderance of
verbs (fourteen) over epithets (two).

Shelley commended Peacock's prose in *Nightmare Abbey* for its
'lightness, chastity, and strength,' and these admirable qualities he
himself strove for and, in his best poetry, attained. They are also the
qualities which Bradley observed in Goldsmith's prose, and caused
him to compare his use of the English language with Shelley's. Since it
is one of the properties of such a style that it does not draw the reader's
attention to itself but allows, or induces, his mind to move, as of its
own volition, 'with perpetual ease and grace', it suggests no easy
definition; and it is not susceptible to parody.

Now the visual arts in the Age of Neo-Classicism had as strong a
literary propulsion behind them as the art of Raphael—that is one of
the reasons why Raphael was then universally regarded as supreme
among the world's painters. An illustration for Shelley's style may
therefore be sought in the art of the most admired of English neo-
classical artists, John Flaxman. Both Shelley and Flaxman held that
the style of one art may be reflected in another: indeed, this was
scarcely questioned by the two generations that succeeded Winckelmann. The emphasis on precision of contour, which to Winckelmann
was 'the characteristic distinction of the ancients', was for Blake, no
less than for Flaxman or George Cumberland, the golden rule of art.
(It is not relevant to literature, since, as Lessing observed, 'the poet is
not compelled to concentrate his picture into the space of a single
moment.') The widespread acceptance of this ideal of draughtsman-
ship led to the extraordinary success of Flaxman's illustrations of the
poems of Homer, Hesiod, Aeschylus and Dante, which were

regularly reprinted throughout the nineteenth century, and which attained a European fame. In these the purity of outline and the disregard of shading or colour seemed to fulfil Winckelmann's requirement of 'a sublime simplicity of contour'. The illustrations for Dante would not at the time have seemed extrinsic to the pure classicism of Flaxman's work for, as Shelley himself observed, Dante more than any other modern poet had succeeded in the Sophoclean type of imagery which he himself attempted in *Prometheus Unbound*. That is why his poetry 'may be considered as the bridge thrown over the stream of time', which unites the modern and ancient world'.

Flaxman's drawing of *The Chained Prometheus visited by the Oceanides* was designed to illustrate the *Prometheus Vinctus* of Aeschylus, but it could serve equally well to illustrate the first act of *Prometheus Unbound*. Indeed, it might now be thought better suited to Shelley than to Aeschylus, for Flaxman did not attempt the rugged and heroic grandeur of Aeschylus' own conception, nor could he suggest in line drawings anything of the epithet-laden density of Aeschylus' verse. His *Compositions from the Tragedies of Aeschylus* are as devoid of ὄγκος as the *Oedipus Coloneus*, and their manner would have been more appropriate to illustration of the plays of Sophocles. His linear treatment of these classical designs derives from Greek vase-painting—his first essays in this kind had been undertaken for Josiah Wedgwood in the 1770s—and the treatment is narrative, not descriptive. So it is with Shelley's poetry, which creates the effect of onward impulsion which any rich colouring of epithet would delay. This Grecian simplicity in Shelley's poetic expression has been the source of much perplexity to those who are unwilling, or unable, to see it for what it is.

This is not to be wondered at, for Shelley does not use the English language as most of us use it, as Keats or Shakespeare used it; he uses it as a Greek used Greek. Shelley makes the verbs, not the epithets, do all the work. This is not what most Englishmen do: we use verbs mainly to stitch epithets to their nouns, to link metaphor and simile to what these illuminate, to confront subject and object; we use them to satisfy the demands of syntax. In a telegram of congratulation we omit the verbs, not the adjectives. Keats addressing a Grecian urn is not in the least Grecian in his use of language.

> Thou still unravish'd bride of quietness,
>   Thou foster-child of silence and slow time,
> Sylvan historian, who canst thus express

> A flowery tale more sweetly than our rhyme:
> What leaf-fring'd legend haunts about thy shape
>   Of deities or mortals, or of both,
>   In Tempe or the dales of Arcady?
>   What men or gods are these? What maidens loth?
> What mad pursuit? What struggle to escape?
>   What pipes and timbrels? What wild ecstasy?

Here are but four verbs in a welter of epithets. In the last three lines of the stanza a series of questions is strung together, and the expressed plural verb has to be understood in the singular in half of them! Verbs, being mere grammatical convenience, can be disregarded. Not only the sentiment but the expression is as unlike Greek poetry as could be devised; but it is not at all strange to English taste, since we habitually make substantives and epithets carry the main weight of expression, where the Greeks employed verbs.

If we recall a famous passage in English poetry, what chiefly strikes us are the epithets: 'unravish'd', 'sylvan', 'leaf-fring'd', 'loth'. These seem to us the stuff of poetry. So with G. M. Hopkins:

> Towery city and branchy between towers;
> Cuckoo-echoing, bell-swarmed, lark-charmed,
>   rook-racked, river-rounded;
> The dapple-eared lily below thee; that country
>   and town did
> Once encounter in, here coped and poised powers.

We do not even object to the feeble verbal expletive 'did'; we are too used to it, in some of the most quoted passages in the language.

> What wond'rous Life is this I lead!
> Ripe Apples drop about my head;
> The Luscious Clusters of the Vine
> Upon my Mouth *do* crush their Wine;
> The Nectaren, and curious Peach,
> Into my hands themselves *do* reach;
> Stumbling on Melons, as I pass,
> Insnar'd with Flow'rs, I fall on Grass.

Or again, ensnared by Enobarbus' epithets, we overlook an almost self-parodying succession of expletives.

For her own person
It beggarded all description; she *did* lie
In her pavilion, cloth-of-gold of tissue,
O'erpicturing that Venus where we see
The fancy outwork nature: on each side her
Stood pretty dimpled boys, like smiling Cupids,
With divers-coloured fans, whose wind *did* seem
To glow the delicate cheeks which they *did* cool,
And what they undid did.

Such writing implies the normal English lack of concern with verbs; it is totally un-Hellenic, and it is very unlike Shelley.

The lack of inflections in English and the resultant fixity of word-order make it impossible for English style to come close to Greek, but it is possible to make verbs and verbal forms such as participles dominant, and this is what Shelley does. Since verbs convey ideas of action, movement, change, a style in which they are conspicuous is especially suited to narrative and drama, which are concerned with these things; but it is also very well suited to lyric poetry, since some progression is required here too. It is no accident that the finest achievements of Greek poetry are in narrative, drama, and lyric, or that there is almost no descriptive poetry, and none of reverie. The pastoral poems of Theocritus are given a dramatic framework of dialogue, in which pure description, as of the cup in the first Idyll, seems disproportionate. One of the most celebrated of Greek lyrics, Sappho's

$$\varphi\alpha\acute{\iota}\nu\varepsilon\tau\alpha\iota \ \mu o\iota \ \kappa\hat{\eta}\nu o\varsigma \ \acute{\iota}\sigma o\varsigma \ \theta\acute{\varepsilon}o\iota\sigma\iota\nu,^{*}$$

achieves its effect almost without recourse to epithet. 'At her most passionate,'(says Bowra,) 'she has passed beyond imagery and essays with triumph the last difficulties of poetry, where sublimity is reached in the nakedness of common words.' Again, the 'imaginative bareness' of Sophocles' mature style is seen as the perfection of Greek poetry. Shelley, who was narrative poet and dramatist, but perhaps greater still as a lyric poet, could also essay with triumph the last difficulties of poetry

---

* Blest as the gods is he.

Ariel to Miranda: Take
This slave of Music, for the sake
Of him who is the slave of thee,
And teach it all the harmony
In which thou canst, and only thou,
Make the delighted spirit glow,
Till joy denies itself again,
And, too intense, is turned to pain;
For by permission and command
Of thine own Prince Ferdinand,
Poor Ariel sends this silent token
Of more than ever can be spoken;
Your guardian spirit, Ariel, who,
From life to life, must still pursue
Your happiness;—for thus alone
Can Ariel ever find his own.

Here too, as in Sappho's lyric, the verbs scarcely need supplementing; and there is not a word that would seem strange in a prose letter, in a letter written today.

The Cloud is as well known as any poem by Shelley, and it exhibits what has been called his 'speed' most appositely. There are various ways of looking at clouds, as Polonius discovered. When Keats looked at them he wished to arrest their ceaseless movement, to capture for ever the fleeting instant by describing it in elaborate detail, as if refusing to let it go. He tells you what the cloud looks like, its shape and colour and brightness; his description resembles one of Constable's meticulously timed and dated studies. He does not tell you what the clouds are doing, or how they got there; he is not concerned with the perpetual flux of weather. But that is what interests Shelley: the activity of clouds, and the scientific theory of their formation by the processes of condensation and precipitation. When he writes of the 'sunbeams with their convex gleams' he is thinking of atmospheric refraction seen from above. His poems are full of such images, drawn from contemporary scientific thought, which, though sometimes abstruse (since not many of us are familiar with early nineteenth century science), are never imprecise; but they are not at all Keatsian. When Shelley writes of clouds we think of the shimmering movement of light in a Turner, most of all in his description in *Julian and Maddalo* of sunset over Venice, which he wrote there the year before Turner's first visit. No one would consult

Turner if he wished to know what the weather was like at Brighton on New Year's Day, 1826, or at Hampstead at noon on 15 September 1830; but Constable will tell him. That is no reason for regarding Constable as the greater artist.

Shelley's method in *The Cloud* deserves careful examination.

> I bring fresh showers for the thirsting flowers,
>   From the seas and the streams;
> I bear light shade for the leaves when laid
>   In their noonday dreams.
> From my wings are shaken the dews that waken
>   The sweet buds every one,
> When rocked to rest on their mother's breast,
>   As she dances about the sun.
> I wield the flail of the lashing hail,
>   And whiten the green plains under,
> And then again I dissolve it in rain,
>   And laugh as I pass in thunder.

In this opening section of twelve lines there are six epithets: fresh showers, thirsting flowers, light shade, sweet buds, lashing hail, green plains. It is easy to see what Keats meant: there is no weight of ore here. Anyone might write of fresh showers, light shade, sweet buds, green plains. When Shelley needs a more vivid epithet he uses a verbal form: thirsting flowers, lashing hail. But if we look at the verbs in these twelve lines we not only find that there are twice as many but that they are contributing more: bring, bear, laid, are shaken, waken, rocked, dances, wield, whiten, dissolve, laugh, pass. So it is throughout the poem: there are more than seventy verbs, and less than fifty epithets, and of these about one in three is participial.

Even where we might expect a Keatsian, or Spenserian, luxury of epithet, in *Adonais*, Shelley's manner is still the same, with the verbs outnumbering and dominating the epithets as in the poem's Greek antecedents but not as in *Astrophel* or *Lycidas*. And it is so throughout his mature work, in the famous lyrics of *Prometheus Unbound* and of *Hellas*, in *To a Sky-lark*, or the *Ode to the West Wind*, or the *Hymn of Pan*. The swift movement imparted by the vigorous verbs is enjoyable without our pausing to observe how it is produced, and it has led to Shelley's reputation as above all a writer of lyric. This is in keeping with the love of music which took him to the opera or ballet whenever possible, and which is often disclosed in his poetry. He wrote *To Constantia singing* in compliment to Claire Clairmont's voice; he wrote several songs for Sophia Stacey, the ward of his uncle whom he met in Florence; he bought a guitar for Jane Williams, and accompanied his gift with one of his most exquisite poems. His sensitivity to the song of the sky-lark is shown in the stanza which he devised to imitate the pattern of clear, ringing notes followed by rapid trilling. And he draws imagery from this most abstract of the arts no less than from scientific theory, for his mind, unlike the minds of most poets, could range easily about the realms of speculation.

This quality of his mind affected his response to the visual arts. He spent the winter of 1819–20 in Florence where, as he told Maria Gisborne, he intended to study the works in the Galleria degli Uffizi, 'one of my chief aims in Italy being the observing in statuary and painting the degree in which, and the rules according to which, that ideal beauty of which we have so intense yet so obscure an apprehension is realized in external forms'. One of the results of these studies was the series of some sixty *Notes on Sculptures in Rome and Florence* which Medwin, on first publishing a few of them, compared to Winckelmann's appreciations. The longest of these *Notes* is on the 'Niobe', whose ideal beauty Winckelmann compared to a Madonna by Raphael. (Shelley had read the *History of Ancient Art* in Naples the previous winter.) 'No production of sculpture, not even the Apollo, ever produced on me so strong an effect as this Niobe,' he wrote to Hogg. Winckelmann also compared the 'Niobe' with the 'Apollo Belvedere' and the 'Venus de' Medici', as 'the finest ideal heads'.

A year after his studies in the Uffizi, early in 1821, Shelley wrote his *Defence of Poetry*, in which he compares the experience of the poet with that of the sculptor or painter. 'A great statue or picture grows under the power of the artist as a child in the mother's womb, and the very mind which directs the hands in formation is incapable of accounting to itself for the origins, the gradations, or the media of the process.' This is the Neo-Platonic doctrine of ideal beauty, which had been developed by Proclus in answer to Plato's strictures on the creative power of the artist, and which had been expressed by Raphael in the often quoted letter to Castiglione. It had again found favour with the neo-classical painters of the later eighteenth century, in its most extreme form with Blake, and in more judicious expression with Sir Joshua Reynolds. The phrase 'intellectual beauty', which was used by both Blake and Reynolds, was used by Shelley in his translation of the *Symposium* for Plato's τὸ καλόν.

Shelley sees the poet's experience as moving always from 'the yellow bees in the ivy-bloom' to the intellectual, ideal world of Platonic forms 'more real than living man'. This idealism leads to the tenuous quality of many of Shelley's epithets, but also, beyond this, to an idiosyncratic liking for negative epithets. By this means he strips away the sensuous character of experience, which he regards as a hindrance to the perception of truth, just as Blake did; for to him

> The deep truth is imageless.

A negative epithet denies the presence of the attribute which the positive describes, and is far more effective than mere omission. In the first act of *Prometheus Unbound*, in a Chorus of Spirits,

> Cloudless skies and windless streams

means something different from 'skies and streams', and so reinforces the next line,

> Silent, liquid and serene.

By these negatives Shelley breaks down

> the veil and the bar
> Of things which seem and are,

the veil—it is one of his favourite images—suspended by the senses between *videri* and *esse*, appearance and reality. When Prometheus, after his renunciation of the Curse, is at last about to be united with Asia, the Mind of Man with Love,* Panthea says to her,

> some good change
> Is working in the elements, which suffer
> Thy presence thus unveiled.

For Shelley the veil was the interposition of the material world between finite mind and Platonic idea; it was also the obscuring effect of concrete imagery, with its appeal to our senses, which his negative epithets were intended to remove. They withdraw the veil of sense-perception. Just so Blake appealed from Wordsworth's complacent

---

* Cf. plate 99 of Blake's *Jerusalem*.

acceptance of the influence of natural objects on the imagination to the Platonic idealism of that sonnet by Michelangelo which Wordsworth himself translated.

Shelley's negative epithets accentuate the liquid purity of his style, its lack of taste, which was the neo-classicists' ideal. But not only spring water: the sea itself provided an apt image. In the most often quoted passage in all Winckelmann's writings, where he claims 'noble simplicity and calm grandeur' as the especial qualities of Greek sculpture, he goes on: 'As the bottom of the sea lies peaceful beneath a foaming surface, a great soul lies calm beneath the strife and passions in Greek figures.' And he repeats the image with reference to the 'Niobe'. Again, he says, 'Quietness and calm, as with the sea, are expedient to beauty.' This association came naturally to Shelley, whose 'passion was the Ocean', as Mary said. His delight in sailing was a delight in feeling at one with wind and wave and tide. To him, as to Spenser, water was a metaphor of life, always changing yet always the same; the continuity between its foaming surface and calm depths gave him a perfect image with which to reconcile delight in the impermanent world of matter with a belief that the real world is the world of thought, beyond time and change. Often, as he peered over the side of his boat into the clear waters of the Mediterranean, this impressed him. 'We set off an hour after sunrise one radiant morning in a little boat,' he wrote to Peacock; 'there was not a cloud in the sky, nor a wave upon the sea, which was so translucent that you could see the hollow caverns clothed with the glaucous sea-moss, and the leaves and branches of those delicate weeds that pave the unequal bottom of the water'. Panthea echoes these words, as well she might, since she was a Nereid who must have had an intimate knowledge of her ancestral domains.

> Erewhile I slept
> Under the glaucous caverns of old Ocean
> Within dim bowers of green and purple moss.

Shelley often alludes to this remote, submarine world, to its stillness, but also to the motion and change that might be found there; for the West Wind that stirs the needles of the pines in the Cascine is felt even beneath the surface of the sea.

> Thou
> For whose path the Atlantic's level powers
> Cleave themselves into chasms, while far below

The sea-blooms and the oozy woods which wear
The sapless foliage of the ocean, know
Thy voice, and suddenly grow gray with fear,
And tremble and despoil themselves.

Shelley, gazing below the ruffled surface of the water, has observed
the silvery greyness that comes upon the weeds when the light is
broken above them. The sea provided a better image than Plato's
Cave, since the poet cannot, like the philosopher, discard any part of
experience, but must preserve the continuity of it all; he must
maintain the concreteness of his sensuous image at the same time as he
allows it to operate in the reader's imagination.

Shelley was always aware of the difficulty for the poet in opening
'the channels of communication between thought and expression' (as
he put it). 'The mind in creation is as a fading coal, which some
invisible influence, like an inconstant wind, awakens to transitory
brightness. . . . When composition begins, inspiration is already on
the decline, and the most glorious poetry that has ever been
communicated to the world is probably a feeble shadow of the
original conceptions of the poet.' It was in part due to his attempt to
overcome this difficulty that he developed the style whose characters I
have been attempting here to define. The Grecian taste of the society
into which he was born, and the Greek literature which he read with
such admiration, determined the lines of its development.

So far I have been considering Shelley mostly as a lyric poet, but
although, in that kind, he is without a rival in English, he is, in fact,
the most versatile of all our poets, and his achievements in drama and
narrative (of several species in each), in satire and invective and
parody and burlesque, in elegy and familiar epistle, in Pindaric ode
and Dantesque *terza rima*—to say nothing of his translations—are not
less remarkable. He himself was aware of this versatility and, with his
usual modesty, wondered 'whether the attempt to excel in many
ways does not debar from excellence in one particular kind'. The
poetry which he left sufficiently answers any such doubt; yet it may
properly be asked whether a manner that is so well suited to lyric is
also suited to so many other kinds. Or did Shelley run the risk that
other great lyric poets—Ronsard, for example—have run when
attempting poetry that is not lyrical?

Now a style that successfully achieves the irresistible onward
movement of the famous lyrics would not be appropriate to a poem
of meditation or reverie, or to poetry of pure description. The

Grecian style is suited to the kinds of poetry in which the Greeks
excelled. Narrative poetry must be kept moving forwards, as Spenser
kept *The Faerie Queene* moving from the first line of the first canto.
Endymion fails because, as Keats himself acknowledged, it was
a test to 'make four thousand lines of one bare circumstance'.
Shelley's dominant verbs impel his narrative ever forwards; it is never
clogged and hindered by a superabundance of epithet. So it is with
drama, which is concerned with action. Alone of the Romantic poets
Shelley wrote drama that is viable on the stage; Wordsworth,
Coleridge, Byron, Keats, and later Tennyson, Browning, Arnold,
Swinburne and Bridges all wrote plays; but their plays cannot hold
the attention of a theatre audience. Shelley's manner certainly gave
him an advantage in keeping the action in progress. What is true of
The Cenci and of the fragmentary *Charles I* is true also of the lyrical
dramas, *Prometheus Unbound* and *Hellas*.

To satire Shelley's manner was peculiarly apt, for the swiftness here
gives incisiveness, which the Augustan satirists attained by the rapid
satisfaction of the expected rhyme in the heroic couplet. The fierce,
relentless energy of *The Mask of Anarchy* results from Shelley's
preference for narration rather than description, as in his portrayal of
Castlereagh and Eldon.

> I met Murder on the way—
> He had a mask like Castlereagh—
> Very smooth he looked, yet grim;
> Seven blood-hounds followed him.
>
> All were fat; and well they might
> Be in admirable plight,
> For one by one, and two by two,
> He tossed them human hearts to chew,
> Which from his wide cloak he drew.
>
> Next came Fraud, and he had on,
> Like Eldon, an ermined gown;
> His big tears, for he wept well,
> Turned to mill-stones as they fell;
>
> And the little children, who
> Round his feet played to and fro,
> Thinking every tear a gem,
> Had their brains knocked out by them.

He chose the ballad stanza for his poem, and drove it onwards with the ballad's economy; and he has the ballad's conventionality of epithet—wide cloak, ermined gown, little children.

Where indignation gives way to merriment, as in *Peter Bell the Third*, Shelley's preference for narration rather than description is again apparent.

> But from the first 'twas Peter's drift
> To be a kind of moral eunuch;
> He touched the hem of Nature's shift,
> Felt faint—and never dared uplift
> The closest, all-concealing tunic.

And although, since this is parody, the form derives from Wordsworth's poem, Shelley makes it his own by using verbs rather than the epithets of Wordsworth's preference, in order to describe what Peter is doing, or failing to do, not what he seems to be.

The easy familiarity of style which *Peter Bell the Third* exhibits is obviously suitable for epistolary verse, whether in the *Letter to Maria Gisborne* or in later poems addressed to Jane and Edward Williams, in *The Boat on the Serchio*, in the dedication to Mary of *The Witch of Atlas* or, at its most serious and comprehensive, in *Julian and Maddalo*. The manuscript of this last poem shows that Shelley was recalling certain words or phrases used by Byron in their conversation on that August day in Venice, when they met again after nearly two years' separation, and that he strove to retain them through repeated revisions. The subtitle, 'A Conversation', correctly describes the opening section of the poem before the Maniac, representing Tasso, is introduced: it is written, as Shelley said, in 'a certain familiar style of language to express the actual way in which people talk with each other whom education and a certain refinement of sentiment have placed above the use of vulgar idioms'. It is written in the Horatian plain style of Ben Jonson's preference, rather than in the slangy colloquialism of *Beppo* or parts of *Don Juan*. It is the record of that momentous reunion of the two poets which was to set them both immediately, within a matter of days, on the chief work of their lives, on *Prometheus Unbound* and on *Don Juan*. (For this Byron chose as superscription Horace's *Difficile est proprie communia dicere.**) *Julian and Maddalo* is also the first completed poem of Shelley's maturity,

---

* 'Tis hard, to speak things common, properly. (Jonson)

and the conversational tone so well achieved in it was to be repeated in other poems of the four years that remained. The only other conversation is the fragmentary poem known as *The Boat on the Serchio*, which describes a sailing trip with Edward Williams.

A style suited to conversation between friends is equally suited to their letters, those conversations at a distance. Shelley and Byron in their letters convey the very tones of their voices: we might be in the room with them, overhearing their talk. The *Letter to Maria Gisborne*, written nearly two years after *Julian and Maddalo*, is Shelley's best epistolary poem, informal, affectionate, full of lively sketches of Shelley's friends in London whom Mrs Gisborne may expect to see, lit with flashes of humorous observation of them and of himself, and ending with happy anticipation of the pleasures they will share again on her return to Italy.

> We will have books, Spanish, Italian, Greek;
> And ask one week to make another week
> As like his father as I'm unlike mine,
> Which is not his fault, as you may divine.
> Though we eat little flesh and drink no wine,
> Yet let's be merry: we'll have tea and toast;
> Custards for supper, and an endless host
> Of syllabubs and jellies and mince-pies,
> And other such lady-like luxuries,—
> Feasting on which we will philosophize!

Earlier in the poem Shelley had reminded Maria Gisborne of occasions when she had

> listened to some interrupted flow
> Of visionary rhyme,—in joy and pain
> Struck from the inmost fountains of my brain.

Two or three weeks later, after a walk by himself up Monte S. Pellegrino, near Lucca, Shelley dashed off 'a fanciful poem' (as he called it), *The Witch of Atlas*. Mary thought little of it: he should be writing more serious poetry, and in a manner more likely to win popular acclaim, which he had recently shown, in *The Cenci*, he could accomplish. He should eschew 'the abstract and dreamy spirit' of such poems as *The Witch of Atlas* and, perhaps, of *Prometheus Unbound*. Mary was correct in judging that *The Cenci* had more appeal than most of Shelley's poetry—it was the only poem of his to reach a second edition in his life-time; and though she realized that he did not expect public approbation she knew, as she said, that 'the want of it took away a portion of the ardour that ought to have sustained him while writing'. Here too, as Shelley's letters show, she was right. But Shelley was incorrigible: Mary, he thought, was talking like Wordsworth who, in his dedication to Southey of *Peter Bell*, had acknowledged that the poem had 'nearly survived its *minority*—for it first saw the light in the summer of 1798'. He went on to claim that throughout this long time 'pains have been taken at different times to make the production less unworthy of a favourable reception'. Such pomposity provoked Shelley into making a comparison of his poem with *Peter Bell*, and perhaps, by implication, of Mary with Wordsworth. His seriousness might be worthy of respect; but what if it issued in such a poem as *Peter Bell*? Besides, a poet, surely, is entitled sometimes to take a holiday, and to indulge himself with writing the kind of poetry which he finds most fun to write. So Shelley teases Mary by dedicating to her a poem which she had too solemnly rejected.

> How, my dear Mary,—are you critic-bitten
>   (For vipers kill, though dead) by some review,
> That you condemn these verses I have written,
>   Because they tell no story, false or true?
> What, though no mice are caught by a young kitten,
>   May it not leap and play as grown cats do,
> Till its claws come? Prithee, for this one time,
> Content thee with a visionary rhyme;

with a poem of the sort that he had read to Maria Gisborne, and which she had enjoyed.

Shelley intended *The Cenci*, unlike the two lyrical dramas, for the stage and indeed wrote the part of Beatrice with the celebrated actress Eliza O'Neill in mind, as he told Peacock. He had seen her play several parts while he was in London, and had been much moved by her acting. But a play on the theme of incest (the theme of *Oedipus Tyrannus*) was not acceptable for public performance in Regency London, and many years were to pass before it was put on the stage. *The Cenci* owes something to early seventeenth century drama— Ford, as well as Sophocles, wrote of incest—but Shelley's manner is still Grecian rather than Jacobean and has those qualities which I have

already noted as characteristic of all his mature work. A poet who in
Julian and Maddalo had succeeded in expressing 'the actual way in
which people talk with each other' could write convincing dialogue,
even when the dramatic situation demanded an intensity which
conversation with Lord Byron did not. The final scene of all, where
Cardinal Camillo comes with the guards to lead Beatrice away to
execution (which takes place off-stage, in the Greek tradition), is
masterly in its restraint. Her brother Bernardo has just rushed in,
distraught, to take his leave of her. She seeks to calm him.

And though

Ill tongues shall wound me, and our common name
Be as a mark stamped on thine innocent brow
For men to point at as they pass, do thou
Forbear, and never think a thought unkind
Of those, who perhaps love thee in their graves.
So mayest thou die as I do; fear and pain
Being subdued. Farewell! Farewell! Farewell!
   Bernardo. I cannot say, farewell.
   Camillo.   Oh, Lady Beatrice.
   Beatrice. Give yourself no unnecessary pain,
My dear Lord Cardinal. Here, Mother, tie
My girdle for me, and bind up this hair
In any simple knot; aye, that does well.
And yours I see is coming down. How often
Have we done this for one another; now
We shall not do it any more. My Lord,
We are quite ready. Well, 'tis very well.

This last speech is based on the group of the Niobe and her youngest
daughter in the Uffizi, and though, when he wrote *The Cenci*, Shelley
had not yet seen the original statues he must have known them from
casts or engravings. When he did see them a few months later he
wrote, 'there is no terror on the countenance, only grief—deep
remediless grief. There is no anger: of what avail is indignation
against what is known to be omnipotent?' The same group had
moved Winckelmann also as a perfect example of restraint, of that
'noble simplicity and calm grandeur' which he had taken to be the
marks of the greatest works of the Greeks.

The two lyrical dramas, *Prometheus Unbound* and *Hellas*, derive
more obviously from Greek tragedy, although they were never

intended for the stage. (In this respect we should perhaps associate them with *Samson Agonistes* rather than with the plays of Aeschylus.) In his preface to *Prometheus Unbound* Shelley disclaimed any attempt 'to restore the lost drama of Aeschylus', which is known to us from fragments, from a passage translated by Cicero, and from other ancient references. *Hellas*, which was 'written at the suggestion of the events of the moment', that is, of the outbreak of the Greek War of Independence in 1821, was modelled on the *Persae*, the one great tragedy ever written which had for its theme contemporary political events. There are occasional quotations from Aeschylus in both dramas, but Shelley's style has none of the high-flown language whose decorum Aeschylus is called upon to defend in the *Frogs* of Aristophanes: even where Shelley is taking Aeschylus for a model, his style remains Sophoclean.

Nowhere is the headlong speed of Shelley's verse more apparent, or more appropriate. The drama of *Hellas* shows the inexorable rapidity of the collapse of Turkish power in Greece, and the futility of all attempts to restore it. If at the time when he wrote Shelley's optimism for the success of the Greeks was unjustified by facts, it was sustained by the ardour of his hope. 'I have,' he wrote in the preface, 'contented myself with exhibiting a series of lyric pictures, and with having wrought upon the curtain of futurity, which falls upon the unfinished scene, such figures of indistinct and visionary delineation as suggest the final triumph of the Greek cause.' The sombre news which Hassan and a succession of messengers bring to the despairing Mahmud in Constantinople may be, as Shelley said, no more than a 'display of newspaper erudition', and the most memorable parts of the drama are the lyrics given to the Chorus of Greek captive women. The final chorus, which is among Shelley's most famous lyrics, is the consummation of that love for Greek poetry and Greek thought which had inspired so much of his best work, and it is written in the manner of Greek lyric. There is a prelude in an earlier chorus:

> But Greece and her foundations are
> Built below the tide of war,
> Based on the crystalline sea
> Of thought and its eternity;
> Her citizens, imperial spirits,
>   Rule the present from the past,
> On all this world of man inherits
>   Their seal is set.

This is a concise statement of Shelley's creed, which was also the creed of the neo-classical movement with which I have been concerned in this book.

If Thomas Taylor's sacrifices to the gods of Olympus ever took place at Walworth they were absurd not because his devotion to Greek civilization went too far, but because it did not go far enough. The response of a modern visitor to the Parthenon would not be enhanced if he struggled to recover the mood of Athena's worshippers; the effort would distract his mind from the aesthetic appreciation which the ruined and empty temple still exacts. In *Prometheus Unbound* Earth calls up such an image, of a temple reflected in water:

> Beside the windless and crystalline pool,
> Where ever lies, on unerasing waves,
> The image of a temple; built above,
> Distinct with column, arch, and architrave,
> And palm-like capital, and over-wrought,
> And populous with most living imagery,
> Praxitelean shapes, whose marble smiles
> Fill the hushed air with everlasting love.
> It is deserted now, but once it bore
> Thy name, Prometheus; there the emulous youths
> Bore to thy honour through the divine gloom
> The lamp which was thine emblem.

The reference to the opening passage of Plato's *Republic*, where a sort of equestrian relay race with torches in honour of Athena is described, provides Shelley with a characteristic adaptation to the theme of Prometheus. The forms of worship are obsolete, but the imaginative power of man's mind, which brought into existence the temples and statues of Athens, survives. They may be considered therefore as erected to the mind of man, and are evidence of that power which man can never lose, though it may be suppressed by religious bigotry or political tyranny. Liberty is the necessary condition for its full development, and Shelley looks forward to a new age of more perfect liberty than Athens had known, when there would be an end to slavery and to the inequality of the sexes. Then at last man would rival the ancient Greeks:

> Another Athens shall arise,
> And to remoter time

> Bequeath, like sunset to the skies,
> The splendour of its prime.

The supreme artistic achievements of the Greeks were not unattainable again; rather they provided an assurance that if the conditions were restored the achievement would be repeated. The history of Greece showed what still lay within man's power to accomplish.

Shelley's continuing concern with politics was not unique: he shared it with others who responded to the Grecian ideals of the age, with Akenside, whose radicalism had offended Dr Johnson, with Blake and Peacock and James Barry and Goya. I have not taken much account here of political opinions, since these are not more relevant to a literary judgment than religious belief: no one is inhibited from appreciating the *Iliad* or the *Oresteia* because he does not share the religious beliefs of Homer or Aeschylus and their first audiences, any more than he is hindered from admiring the Parthenon because he is not a devotee of Athena. Shelley was not a political propagandist, but a poet, and the greatest of the English poets who responded to that phase in European taste to which Winckelmann gave memorable formulation. 'The Taste is not to conform to the Art, but the Art to the Taste,' Addison had written long before, in the Augustan age, and though Wordsworthian Romantics might reverse the priorities there is no reason to suppose that Shelley would have done so. He wrote very little personal poetry, and published less; but as Wordsworth recognized, he was 'one of the finest *artists* of us all: I mean in workmanship of style'.

This style was fundamentally Grecian: Shelley perfected a style towards which Collins and Goldsmith and Peacock, in their various ways, had been striving. It is not in the English tradition, the common tradition of English usage, and has therefore generally been misunderstood; it is the consummation of the style of the Age of Neo-Classicism, and was developed in response to the taste of the age by the finest literary artist of the age. 'His affinity with Hellenism was not merely intellectual,' Walter Pater said of Winckelmann, 'the subtler threads of temperament were inwoven in it.' The same may be said of Shelley. That is why his poetry, better than any other, exhibits the response of English literature to the ideals of the age and most of all conforms to the Grecian Taste.

References

Chapter 1
Page

1 The Society of Dilettanti: Lionel Cust and Sidney Colvin, *History of the Society of Dilettanti*, 1898; Sir Cecil Harcourt-Smith, *The Society of Dilettanti, its Regalia and Pictures*, 1932, pp. 15–17.

2 Walpole: *Anecdotes of Painting*, 1762.
 Lord Kames: *Elements of Criticism*, 1762.
 Thomas Warton: *Verses on Sir Joshua Reynolds's Painted Window at New-College Oxford*, 1782. Cf. correspondence quoted in C. Woodforde, *The Stained Glass of New College, Oxford*, 1951, pp. 53–4.
 William Blake: *Complete Writings*, ed. G. Keynes, 1969, p. 778. (Quotations from Blake all given from this edition, and indicated by K with page number, e.g. K778.)
 Sir Walter Scott: *The Lady of the Lake*, 1810, I, xvii.
 In India: Philip Mason, *A Matter of Honour*, 1974, p. 21.

3 Wyatt's satires: Patricia Thomson, *Sir Thomas Wyatt and his Background*, 1964, ch. VIII.
 Spenser: A. C. Judson, *Life of Spenser*, 1945, p. 40; H. Tonkin, *Spenser's Courteous Pastoral*, 1972, p. 6.
 Campion: C. W. Peltz, 'Thomas Campion, an Elizabethan Neo-Classicist', *MLQ* XI (1950) 3–6.
 Milton: Tulsi Ram, *The Neo-Classical Epic*, 1971.
 Milton: note on *The Verse* added to *Paradise Lost* in 1668.
 Evelyn: *Account of Architects and Architecture*, 1664.
 Praz: *On Neoclassicism*, tr. Angus Davidson, 1969, p. 13.

4 Atterbury: Preface to *The Second Part of Mr Waller's Poems*, 1690.
 Walpole to Richard West: *Correspondence*, ed. W. S. Lewis, George L. Lam and Charles H. Bennett, 1948, XIII, 248.

5 Gray to his mother: *Correspondence* ed. Paget Toynbee and Laurence Whibley, 1935, I, 163–4.

6 One play of Sophocles and one of Euripides: the *Electra* of Sophocles, tr. Christopher Wase, published at The Hague, 1649; the *Phoenissae* was ancestral (through Lodovico Dolce's adaptation of Seneca's version of Euripides) to George Gascoigne's *Jocasta*, acted at Gray's Inn, 1566, published 1572. Lady Lumley's partial translation of Euripides' *Iphigeneia in Aulis*, made *c.* 1555, was not published until 1909.

translation of Pausanias used by Byron: *Letters and Journals*, ed. Rowland E. Prothero, 1922, V, 574.

Stuart and Revett: *Proposals for publishing an accurate description of the Antiquities of Athens*, 1751.

7 Winckelmann knew Pope's *Essay on Man:* M. Praz, *op. cit.*, p. 47.

8 Goethe: *Conversations with Eckermann* (Everyman's Lib. ed.) p. 173.

Berkeley to Pope: *Correspondence of Alexander Pope*, ed. George Sherburn, 1956, I, 222.

Shaftesbury: *Characteristicks*, VI, iii, 1.

Shaftesbury: *op. cit.*, III, i, 3, quoting Horace, *Ars Poetica*, 268—9.

9 'eine edle Einfalt': *Gedanken über die Nachahmung der griechischen Werke*, 1755.

the Niobe group: *History of Ancient Art*, tr. G. H. Lodge, 1881, IV, iii, 13.

Wheler: *A Journey into Greece*, 1682.

Lord Sandwich: *A Voyage performed by the late Earl of Sandwich round the Mediterranean in the years 1738 and 1739*, 1799.

10 Lord Charlemont: Francis Hardy, *Memoirs of the Political and Private Life of James Caulfeild Earl of Charlemont*, 1810.

Dalton: *Antiquities and Views in Greece and Egypt*, 1752.

Wood played a leading part: Cust and Colvin, *op. cit.*

11 about fifty Greek vases: *Winckelmann, Writings on Art*, ed. D. Irwin, 1972, p. 21.

Sir William Hamilton: Brian Fothergill, *Sir William Hamilton, Envoy Extraordinary*, 1969, for the facts of his career.

vases bought by Thomas Hope: David Watkin, *Thomas Hope and the Neo-Classical Idea*, 1968, pp. 35—6.

12 Goethe: *Italian Journey*, tr. W. H. Auden and Elizabeth Mayer, 1970, p. 208.

13 Emma to Sir William: quoted by Fothergill, *op. cit.*, p. 226.

Walpole to Miss Berry: *Correspondence*, ed. W. S. Lewis and

A. Doyle Wallace, 1944, XI, 349.

13 Josiah Wedgwood: Fothergill, *op. cit.*, p. 68.

'the characteristic distinction': *Winckelmann, Writings on Art*, pp. 68–9 (Fuseli's translation).

Flaxman to Romney: quoted by W. G. Constable, *John Flaxman*, 1927, p. 31.

14 Ingres kept his drawing: W. G. Constable, *op. cit.*, p. 74.

Blake to Cumberland: K795.

Blake to Trusler: K792.

Dr Johnson: Boswell, *Life of Dr Johnson*, ed. R. W. Chapman, 1969, p. 742.

15 Goethe: *Italian Journey*, p. 218.

Goethe to Herder: *Italian Journey*, p. 309.

Shelley to Peacock: *Letters*, ed. F. L. Jones, 1964, II, 74–5, 79–80.

16 Goethe: *Conversations with Eckermann*, p. 173.

Pater: *The Renaissance*, 1873.

17 Goethe on Fuseli: quoted from Diary, 2 May 1800, by Herbert von Einem, *Goethe and the Contemporary Fine Arts*, in catalogue of '*The Age of Neo-Classicism*', 1972, p. xxxvii.

Goethe on Raphael: *Italian Journey*, p. 433.

Hayley: *Essay on Painting*, 1781, I, 259.

Shelley to Hunt: *Letters*, II, 112.

Goethe: *Italian Journey*, p. 108.

18 Shelley to Peacock: *Letters*, II, 51.

Pope-Hennessy: *Raphael*, n.d., p. 34.

Berenson: *Italian Painters of the Renaissance*, 1948, pp. 209–22.

Blake: K472.

Winckelmann: *Writings on Art*, p. 61.

19 Berenson: *op. cit.*, p. 213.

Shelley to Hunt: *Letters*, II, 112.

Michelangelo claimed: Pope-Hennessy, *op. cit.*, p. 31.

20 Raphael to Castiglione: V. Golzio, *Raffaello nei documenti, nelle testimonianze dei contemporanei, e nella letteratura del suo secolo*, 1936, pp. 30–31.

Proclus: Εἰς τὴν πολιτείαν Πλάτωνος, II.

Cicero: *De Inventione*, II, i, 1.

Pliny: *Historia Naturalis*, XXXV, 36.

21 Byron to Murray: *Byron's Letters and Journals*, ed. Leslie A. Marchand, 1976, V, 133.

Winckelmann: *History of Ancient Art*, ed. cit., IV, ii, 25, 33.

21 Shelley to Maria Gisborne: *Letters*, II, 126.
Medwin: *The Shelley Papers*, 1833, p. 56.
22 Shelley: *Letters*, II, 50, 52.
Shaftesbury: *Characteristicks*, VII, *ad fin*.
Winckelmann: *History of Ancient Art*, ed.cit., IV, ii, 19.
Blake: K469.
Reynolds: *Discourses on Art*, ed. Stephen O. Mitchell, 1965,
pp. 143, 27.
23 Shelley: *Defence of Poetry* in *Complete Works*, ed. R. Ingpen and
W. E. Peck, 1930, VII, 135.
Blake: K459.
Barry: *A Letter to the Dilettanti Society*, 1793, in *Works*, 1809, II,
491.
Hayley: *Essay on Sculpture*, 1800, I.
Flaxman: *Lectures on Sculpture*, 1829, p. 201.
24 Peacock: *Crotchet Castle*, 1831, ch. VII.
Peacock: *Gryll Grange*, 1860, chs. IX, XI, IV.

Chapter 2

26 Dr Johnson: *Life of Akenside*, in *Lives of the Poets*.
28 Pope advised Dodsley: quoted by Johnson, *Life*.
30 Blake: *Milton*, II, 41.5; *Jerusalem*, 54.17.
Haydon: *Autobiography and Journals*, ed. M. Elwin, 1950, p. 317.
Dryden: *Apology for Heroic Poetry*, 1677.
31 Wotton: *The Elements of Architecture*, 1624.
33 *The Choice of Hercules*: *v. inf.*, p. 37.
35 Letitia Barbauld: *Essay on the Pleasures of Imagination*, 1794.
Addison: *Spectator*, 412.
Burke: *A Philosophical Enquiry into the Origin of our Ideas of the
Sublime and the Beautiful*, 1756.
37 Lowth: *The Choice of Hercules*, in J. Roach, *Beauties of the Poets*,
1794, VI.
Spence: *Polymetis*, 1747.
38 Shaftesbury: *Characteristicks*, V, iii, 1.
39 Congreve: *A Discourse of the Pindarique Ode*, 1706.
43 Severn: *The Keats Circle*, ed. H. E. Rollins, 1965, II, 133.
'load every rift': Keats *Letters*, ed. R. Gittings, 1970, pp. 390–1.
Ode to a Nightingale: Arthur Pollard noted the similarity between
the seventh stanza of Akenside's ode and the fourth and fifth

of Keats'; but the reminiscence goes further than this: *v.* 'Keats and Akenside; a Borrowing in the Ode to a Nightingale', *MLR*, LI (1956) 75—7.

44 decomposition: Letter to B. R. Haydon, 8 April 1818; *ed. cit.*

Gibbon: *Autobiography*, ed. Lord Sheffield *World's Classics* ed., J. B. Bury, p. 3.

too much liberty: Sonnet, 'Nuns fret not at their convent's narrow room.'

45 Bagehot: *Literary Studies* (Everyman's Lib. ed.) I, 82.

Hunt: *A Day by the Fire*, ed. J. E. Babson, 1870, p. 179.

47 clear, pure water: *v.* note on p. 150.

Chapter 3

48 *A Review of the Advancement of Learning*: H. O. White, 'The Letters of William Collins', *RES* (January 1927) p. 16.

49 Mrs Barbauld: *Essay on The Pleasures of Imagination*, 1794.

Gray: *Correspondence*, ed. Paget Toynbee and Leonard Whibley, 1935, I, 261.

Salmon's *Modern History*: Joseph Warton in his ed. of *The Works of Alexander Pope*, 1797, I, 61.

51 Joseph Warton's letter: in John Wooll, *Memoirs of Joseph Warton*, 1806, pp. 14—15.

Congreve: *Discourse of the Pindarique Ode*, 1706.

Millar offered Collins his fee: Ralph Griffiths, review of John Langhorne's ed. of the *Poems*, 1765, in *The Monthly Review*, 1765, XXXII, 294.

52 contract with Akenside: quoted by Dyce in his *Life* prefixed to his ed. of *The Poetical Works*, 1834, p. xxxiii, n. 3.

54 Ragsdale: quoted by P. L. Carver in *The Life of a Poet*, 1967, p. 66.

55 memorial to Otway: Carver, *op. cit.*, pp. 13, 21.

56 passages on the nightingale: *Electra*, 147—9; *Oedipus Coloneus*, 668—93.

Bagehot: essay on Shelley in *Literary Studies* (Everyman's Lib. ed.) I, 105.

57 Fanshawe: *Selected Parts of Horace, Prince of Lyricks*, 1652.

Dryden: dedication to the *Pastorals* in *The Works of Virgil*, 1697.

Addison: *Spectator*, 411.

Praz: *Mnemosyne*, 1970, pp. 15—17.

contemporary reviewer: *The Monthly Review*, 1764, XXX, 24.

57 Blake: *A Descriptive Catalogue,* 1809, K585.
58 the fairy kind: Dryden, dedication to *King Arthur.*
59 Blunden: in his ed. of the *Poems,* 1929, p. 170.
   Walpole: letter to J. Chute, 4 August 1753. *Correspondence,* ed.
      W. S. Lewis, 1973, XXXV, 77.
   Die Vernon: Scott, *Rob Roy,* ch. VII.
61 Gray: *Correspondence,* I, 258.
   White: quoted by Carver, *op. cit.,* p. 23.
   Dryden: *The Grounds of Criticism in Tragedy,* prefixed to *Troilus
      and Cressida,* 1679.
   Collins told Hayes: W. Seward, *Supplement to the Anecdotes of
      some Distinguished Persons,* 1797, pp. 123–4.
62 *Great Expectations*: bk I, ch. VII.
   Ode to Horror: first published in *The Student,* 1751.
   Scott and Home: J. G. Lockhart, *Life of Sir Walter Scott*
      (Everyman's Lib. ed.) p. 49.
65 *Childe Maurice* is F. J. Child's title, *Gil Morrice* is James Kinsley's
      in the *Oxford Book of Ballads,* 1969, following Percy's
      Reliques.
66 *Biographia Literaria*: ch. I.
   Hazlitt: *Lectures on the English Poets,* 1818, VI.

Chapter 4

67 Dr Johnson: letter to Bennet Langton, 5 July 1774, in Boswell's
      Life, ed. R. W. Chapman p. 564. (The Greek epigram is
      quoted here also. The Latin epitaph is given at pp. 778–9.)
68 Johnson defended: *Life, ed. cit.,* pp. 527–8.
   'Is there a man . . .': Memoir prefixed to *Miscellaneous Works of
      Goldsmith,* ed. T. Percy, 1809, pp. 102–3.
   comprehensive praise: *Life,* p. 512.
   'To copy Nature . . .': *Life of Dr Parnell,* 1770. *Collected Works,*
      ed. A. Friedman, 1966, III, 423.
   Shelley: Preface to *The Revolt of Islam.*
69 suggested that Dr Johnson had written: *Life,* p. 355.
   Johnson denied: *Life,* p. 512.
   Akenside: Sir James Prior, *Life of Malone,* 1860, pp. 413–14.
   review of Gray's *Odes*: *Monthly Review,* September 1757.
      Collected Works, I, 112–17.
   Boswell: *Life,* p. 292.

69 Dr Johnson got him 60 gns.: *Life*, p. 294.
   'brought him into high reputation'. *Life*, p. 917.
70 Dr Johnson told Boswell: *Life*, pp. 355–6.
   Hazlitt: *Lectures on the English Poets*, VI, 1818. *Complete Works*, ed. P. P. Howe, 1930, V, 119.
74 Pope: *The Rape of the Lock*, III, 157–8.
76 Dr Johnson contributed: *Life*, p. 356.
77 'the state of a man confined . . .': *Rambler*, 36. Yale ed. of the *Works*, ed. W. J. Bate and A. B. Strauss, 1969, III, 198.
79 Scott: *Oliver Goldsmith*, 1821. *Miscellaneous Works*, 1870, III, 256.
   Goethe: *Truth and Fantasy*, ed. J. M. Cohen, 1949, pp. 121, 124.
80 Bradley: *A Miscellany*, 1929 p. 147.
81 'the inflated style . . .': *Enquiry into the Present State of Polite Learning. Collected Works*, I, 322.
   The Beauties of English Poesy: Collected Works, V, 320, and note.
82 'This was a very grave personage': *Collected Works*, I, 447–8 (*The Bee*, V, 1759).
83 'My house consisted of . . .': *Vicar of Wakefield*, ch. IV. *Collected Works*, IV, 32–3.
   History of England, 1764: *Collected Works*, V, 297.

Chapter 5

Biographical data from *Blake Records*, ed. G. E. Bentley, 1969, quoted as BR followed by page no.; quotations from Blake's *Complete Writings*, ed. G. Keynes, 1969, quoted as K followed by page no.

85 'Grecian is mathematic form': K778.
   could read Greek: K821.
86 William Pars' water-colours are reproduced in Richard Chandler, *Travels in Asia Minor*, ed. Edith Clay, 1971.
   Blake to Reveley: K790.
87 Blake and Goldsmith: BR13.
   Blake's copy of *Reflections* etc.: BR12.
   Descriptive Catalogue: K585.
   Winckelmann: *v.* Fuseli's translation of the *Reflections* in *Winckelmann, Writings on Art*, ed. David Irwin, 1972, pp. 68, 69, and G. H. Lodge's translation from the *History of Ancient*

Art in the same work, p. 118.

89 epigram on Parrhasius' painting: *Anth. Pal.*, IV, 111. cf. Xenophon, *Memorabilia Socratis*, III, 10.

Blake to Cumberland: K795.

'a little cracked': quoted in Sir Geoffrey Keynes, *Blake Studies*, 1971, p. 245.

90 Blake owned Potter's translation: Keynes, *op. cit.*, p. 159.

Tiriel: extant drawings reproduced in the facsimile and transcript, ed. G. E. Bentley, 1967.

91 'By Bacchus . . .': *Thomas Taylor the Platonist, Selected Writings*, ed. Kathleen Raine and G. M. Harper, 1969, pp. 408–9.

Blake's marginal note: K452.

'No man of sense': K597.

92 W. M. Rossetti: quoted in *Tiriel, ed. cit.*, p. 42.

'the immense flood': K797.

'I think that Barry': K463.

93 Bacon, Locke and Newton: K533, 685, 772.

Proclus: Εἴς την πολιτείαν Πλάτωνος, II.

Descriptive Catalogue: K579–80.

marginal note: K459.

Reynolds: *Discourses on Art*, ed. Stephen O. Mitchell, 1965, p. 27.

94 note on Wordsworth's *Poems*: K783.

Raphael's letter: V. Golzio, *Raffaello nei documenti* etc., 1936, pp. 30–31.

'It is not only nature:' *Reflections*, in *Winckelmann, Writings on Art*, p. 62.

96 'But this name': *The Cratylus, Phaedo, Parmenides and Timaeus of Plato*. Translated from the Greek by Thomas Taylor with notes on the Cratylus, 1793, p. 37.

James Barry and Mary Wollstonecraft: *Works*, 1809, II, 594.

97 'Man has no Body': *Marriage of Heaven and Hell*, K149.

98 poem to Blake: Gilchrist, *Life*, ed. R. Todd, 1942, p. 125.

Hayley to Lady Hesketh: BR71.

'to be no longer Pester'd': K825.

December 1805: K862.

99 'the new Grecian': M. Bishop, *Blake's Hayley*, 1951, p. 276.

100 Lessing: *Laokoon*, I.

praise of Parrhasius: *Winckelmann, Writings on Art*, p. 69.

'all who endeavour': K573, 585.

100 'pure Design the very Soul of Art': *Essay on Painting*, 1779, I, 351.
   'all depends on Form': *Descriptive Catalogue*, K563.
   Hayley's note: *Essay on Painting*, 1779, note XVI, p. 63.
   Such idiots: K464.
101 Winckelmann: *Writings on Art*, pp. 73-4.
102 Blake: K472.
103 'Imagination is the Divine Vision': K783.
   Blake to Butts: K825.
104 Landor: Henry Crabb Robinson, *On Books and their Writers*, ed. Edith J. Morley, 1938, II, 549-50.

Chapter 6

105 'So early in life . . .': Post-Script to *Gebir. Complete Works*, ed. T. Earle Welby, 1927-36, XIII, 352-3.
   Rose Aylmer lent: J. Forster, *Life*, 2nd ed., 1876, I, 50-51.
106 'Poetry was always . . .': *Last Fruit off an Old Tree*, 1853.
   'constructive faculty': *Diaries of W. C. Macready*, 1912, I, 319.
107 Swinburne: *Letters*, ed. Cecil Y. Lang, 1960, IV, 221.
   Sappho: Σάπφους Μελη, ed. E. Lobel, 1925, p. 102.
   Plato: *Anth. Pal*, V, 78.
108 'The thoughts of our poets': *The Idyls of Theocritus, Complete Works*, XII, 22.
   'They are hot and pothery': *Imaginary Conversations, Southey and Landor*, II, *Complete Works*, V, 318.
109 'Incomparably the best poetry': Letter to Southey, 1811, in Forster, *Life*, I, 2.
110 fit audience: *P.L.* VII. 31.
111 'I sometimes thought': Post-Script to *Gebir, Complete Works*, XIII, 352.
   Epicurus: ed. C. Bailey, 1926, V, 43; translation from *The Mission of Greece*, ed. R. W. Livingstone, 1928, p. 24.
112 Mr Burchell condemned: *The Vicar of Wakefield*, ch. VIII.
   Landor had shocked Parr: R. H. Super, *Walter Savage Landor*, 1954, p. 12.
   he told Forster: *Life*, II, 537.
   'Tasso gave to a prince': *Reason of Church Government*, 1642.
113 'Some passages . . . rival Pindar': *Poemata et Inscriptiones*, 1847.
   A distinguished critic: Douglas Bush, *Mythology and the Roman-*

tic Tradition in English Poetry, 1937, ch. VII.

113 Landor ridiculed: in his *Imaginary Conversation* between Addison and Lord Somers, which he destroyed because 'it was composed maliciously'. Forster's *Life*, I, 510—11.

114 Joseph Warton's assessment: quoted in Chapter 1, p. 2.

117 Fragonard: Georges Wildenstein, *The Paintings of Fragonard*, 1960, cat. nos 221—5, especially the last.

Dr Johnson's advice: Boswell, *Life*, ed. R. W. Chapman, p. 480.

'Thomson, in the Seasons': *The Idyls of Theocritus, Complete Works*, XII, 22.

118 cedars of Lebanon: Super, *op. cit.* p. 92.

Bagehot: essay on Shelley in *Literary Studies* (Everyman's Lib. ed.) I, 83.

'of that order of simplicity': *Complete Works*, XIV, 382.

Swinburne: quoted in M. Elwin, *Landor a Replevin*, 1958, p. 380.

Sidney Colvin: *Landor*, 1881, p. 62.

119 Swinburne: *Miscellanies*, 1886, p. 203.

he told Southey: Forster, *Life*, I, 298.

he wrote to Lady Blessington: Super, *op. cit*, p. 288.

Lessing: *Laokoon*, III.

120 letter to Southey: M. Elwin, *op. cit.*, p. 205.

121 Dickens: *Letters*, ed. W. Dexter, 1958, II, 488.

Wordsworth: *The Letters of William and Dorothy Wordsworth: The Later Years*, ed. E. de Selincourt, 1939, I, 166.

Hare: quoted by Elwin, *op. cit.*, p. 408.

122 Seymour Kirkup: quoted by Elwin, *op. cit.*, p. 215.

124 Epicurus' famous precept: *ed. cit.*, V, 86.

'We aim at self-sufficiency': *ed. cit.*, III, 130; translation from *The Mission of Greece*, ed. R. W. Livingstone, 1928, p. 22.

125 letter to Southey: quoted by Elwin, *op. cit.* p. 273.

126 to give Mary some idea: letter to John and Maria Gisborne, 10 July 1818, *Letters*, ed. F. L. Jones, 1964, II, 20.

'Pericles was somewhat less amiable: quoted by Elwin, *op. cit.*, p. 288.

127 'Vite, vite, mon ami': quoted by Kenneth Clark, *The Romantic Rebellion*, 1973, p. 21.

Chapter 7

128 Leigh Hunt: *Shelley and Mary*, II. 390.
   'There is nothing perfect': 'Mozart', *The Examiner*, 2 June 1833.
   Peacock recalled: *Memoirs of P. B. Shelley*, ed. H. F. B. Brett-Smith, 1909, p. 68.
129 Shelley sent Peacock: *Letters*, ed. F. L. Jones, 1964, II, 27.
   'I am delighted': *Letters*, II, 98.
   review of *Rhododaphne: Shelley's Complete Works*, ed. R. Ingpen and W. E. Peck, 1929, VI, 273–6.
130 Shelley wrote: *Letters*, II, 192.
   Wickes: *Peacock's Complete Works*, ed. H. F. B. Brett-Smith and C. E. Jones, 1924–34, I, xxiii.
133 Scott said: introduction to *Rokeby*, ed. of 1830.
136 Landor's dislike of Plato: cf. *Imaginary Conversations, Diogenes and Plato*.
137 Thackeray: *The Great Hoggarty Diamond*, 1849, ch. II.
138 Of Bellini's *La Sonnambula*: *Peacock's Complete Works*, ed. cit., IX, 437.
   'Peacock dines here': *Letters of M. W. Shelley*, ed. F. L. Jones, 1944, I, 30.
   'I think one is always in love': *Letters*, II, 434.
139 Shelley to Hunt: *Letters*, II, 66.
141 Raleigh: *On Writing and Writers*, 1926, p. 153.
   Goldsmith: *Vicar of Wakefield*, ch. VII.
144 Priestley: *Thomas Love Peacock*, 1966, p. 141.
   'where every wonder': *Melincourt*, ch. XXV.
145 'that on the Velenrhyd': letter to Thomas L'Estrange, 11 July 1861. *Complete Works*, VIII, 253.

Chapter 8

147 Shelley: Preface to *Hellas*.
   'where in her Mediterranean mirror': Robert Bridges, *The Testament of Beauty*, 1929, I, 657–8.
148 the solid fabric: Gibbon, Preface to *The History of the Decline and Fall of the Roman Empire*, 1771.
   Vitruvian: cf. Colen Campbell, *Vitruvius Britannicus*, 1717–25.
   Walpole: *v. supra*, Ch. 1, p. 4.
   Castle Goring: Ian Nairn and N. Pevsner, *Sussex* (The Buildings

of England) 1965, pp. 125—7.

148 Goethe: *Italian Journey*, tr. W. H. Auden and Elizabeth Mayer, 1970, p. 218.

'Grecian literature': *On the Revival of Literature*, 1818, in *Complete Works*, ed. R. Ingpen and W. E. Peck, 1929, VI, 214.

The Symposium took eight or nine days: *Mary Shelley's Journal*, ed. F. L. Jones, 1947, pp. 101—2.

149 Sophocles: *Oedipus Tyrannus*, 67.

Bagehot: *Literary Studies* (Everyman's Lib. ed.) I, 105.

Oedipus Coloneus, 337—52.

150 Plutarch: *Moralia*, 79B.

two unusual words: ἱστουργοῦντες, γεροντάγωγεῖ. cf. F. R. Earp, *The Style of Sophocles*, 1944, p. 24; S. H. Butcher, *Some Aspects of the Greek Genius*, 1891, pp. 88—9.

Bagehot: *op. cit.*, I, 109.

History of Ancient Art, IV, ii, 23.

Keats' advice: *Letters*, ed. R. Gittings, 1970, p. 390.

151 the same has been said of Sophocles: F. R. Earp, *op. cit.*, p. 2.

'So Gherardi's hall': *Ginevra*, 131—44.

152 'unbeheld': used again by Shelley, *Prometheus Unbound*, III, i, 23, 45; iii, 8; *The Cenci*, II, i, 192; ii, 155; *Zucca*, IX, 8.

'lightness, chastity, and strength': *Letters*, ed. F. L. Jones, 1964, II, 98.

Bradley: *A Miscellany*, 1929, p. 147.

'the characteristic distinction': *Reflections*, tr. Fuseli, in *Winckelmann, Writings on Art*, ed. D. Irwin, 1972, p. 68.

Lessing: *Laokoon*, IV.

153 Dante's poetry 'may be considered': *Defence of Poetry*, in R. Ingpen and W. E. Peck, *Complete Works*, 1930, VII, 129.

154 G. M. Hopkins: *Duns Scotus's Oxford*, 1—3.

'What wond'rous Life': Marvell, *The Garden*, 33—40.

155 'For her own person': *Antony and Cleopatra*, II, ii, 205—13.

Sappho: Σάπφους μέλη ed. E. Lobel, 1925, 31.

'At her most passionate': C. M. Bowra, Introduction to *Oxford Book of Greek Verse*, 1930, p. xiv.

156 Ariel to Miranda: *With a Guitar to Jane*, 1—16.

Julian and Maddalo: 65—76.

157 Constable: the two paintings referred to were nos 244 and 270 in the Constable Exhibition at the Tate Gallery, 1976.

158 he told Maria Gisborne: *Letters*, II, 126.

158 Medwin: *The Shelley Papers*, 1833, p. 56.
     Winckelmann: *History of Ancient Art*, tr. G. H. Lodge, 1881, IV,
         v, 23.
     Shelley to Hogg: *Letters*, II, 186.
     Defence of Poetry: *Complete Works*, 1930, VII, 136.
     Raphael: V. Golzio, *Raffaello nei documenti* etc. 1936, pp. 30–31.
     Blake: e.g. *Descriptive Catalogue* K580.
     Reynolds: *Discourses on Art*, ed. Stephen O. Mitchell, 1965,
         p. 143.

159 'The deep truth': *Prometheus Unbound*, II, iv, 116.
     'the veil and the bar': *Prometheus Unbound*, II, iii, 59–60.
     'some good change': *Prometheus Unbound*, II, v, 18–20.
     Blake: K783.

160 Winckelmann: *Reflections* in *Writings on Art*, p. 72.
     Mary said: Note on *Poems* of 1821.
     letter to Peacock: *Letters*, II, 61.
     'Erewhile I slept': *Prometheus Unbound*, II, i, 43–5.
     'Thou for whose path: *Ode to the West Wind*, 36–42; cf.
         Prometheus Unbound, III, ii, 41–7.

161 'The mind in creation': *Defence of Poetry*, in *Complete Works*, ed.
         cit., VII, 135.
     'whether the attempt': *Letters*, II, 219.

162 Keats acknowledged: *Letters*, ed. cit. 27.

163 'a certain familiar style of language': *Letters*, II, 108.
     Difficile est': *Ars Poetica*, 128.

164 'We will have books': *Letter to Maria Gisborne*, 298–307,
         167–9.
     'a fanciful poem': *Letters*, II, 257.
     'the abstract and dreamy spirit': Mary Shelley's Note on *The
         Witch of Atlas*.

165 Shelley's letters show: *Letters*, II, 245, 262, 290, 366, 374, 382,
         406.
     Shelley to Peacock: *Letters*, II, 102.

166 'And though ill tongues: *The Cenci*, V, iv, 149–65.
     'there is no terror': *Notes on Sculptures* in *Complete Works*, ed. cit.
         VI, 331.

167 'written at the suggestion': Preface to *Hellas*.
     'display of newspaper erudition': Preface to *Hellas*.
     'But Greece and her foundations are': *Hellas*, 696–703.

168 'Beside the windless': *Prometheus Unbound*, III, iii, 159–70.
     Plato's *Republic*: 328.

168 'Another Athens': *Hellas*, 1084—7.
169 Addison: *Spectator*, 29.
   Wordsworth: C. Wordsworth, *Memoirs of William Wordsworth*,
      1851, II, 474.
   Pater: *The Renaissance*, 1873.

Index